Comparative Stud

and

Growth of Automotive Industry in India

By,
Soman, Prasad Prabhakar

ACKNOWLEDGEMENT

This Research work would not have seen the light of the day without the invaluable guidance and active kind help of Dr. Padmawati Sanjay Ingole, Research Guide, Department of Commerce, Prof. Ramakrishna More College, Akurdi, Pune SAVITRIBAI PHULE PUNE UNIVERSITY. I feel extremely honored for the opportunity best owed upon me to work under her guidance. I will always be indebted to our Head of Department, Dr. Nannaware Sir and Dr. Archana Mali madam for their guidance, inspiration and knowledge given to me. My family members have always been a source of inspiration to me in my endeavor of completing this research work. Lastly I would like to thank my colleagues from previous employer 3M India Ltd and current employer Unifrax India Pvt Ltd., well-wishers from the Automotive Industry in India, I would also like to thank Dr Sanjay Kaptan , Head DCRC, SPPU, Mrs. Neha Kurhade DCRC Pune & Dr. Dhananjay Pingale , Director, Sri Balaji International School of Management and Research for their valuable support.

Date: 25/02/2022

Place: Pune

(Mr. Prasad Prabhakar Soman)

INDEX

Sr. No.	Particulars	Page No.
	Chapter 1 - Introduction	
1.1	Overview of Automotive Industry	1
1.2	Classification of the Indian Automotive Industry	2
1.3	Two Wheelers	3
1.4	Three Wheelers	3
1.5	Passenger vehicles	4
1.6	Commercial vehicles	4
1.7	Mining equipment's and earthmovers	4
1.8	OFF Road vehicles	5
1.9	Segment level classification	6
1.10	International Automotive Classification	8
1.11	Indian Automotive Industry at a Glance (2017)	9
1.12	Automotive Industry status	14
1.13	Revolution in the mobility of vehicles in India	15
1.14	Affordability of the passenger vehicle	15
1.15	Fuel Economy Logic	16
1.16	Alternate fuel usage	16
1.17	High-end products	17
1.18	Rural Market demand	17
1.19	Automotive Market consolidation	17
1.20	Indian Auto industry is at the junction	18
1.21	Major Trends in the India Auto space	18
1.22	Key players and expansion plans	24
1.23	Nationwide Industry footprint	25

1.24	India investments	25

	Chapter 2- Research methodology &Review of the literature.	
2.1	Introduction	27
2.2	Need of the Study	27
2.3	Relevance & importance of Study	28
2.4	Limitation of Study	28
2.5	Objectives of Study	29
2.6	Justification of Objectives	29
2.7	Assumptions	29
2.8	Statement of the problem.	29
2.9	Statement of Hypothesis	30
2.10	Scope of study	30
2.11	Universe and sample size	30
2.12	Justification of the sample size	30
2.13	Methods of data collection	38
2.14	Research Design	38
2.15	Study of Literature	38

	Chapter 3- Profile of Indian Auto Industry	
3.1	Asia Motor Works (AMW)	46
3.2	Atul Auto Ltd (AAL)	46
3.3	Bajaj Auto Ltd	47
3.4	BMW	47
3.5	Daimler India commercial vehicles (DICV)	48
3.6	Fiat Chrysler Automobiles (FCA)	48

3.7	Force Motors Ltd	48
3.8	Ford Motors Pvt. Ltd	49
3.9	Harley Davidson India	49
3.10	Hero MotoCorp Ltd	49
3.11	Hindustan Motors Limited (HM)	50
3.12	Honda Cars India Ltd., (HCIL)	50
3.13	Honda Motorcycle & Scooter India Pvt. Ltd. (HMSI)	50
3.14	Hyundai Motor India Limited (HMIL)	51
3.15	India Kawasaki Motors Pvt. Ltd (IKM)	51
3.16	Yamaha Motor (IYM)	52
3.17	Isuzu Motors Limited	52
3.18	JCBL Limited	52
3.19	Mahindra & Mahindra Ltd. (M&M)	53
3.20	Maruti Suzuki India Limited (MSIL)	53
3.21	Mercedes-Benz India Pvt. Ltd (MBIL)	54
3.22	Nissan Motor India Pvt. Ltd	54
3.23	Piaggio Vehicles Private Limited (PVPI)	54
3.24	Royal Enfield Motors (REM)	55
3.25	Scania Commercial Vehicle's	55
3.26	SKODA Auto India	56
3.27	Suzuki Motorcycle India Private Limited (SMIPL)	56
3.28	Tata Motors Limited (TML)	56
3.29	Toyota Kirloskar Motor Ltd. (TKML)	57
3.30	Triumph Motorcycles India	57
3.31	TVS Motor Company	57
3.32	VE Commercial Vehicles Limited (VECV)	58

3.33	Volkswagen India Pvt. Ltd (VW)	58
3.34	Volvo	59
3.35	Automotive Segment Profile	59
3.36	Two Wheelers in India	59
3.37	Types of Two Wheelers	61
3.38	Technical Classification 2W	64
3.39	Overview of the Motorcycle Industry	64
3.40	Major Manufacturers of Two Wheelers	65
3.41	Electric Two-Wheelers	66
3.42	Evolution Stage 1-2W	67
3.43	Evolution Stage 2-2W	68
3.44	Driving forces -2W	69
3.45	Business Design-2W	70
3.46	Why scooters had dominated pre-1990	70
3.47	A rise in India's Young Working Population	74
3.48	Rise of India's Rural Economy and Growth in Middle Income Households	75
3.49	Greater Affordability of Vehicles	75
3.50	Rapid Product Introduction and Shorter Product Life Cycle	75
3.51	Inadequate Public Transport Systems in most Urban Areas	75
3.52	Challenges faced by the industry	75
3.53	Rising Customer Expectations	76
3.54	Environmental and Safety Concerns	76
3.55	Creation of Distribution Infrastructure	76
3.56	Lower penetration to improve growth	77
3.57	Profile of Three-wheelers segment	77
3.58	Market Profile of Three Wheeler	77

3.59	Types of Three Wheelers	79
3.60	Major Manufacturers of Three Wheelers	80
3.61	Fuels Used in Three Wheelers	80
3.62	Three-wheeler vs four Wheeler Taxi, India point of view	81
3.63	Three Wheeler Vehicles Exports from India	84
3.64	Economically competitive transport infrastructure requirements	84
3.65	Segment profile - Passenger Vehicles	85
3.66	Five Forces Analysis	87
3.67	Entry obstacles	87
3.68	Competitive Competition	88
3.69	Buyers' negotiation power	88
3.70	Bargaining Power of Suppliers	88
3.71	The threat of Substitutes	89
3.72	4w Industry classification	90
3.73	Latest developments	91
3.74	Planned trends	91
3.75	Segment profile - Commercial Vehicles	92
3.76	Exports of CVs from India	94
3.77	Growth in Industrial Production	95
3.78	Enhanced access to low-cost financing	96
3.79	Path emergence as the main form of transport	96
3.80	Implementation of the Overloading Laws and others	96
3.81	Segment profile - Tractors and Off-Road vehicle industry	96
3.82	Segment profile - Off Road Vehicles	100
3.83	The 12th Five Year Plan	103
3.84	Indian Urban Infrastructure	104

3.85	Roads	105
3.86	Airports	105
3.87	Railways	105
3.88	Ports	106
3.89	Indian Earthmoving & Machinery Industry	106
3.90	Construction equipment market share by segment	107
3.91	CE market contracted in 2018	107
3.92	Financing and renting facilities in India	108
3.93	Key Challenges for Infrastructure and Construction Equipment Industry	109
3.94	The Way Ahead: India will become the third largest building sector in the world by 2025	111
3.95	OFF Road/Construction vehicles	112
3.96	Internet sites for secondary data source	112

	Chapter 4 - Data Analysis, Interpretation and Hypothesis Testing	Page No
4.1	Introduction	151
4.2	Automotive segment companies	152
4.3	Analysis of Challenges faced by Automotive Industry	153
4.4	Factors for Growth of Indian Economy	157
4.5	Assessment of Automotive Industry	161
4.6	Economic Growth and Automotive Industry	170
4.7	Challenges faced by Automotive Industry in India	177
4.8	Growth pattern of automotive industry in Indian Economy	181
4.9	Growth of Indian GDP	182
4.10	Road length	183
4.11	Population growth	183
4.12	Fuel prices	184

4.13	Automotive industry growth	185
4.14	Co relation coefficient	186
4.15	Factor analysis	187
4.16	Testing of Hypothesis	188

	Chapter 5 - Findings, Suggestions & Conclusion	
5.1	Summary of Findings based on Primary and secondary data	191
5.2	Factors affecting the growth of respective Auto sector	197
5.3	Suggestions	201
5.4	Data correlation and final conclusion	202
5.5	Key words and their long form	202
5.6	Bibliography	204
5.7	Papers Published with ISSN / ISBN No	209
5.8	ANNEXTURE	210

Chart Index

Sr. No.	Particulars	Page No.
6.1	Classification of Automobile Industry	2
6.2	Off-road vehicles	5
6.3	Segment level classification of the automotive industry	6
6.4	International Classification of the auto industry	7
6.5	Snapshot of the Indian auto industry	9
6.6	Production statistics of Indian Automotive Industry	11
6.7	Automotive production chart	11
6.8	Tractor and Off road vehicle production	12
6.9	Total automotive production for all the six segments	12
6.10	Key players and spread of Auto Industry in India	24
6.11	Consolidated growth of Auto industry from 2004 to 2017	25
6.11-A	Automotive industry segment share 2004	32
6.11-B	Automotive industry segment share 2017	32
6.11-C	Top manufacturers of automotive space	33
6.11-D	Passenger vehicle Pareto	34
6.11-E	Commercial vehicle Pareto	35
6.11-F	Three Wheeler vehicle Pareto	36
6.11-G	Two wheeler vehicle Pareto	37
6.12	Two-wheeler Industry production	60
6.13	Graphical representation 2W segment	74
6.14	Global 2W industry penetration per 1000 person	76
6.15	3W industry production	78
6.16	3W city level penetration	83
6.17	4W industry production	86
6.18	4W industry Classification	89
6.19	4W segments	92
6.20	Commercial vehicles production statistics	94
6.21	Global Commercial vehicles penetration per Km	95
6.22	Tractor sales statistics	99
6.23	state-wise tractor sales	99
6.24	share of Business (Tractors – India)	100
6.25	Off-Road vehicles statistics	101
6.26	Five-year plan spending	102
6.27	Five-year plan center vs state spending	104
6.28	Market share of earthmoving equipment's	106
6.29	Construction Equipment market in 2018	108

6.30	Types of Off-Road Equipment's	112
6.31	India population1985-2019	113
6.32	Per capita income 1985-2020 India	113
6.33	Average Per Capita income Vs Automotive Hubs -India	114
6.34	Infrastructure spend-India 1985-2020	115
6.35	Sector wise GDP contribution 1950-2014	116
6.36	Job creation logic by Automotive Industry	117
6.37	Infrastructure investment spread -India	118
6.38	Auto industry plants- state level	120
6.39	Snapshot by Auto component industry	123
6.40	Broad level component break up-Auto comp	124
6.41	Global Export statistics-Auto components	126
6.42	Export revenue USDB –Auto Comp	127
6.43	Auto component imports	129
6.44	Population of India and growth rate 1950-2014	130
6.45	Population density chart –world	130
6.46	India population share in world population (top 50)	132
6.47	35 years data for the GDP of India 1985-2020	133
6.48	India GDP graph for 35 years 1985-2020	134
6.49	World GDP (Regional GDP)	134
6.50	USD to INR exchange rate from 1985 to 2019	135
6.51	Global Commercial vehicles sales Vs Road network	136
6.52	Distribution of workforce per economic sector	137
6.53	Fuel price comparison from 1989 -2018	138
6.54	Petroleum import and production 2017	139
6.55	Foreign exchange USD vs INR 1985 - 2019	140
6.56	Crude oil price study 1989-2021	140
6.57	Automotive production and Economic factors comparison	141
6.58	Road length snapshot 2017	143
6.59	Various road length -India 2017	145
6.60	Road infra development over 50 years(1970-2017) -India	146
6.61	State-wise Road % share of National highway 2017	148
6.62	International Road infrastructure 2018 per 1000 population	149
6.63	Production trend of automotive industry (SIAM data)2010-20	152
6.64	Distribution of respondents as per age	156
6.65	Distribution of respondents as per experience	158
6.66	Economic growth indicators	159
6.67	Impact of industrial growth	160
6.68	Impact of Road infrastructure	161
6.69	Factors responsible for auto industry growth	162

6.70	Factors affecting commercial vehicle sales	163
6.71	Income bracket for 2W Buyer	164
6.72	Income bracket for 3W Buyer	165
6.73	Income bracket for 4W Buyer	166
6.74	Popular use of 2W	167
6.75	Popular use of 3W	168
6.76	Popular use of 4W	169
6.77	Popular use of Bus and Truck	170
6.78	probability of cycle owner to buy 2W	171
6.79	probability of 2W owner to buy 4W	172
6.80	Factors essential for industrial growth	173
6.81	Factors responsible for cyclic nature of auto industry	174
6.82	Relationship between economy and automotive industry	175
6.83	Impact of road infra and disposable income	176
6.84	Challenge faced by 2W Industry	178
6.85	Challenges faced by 3W industry	179
6.86	Challenges faced by 4W industry	180
6.87	Challenges faced by commercial vehicle industry	181
6.88	Comparison between the vehicle production and fuel price fluctuation	186

Table Index

Sr. No.	Particulars	Page No.
Table 4.1	Automotive sub segments players Source	153
Table 4.1-A	Distribution of Respondents according to Age and Education-Numbers	154
Table 4.1-B	Distribution of Respondents according to Age and Education-percentage	154
Table 4.2	Distribution of Respondents according to Age and Experience-Numbers	156
Table 4.2-A	Distribution of Respondents according to Age and Experience (In percent)	156
Table 4.3	Most relevant indicator for economic growth	158
Table 4.4	Growth in industrial production and its impact	159
Table 4.5	Impact of increase in road infrastructure	160
Table 4.6	Factors responsible for growth of Automobile industry	161
Table 4.7	Factors affecting commercial vehicle sales	163
Table 4.8	Most relevant income Bracket for buying 2W	164
Table 4.9	Most relevant income Bracket for buying 3W	165
Table 4.10	Most relevant income Bracket for buying 4W	166
Table 4.11	Popular use of 2W	167
Table 4.12	Popular use of 3W	168
Table 4.13	Popular use of 4W	169
Table 4.14	Popular use of commercial vehicle -Bus & Truck	170
Table 4.15	Probability that the bicycle owner will buy a 2W	171
Table 4.16	Probability that the 2W owner will buy a 4W	172
Table 4.17	Factors essentials for industrial growth	173
Table 4.18	Factors responsible for cyclic nature of the Auto industry sale	175
Table 4.19	correlation between economic growth and growth of automotive industry	175
Table 4.20	Positive impact of Road infra and disposable income on auto industry	176
Table 4.21	Challenges faced by 2W Industry	177
Table 4.22	Challenges faced by 3W Industry	178
Table 4.23	Challenges faced by 4W Industry	179
Table 4.24	Challenges faced by Commercial Vehicle Industry	180
Table 4.25	Growth of Indian GDP	182
Table 4.26	Road length	183
Table 4.27	Population growth in India	184
Table 4.28	Fuel price increase	185
Table 4.29	Automotive production and growth	186

Table 4.30	Comparison of Automotive industry and Growth of Economy ,(Using Correlation Co-efficient)	187
Table 4.31	Technical hypotheses for H1	189
Table 4.32	Descriptive Statistics	189
Table 4.33	One sample test	189

Chapter 1 - Introduction

1.1. Overview of Automotive Industry

Since 1890, cars have been part of the Indian economy, while Baggie was on the roads of Mumbai and Kolkata during the British period, and horses were later used to drive with simple motors having steering wheels. The Indian car industry has made considerable progress since that time in the past 125 years and has played a leading role in the global automotive industry. The only post-1983 Indian government that was more independent than the protection economy. It was Manmohan Singh who put in the required efforts, and then the Indian industry began making good progress, opening the Indian economy to the world. During this protected economic period, many auto industries started business in India, including Hindustan Motors, TATA Motors, Bajaj Auto Ltd and Premier Automobiles. Few companies in the list of companies cultivated during the license period, as they were the only companies to produce and sell cars in India. This resulted in inefficient manufacturing because these companies were not concentrating on the sleek manufacturing process because of their monopolies. The main reason was a secure enterprise and virtually no competition. Some of these companies such as Hindustan Motors have recently shut down since they have not been able to compete. The Indian economy is open to the entire world, where the final consumer of cars can decide what kind of characteristics are required in cars and who can survive in this competitive market in this closely connected world.

Mr. Sanjay Gandhi was the great leader and dreamed of the most economical car for India, which bore the current Maruti Suzuki, a JV between India's government and Japan's Suzuki Motors company. In conjunction with Indian economic work and Japan's best manufacturing technology, the company launched the highly renowned Indian car known as Maruti 800 quickly. In the Indian automotive industry, Maruti Suzuki quickly improved its 50 percent market share. The quality and reliability of Maruti 800 were high; the competition soon collapsed and helped the company gain a maximum share of the business. At the same time, TATA Motors worked on the trucks and buses gained enormous popularity among the world's players and took a top position. TATA Motors has been very reliable in its difficult terrine and its service network has made its very popular brand across India and Globe. Due to product reliability, it started to export trucks and buses around the world. The 1991 liberalization helped Indian economies attract the world's players to India and explore India's business and growth market.

Two, things that were different occurred after the Indian economy liberalization. All the leading brands from Rolse Royse to Hyundai have entered India to gain maximum market share because India has all types of customers. Over time, Indian car manufacturers have also gained strength by creating JVs for technology and other global business excellence with various global players. After liberalization, many car players opened their shops in India like Korea's Hyundai, Ford, and Japanese Nissan. SAIC from China, the Chinese 2nd Highest Auto Manufacturer, have recently opened its factory in India with a look at the lucrative Indian market. Aspiring young people, building new expressways, growing road networks in India, increasing disposable income of the population, and finally, the increasing needs of the young population for faster and point-to-point mobility are some of the key reasons that fuel the growth of the auto industry in India. Still, the motorcycle of the commuter, 3-wheeler and collection carriers are considered mobility. However, High-end bikes and cars have become their image for many young enthusiasts. Therefore, the craze for Image Bikes and Autos also rises among young people with high availability incomes.

1.2. Classification of the Indian Automotive Industry

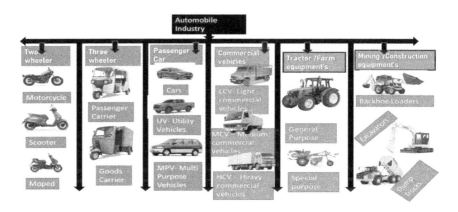

Chart 6.1 - Classification of Automobile Industry (Source SIAM /Self-study)

Source – Self Study /SIAM

Based on the usage type and number of wheels Automotive industry in India is classified in to six classes
1. Two-Wheeler   2. Three-Wheeler   3. Passenger Car
4. Commercial vehicle   5. Tractor   6. Construction equipment's

1.3. **Two Wheelers**-Two wheelers are simply known as two-wheeled cars. While driving .two wheelers, which needs balancing technique, comparative small engines starting from 100 CC to 250 ccs are used, mostly 90 percent of the two vehicles fall in this space. There are, however, mega bikes with higher CC engines, from 250 ccs to 1200 cc. In the following fashion, two-wheelers are further categorized into :

1.3.1. **Motorcycles**-Motor bikes are usually large wheel foundation systems. The seating position is very convenient for the rider and it has a very good grip on the roads since the wheelbase is high. Example - Bajaj Pulsar.

1.3.2. **Scooters** - Scooters usually have a smaller wheelbase, but they are still common with family users with higher CC motors and can accommodate small families on the same very well. It has storage room even to hold any tiny bag. New-generation scooters, such as Vespa scooters and Honda Activa, also have handheld charging points.

1.3.3. **Mopeds**- Mopeds have an extra tiny wheelbase or anything comparable to a scooter wheelbase. Currently used for a very short distance of less than 30-40 km. They usually have very limited engines of between 60 ccs and 80 ccs approx.For instance, TVS Pep.

There is a movement in the industry to get battery-driven scooters and mopeds. The Government of India is also offering several incentives for the usage of this lithium ion-based battery-based technology. This will potentially profit the government by providing a reduced import duty on the importation of crude oil. The highest foreign exchange for crude oil import bill is expended by the Government of India, which is expected to grow every year as the need for mobility goes up.

1.4. **Three-wheelers** – The basic description of the three-wheeler is that the car requires three wheels to drive. Usually, this is for 150 or 200 cc diesel / CNG or gasoline engines, which are further classified into two groups depending on the utilization of cars.

1.4.1. **Goods Carrier** – These vehicles are used to transport commodities to less than 40 km of size, three-wheeler provides advantages of travel in the narrower space, takes sharp turns on narrow roads, which is typical of India. This is referred to as a center and spoken system where a larger truck carries the requisite goods between towns and smaller vehicles such as three-wheeler carries the same goods from factories outside the city to within city limits to prevent traffic jams within city limits due to smaller roads and old city layout.

1.4.2. **Passenger Carrier** – These are the TUKTUK or Rickshaw that we see in every town in India, using in the city for smaller distances. The population of these vehicles is regulated in each city by a permit from the regional traffic offices. Depending on needs, distances and demographic considerations, the regional traffic authority shall settle on the number of permits to be issued in a particular location. Bajaj RE 150, for instance.

1.5 Passenger Vehicles – There is a very simple way of defining a passenger car, based on the size of the vehicle, it is meant to carry passenger's min 2 Max 8. Passenger vehicles are further classified as below in sub-classes.

They are a typical urban way of commuting small and large distances usually owned in urban or semi-urban areas by the small family, such as Maruti Suzuki swift.

1.5.1. **Utility vehicles** – Utility vehicles are the vehicles that are used for different purposes, as the name suggests the use that can be used in urban and semi-urban areas for people's transport, usually large. These types of vehicles are also used by motoring enthusiasts for off-road applications. Example – Scorpio from Mahindra & Mahindra Company.

1.5.2. **Multi-Purpose Vehicles**-Multi-Purpose Vehicles or MUVs are typical classes of vehicles used for people and good transport, both of which are sometimes used for mass transport. Alternatively, they are also used for ambulance applications or other applications, such as TATA Winger is an example.

1.6. **Commercial vehicles** – Commercial vehicles are divided into LCV and M & HCV based on their tonnage carrying capacity. They are often known as trucks or buses, based on their use.

1.6.1. **LCV** – Light or Small commercial vehicles consist of trucks and buses with fewer than 4 tons passing.

1.6.2. **M & HCV** – Medium to heavy commercial vehicles vary from 4 tons to 50 tons.

1.7. **Mining equipment's and earthmovers** – As seen below in the graphic, there are several forms of mining equipment and earth-moving equipment.

Chart 6.2 – Off-road vehicles

Source – JCB PPT /https://dozerin.wordpress.com/

Off road vehicles industry do not contribute to the volumes of the automotive industry, however it is based on the applications and hence the type of vehicles are based on various special applications

1.8. **OFF Road vehicles**– The name itself is enough to explain the class of vehicles, these vehicles are used for the various jobs to be done OFF Road, it has more rugged structure to survive in the rough terrine. Their typical use is based on the function it doses while in the usage. Most of the automobiles are rated based on their mileage. This section of automobile are rated based on the function done by them.

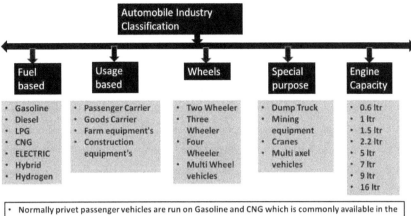

- Normally privet passenger vehicles are run on Gasoline and CNG which is commonly available in the urban areas
- Commercial vehicles , Buses , construction equipment's are run on Diesel , available across the country

Chart 6.3- Segment level classification of the automotive industry

Source –self Study /SIAM /ACMA

Automotive industry can also be classified considering verticals as fuel used, actual usage, wheels used for movement, purpose, engine capacity.

1.9. Segment level classification

1.9.1. Fuel based auto classification – based the economy and various factors like availability etc. the fuel is chosen. Hence this is one of the mail way of classifying the vehicles.

1.9.2. Usage based auto classification–It is also classified depending on what kind of the usage is carried by the vehicles. Based on the design, it could be used for passenger movement, goods movement, farm usage or construction usage.

1.9.3. Wheel based auto classification – Wheel based classification is also one of the popular way of classification. It depends on the wheels used to run the vehicles, normally bikes will have two wheels to run and Multi axel vehicles will have wheels some time more than 16 due to heavy weight.

1.9.4. Engine capacity auto classification- based on the usage and pick up desired, engines are fitted in the automobile. Normally passenger vehicles will have engines with the capacity of 1 liter. To 5 liter. Trucks will have 5 liters and above of the engine capacity.

There are various organisations across the world who represent automotive industry. In the chart of classification which was done based on the way it is done in India by SIAM and various other organisations which represents the component part. However there are many ways of classification. One must understand that the automotive industry is well developed in North America as it has developed its economic based around the automotive industry and hence the huge network across America was developed. It is interesting to note that North America region is bigger than the size of India. However due to low level of population the public transportation system isn't developed. This country more relied on the privet transportation like car. Also due to capitalist view of life it uses lots of good and services hence truck market has also seen growth.

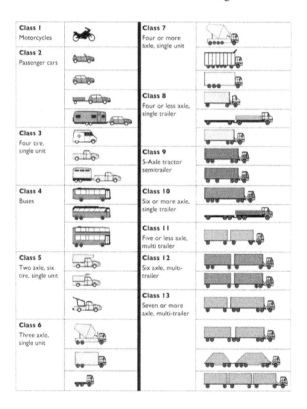

International way of classification of Auto vehicles is given below is self-explanatory.

Chart 6.4 – International Classification of the auto industry

Source – U.S. Department of Transportation Federal Highway Administration **https://highways.dot.gov**

International way of classification of automotive industry is based on the combination of usage and wheels used to run the vehicle.

1.10. INTERNATIONAL AUTOMOTIVE CLASSIFICATION

- **Class 1 – Motorcycles**

  Motorcycles are two wheeled automobiles used by urban class of the users. In the countries like India with lower of capacity of two wheelers. It is used for short distance transport for family or self like going to market and going to office and coming back. For countries like US, it is used more as life style vehicle for going on the long drive; in this case, it is a higher capacity engine.

- **Class 2 – Passenger Cars**

  This class is also well known in India as these vehicles have four wheels and normally act as privet vehicle to carry passenger. The engine capacity vary between 1-Literengines to 5-Liter engine. Used for inter-city and Intracity transport

- **Class 3 – Four Tire single unit**

  These type of vehicles are four tire vehicles but have multiple use,it could be ambulance, pick up van or caravan. They could carry passenger or goods

- **Class 4- Buses**

  The word says everything, its mass level passenger-carrying vehicle. Typically used for public transport system between the city or intercity.

- **Class 5- Two axel, six tire single unit**

  This 2-axel unit with about six tires is used to carry more load.The construction is very similar to the passenger car. As the load requirements are higher, it has two axels and has six tyres to support the load.

- **Class 6- Three-axel single unit**

  Vehicle having more than one axel has higher load requirements, these type vehicles are also used as cement mixers and load carriers

- **Class 7- Four or more axel single unit**

  Four axel offer more load carrying capacity and easy handling of the vehicle to some extent

- **Class 8-Four or less axel single trailer**

  This normally a single trailer with multi axel,

- **Class 9- Five-axel single trailer**

  Five axel trailers are the one with very high load carrying capacity. Multi axel gives driving comfort despite of the load

- **Class 10- six or more axel single trailer**

  This has more load carrying capacity than the five-axel trailer

- **Class 11- Five or less axel Multi trailer**

  The multi trailer function will carry more volume load with similar axel count. It is used for the material, which has more volume but less load as shown in the picture

- **Class 12- Six-axel Multi trailer**

  This carries further more load than the five-axelcarrier does

- **Class 13- Seven or more axel Multi trailer**

  Seven or more axel load carrier has the highest load carrying capacity than any of the denominations above.

1.11. Indian Automotive Industry at a Glance (2017)

Parameter	Value
Importance to Economy	
Turnover	73 USD B
Share in National GDP	6%
Share in Manufacturing GDP	22%
Share in Excise duty collection	21%
Employment	13.1 Million people
FDI inflow	25 USDB from 2010 to 2020
Global Ranking	
Three wheeler	1st Ranking
Two wheeler	2 nd Ranking
Commercial vehicles	5th Ranking
Passenger Cars	7th Ranking
Tractor	1 st Ranking

Chart 6.5 – Snapshot of the Indian auto industry

Source – IBEF.ORG/ SIAM 2017 update

Indian Automotive industry had a turnover of about 73 USD Billion with the contribution of 6% in the national GDP. It provided employment to 13.1 million people directly with highest FDI inflow of 25 USD Billion in 10 years from 2010 to 2020as per IBEF and SIAM

The above chart illustrates the value of the Indian car sector and the auto industry's relation to the Indian economy. The automobile sector contributes a great deal to the Indian economy, which is one of the Indian economy's main pillars. All the figures given above are self-explanatory. This sector explicitly or indirectly funds the Indian economy. The automotive industry is pushing the development of the steel industry, the plastic industry, the petroleum industry, the computer and chemical industry, etc. Each vehicle produced takes between 35,000 to 40,000 parts to be installed. All of these part suppliers use different raw materials to produce them, all of which are sub-assembled for the manufacture of the final car or another car in the automobile industry. This generates massive jobs around the regions wherever the auto hubs are open.

India is ranked No 1 for 3-wheeler production; India produces and exports three wheelers to most of the African nations and Asian nations. India has a strong lower middle class and upper-middle-class community, rendering it the world's second-largest 2W producer after China. It ranks fifth and seventh for commercial vehicles and passenger vehicles, respectively. With the automotive industry's overall turnover reaching USD 73 billion, it contributes more than 6% to the national GDP and 22% to the industrial GDP. This industry is also known to build massive job potential for the country like India, which is getting very large population density. In India, the automobile industry is spread through several clusters, the largest being Pune in Maharashtra, Manesar in Delhi, Chennai in the south, Rudrapur and Jamshedpur in the north, Sanand in Gujrat is the latest emerging center. The decentralization of this sector has addressed several problems faced by countries like India, which mostly have urbanization-related problems. Spread across India, the automotive sector contributes to job growth across the country. Let us research the output of the auto industry around the industries over the last 14 years. This analysis would allow us to consider the partnership between different sectors of the economy and the automotive market. It would also shed some light on the microeconomic variables influencing all sides of the research.

Year	Passenger Vehicles	Commercial Vehicles	Three Wheelers	Two Wheelers	Tractor Industry	Off road vehicles	Grand Total
2004	989560	550080	356223	5622741	179000	12000	7709604
2005	1209876	707406	374445	6529829	242000	15000	9078556
2006	1309300	782166	434423	7608697	254000	23000	10411586
2007	1545223	539989	556126	8436212	311000	38000	11426550
2008	1777583	484141	500660	8009292	304000	45500	11121176
2009	1838593	466393	497020	8395613	303000	40500	11541119
2010	2557411	721939	619194	10510536	383000	59700	14651580
2011	2982772	881144	799553	13349349	440331	72200	18525349
2012	3231058	832649	839748	15744156	545109	66400	21259120
2013	3087973	699035	830108	16883049	526912	55900	22082977
2014	3221419	698298	949019	18489311	634151	60700	24052898
2015	3465045	786692	934104	18830227	612994	68200	24697262
2016	3801670	810253	783721	19933739	570791	76000	25976174
2017	4010373	894551	1021911	23147057	691361	84500	29849753
CAGR	11%	4%	8%	11%	11%	16%	11%
Growth over 2016	5.49	10.40	30.39	16.12	21.12	11.18	14.91

Chart 6.6 – Production statistics of Indian Automotive Industry

Source – SIAM Database and Tractor industry association

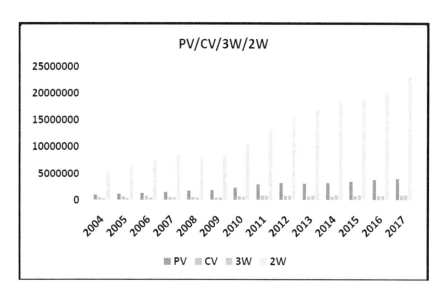

Chart 6.7 – Automotive production chart comparative production volumes for passenger vehicles, commercial vehicles, three wheelers and two wheelers

Source – SIAM Database

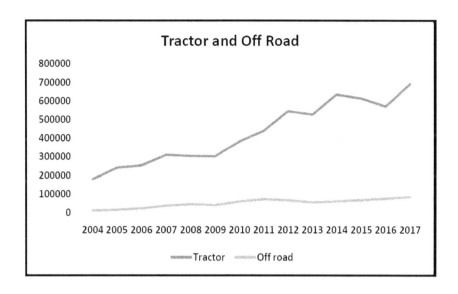

Chart 6.8 - comparative chart for tractor and off road vehicles production

Source – ET Auto, Mahindra and Mahindra

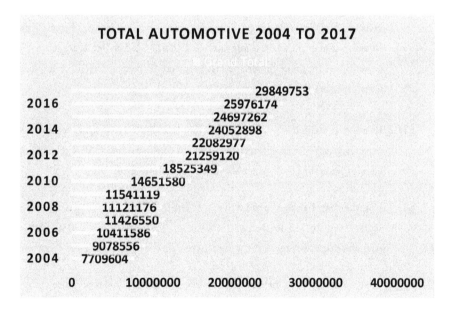

Chart No 6.9 – Total automotive production for all the six segments

Source – SIAM Database

The automotive industry in India is on the growth trajectory, if we study the 14 years period from 2004 to 2017, we will find that total automotive industry experienced growth of CAGR 11%, the sub segments of automotive industry experienced CAGR (compounded annual growth rate) per the number in bracket. Passenger vehicles (CAGR 11%), Commercial vehicles (CAGR 4%), Three wheelers (CAGR 8%), Two wheelers (CAGR 11%), Tractor Industry (CAGR 11%), &off road industry (CAGR 16%).Post study of various category of automotive industry in India one can understand that 2W segment is the largest contributor in terms of volumes exceeding 80% of the total industry volume

- The total automotive production chart on the left clearly indicate the trend of growth
- 2007 to 2009 , the industry witnessed recession due to various economic reasons
- 2011 onwards, industry witnessed huge surge in the segments like 2W, passenger vehicles and commercial vehicles.
- 2017 was the peak of economic activity and exports of the automotive industry to neighboring countries took off and gave the required push to the industry.

1.11.1. **Total auto Production** - In Jan-Dec 2017, the industry generated a total of 29849753 vehicle, including Passenger Vehicles, Industrial Vehicles, Three Wheelers, Two Wheelers and Quadricycles, compared to 25976174 in Jan-Dec 2016, recording 15 percent growth over the same timeframe last year and 11 percent CAGR (Compounded Annual Growth Rate) over 14 years from 2004.

1.11.2. **Passenger Vehicles production** -In Jan-Dec 2017, passenger vehicle manufacturing expanded by 5.49 percent over the same span last year and CAGR (Compounded Annual Growth Rate) rose by 11 percent over 14 years from 2004.

1.11.3. **Commercial Vehicles production** -In Jan-Dec 2017, the total Commercial Vehicles sector rose by 10.40 percent relative to the same period last year and CAGR (Compounded Average Growth Rate) improved by 4 percent across 14 years from 2004.

1.11.4. **Three Wheelers production** -In Jan-Dec 2017, sales of Three Wheelers rose by 30.39 percent over the same period last year. Eight percent CAGR (Compounded Average Growth Rate) estimated over 14 years from 2004.

1.11.5. Two Wheelers production -In Jan-Dec 2017, Two Wheelers sales rose by 16.12 percent over the same period last year and CAGR (Compounded Annual Growth Rate) improved by 11 percent over 14 years from 2004.

1.11.6. Tractor Industry production -In Jan-Dec 2017, revenue in the tractor industry increased by 21.12 percent over the same period last year, and CAGR (Compounded Annual Growth Rate) increased by 11 percent over 14 years from 2004.

1.11.7. Off-Road Vehicles production -In Jan-Dec 2017, off-road vehicle revenues grew 11.18 percent over the same period last year and CAGR (Compounded Average Growth Rate) increased by 16 percent over 14 years from 2004.

1.12. Automotive Industry status —The automobile sector receives the largest sales worldwide. Many industrialized economies such as the US, CHINA, Germany and even underdeveloped economies such as India depend heavily on the wealth generation and job generation of the automotive industry. As the Indian economy is predominantly labor-based, several car firms are now using it as an export center. A skilled worker is much more affordable in India relative to global norms. This pattern is genuinely welcoming and allows India to some degree to solve the trade gap and balance of payments problems with other countries. This business is still heavily based on the global economic cycles, and in the past, it has also experienced many difficulties. The interdependence of the car industry's economic cycles and the economic indices of most countries in the world was seen during the slowdown of 2003 and 2008. This business is often primarily an industry powered by expertise. This encourages the masses to acquire expertise. The Indian government, especially the Ministry of Heavy Industries, is closely monitoring the output of this industry, as this industry helps to increase exports largely. Even, to throw off the import bill for crude oil. The government also takes measures to incorporate electric cars and eco-friendly vehicles to minimize reliance on crude imports and boost the balance of payment-related problems, if this is achieved efficiently, funds used for imports of crude oil may be used for any other government of India welfare schemes.

The government is also taking a lot of action to incorporate electric cars as an alternative option for mobility. Many obstacles have met this, but innovative strategies are available to fix the problems confronting the battery-operated car. The usage of electrically driven 3W, which is largely used, has seen a rise in northern parts of India. Town municipalities are encouraging this as an option and several states are waving off the license costs on these hybrid cars.

1.13. Revolution in the mobility of vehicles in India

Significant reforms are underway in the public transit system in India. BRTS (Bus Rapid Transit Scheme) is designed around big cities with any area seeking to have its metro system. Significant improvements are happening in the rail and flight networks. Therefore, one would assume that there is no need for private transport vehicles to be available. However, if one considers profoundly that every vehicle not only satisfies the need for transportation but also functions as a socio-economic position in society, demand for new advanced cars to be imported and cars to be preserved will therefore still increase. Often, the pace of life requires quicker point-to-point connectivity between the towns, but it is not often easy to use public transport with every use since it will take a lot of time to exchange between public transports and thus it may be a challenge to sustain the speed of life. The modern automobile fulfills the need for quick mobility, there is no other alternative.

There is no justification required on the role that the automobile industry would play in India for the mass transportation of citizens, but it is not necessary to conclude that the usage of private transport and public transport would still be important after the use of railways and airports for the last mile of connectivity. Shared mobility is yet to take off in some cities in India, it is also getting a positive answer, but as pride, the aspiration of citizens to own a car would still stay at the peak. The Indian economy has developed at a pace of 8-9% in the past, which now offers the automotive industry a tremendous opportunity. If people's discretionary income is on the rise, their urge to buy a vehicle may increase. In the country, the ratio of vehicles to the Indian population is the lowest. It suggests that even when people's discretionary income increases, there is always a large opportunity for individuals to purchase automobiles. Therefore, the car sector should dream about happier days ahead. The growth of the automotive industry in India is catalyzed by growing demand for fast and stable mobility, affordability of the automobile, increased disposable income, better infrastructure in the nation.

1.14. Affordability of the passenger vehicle – Car affordability is a big problem in India. India's average bike price is INR 50000, which is also, interestingly, India's per capita revenue. Now the lowest priced car is nearly 3.5 lakhs all-inclusive. That is exactly around 6 times the Indian population's per capita income. In developing nations, where the lowest car rates are approx., the situation is precise. In western countries, this reality keeps automobile sales booming, as it is inexpensive. However, the entire globe is well recognized by Indian power to produce cars at the lowest price in the world and all the

major manufacturers in the world from the US / EU / China and Japan have agreed to have a manufacturing location in India, considering India as a major player in this region.

1.15. **Fuel Economy** - As far as fuel efficiency goes, both Indian companies and foreign players working out of India can follow the highest levels in the industry. India's typical bike offers an average of 60 KM/LITER, while the car provides approx. Fifteen KM/LITER. In the case of passenger cars, petrol accounts for more than 50 per cent of ownership costs. However, over the statistics of the last 30 years of all fuel costs vs. car purchases, it is often found that vehicle sales remain independent of the cost of fuel. It indicates a degree of fluctuation, but it is due to the shift of economic operation and not due to the change in fuel prices. The requirement for hours is gradually becoming the possession of the engine. As mentioned in the last paragraph, quick and efficient mobility powers the automobile industry, thereby being independent of the cost of gasoline. This demand to operate the car at the lowest cost is much greater in India because, in the form of oil, India imports 80% of the fuel requirement. India's payment balance would be impaired. It is easier for India to operate the display to decrease fuel usage.

1.16. **Alternate fuel usage** – India is largely dependent on imported crude oil, as mentioned above. The Government of India is making every attempt to decrease the use of crude-based oils, which would help to boost forex problems. The alternative fuels being used in India are as follows:

- CNG – Compressed Natural Gas
- LPG – Liquefied natural GAS
- Biodiesel
- Hybrid vehicles
- Electrically driven vehicles

India is now attempting to use hydrogen isolated from water for fuel use in automobile applications.

Both alternative fuel use has a long way to go since certain areas are not eligible for these substitute fuels, so use is restricted close to the supply of these fuels. India would have to make massive efforts to make the alternative fuel accessible to the people, due to its population unless the fuel is available at a wide place it will not be used as an alternate. CNG is still the most common substitute fuel because of its availability for the masses; the vehicle's operating cost is much smaller than the usage of gasoline. In India, the cost element drives several things. As the operating expense of CNG fuel is almost half that of oil, several public transport firms have started running a fleet of vehicles running on CNG fuel.

1.17. **High-end products** – In India, the automobile industry is primarily governed by cost and efficiency constraints. There is, however, a high-end or specialty segment where consumers are unique in their perception and preference for goods. Examples of such markets are various. Gearless scooters, luxury vehicles, hi-end race bikes, this demand is less than 1% of the overall value, but it is rising at a pace of 40 percent, which is a rather attractive growth rate, as maximum expenditure on OE goods and their accessories occur in this category.

1.18. **Rural Market demand** - India's rural market plays a major role as cities are saturated with populations and more expansion, so the automotive segment cannot stay away from it. Rural investment is growing as the rural economy stabilizes, relying mostly on India's monsoon cycles, which is very volatile, but farmers can have steady incomes due to the different water storage systems and their spending power is increasing. In large part, farmers require sturdy vehicles that can operate both urban and agricultural, and they will have to treat them in both market places. The players in the industry have recognized the value of the rural market and are introducing suitable goods for the rural market. In today's environment, tractor sales are still booming as management of the livestock is a challenge and it is no longer a feasible business scenario, but it is easier to retain the tractor. This will play a significant role in the future under-tapped sector.

1.19. **Automotive Market consolidation**- With all the favorable conditions of the industry and resources, India is well positioned to become the world leader in automotive development. To do so, the supply chain needs to be established, helping India to compete in the global market place. It is interesting to see how, over the last 20-30 years, India has made the required changes in that space. India's efforts to do so have been respected by many of the world's major companies and markets. Today, every major car brand needs to have a foothold in the Indian market, and everybody knows the future. It is obvious from the post-1983 FDI (Foreign Direct Investment) when world producers were opened up to the Indian sector. Since automotive manufacturing is considered device manufacturing and sub-systems are needed for automotive manufacturing, the Tier 1 industry in this area will continue to grow at a proportionate or even higher pace. As the Indian tier 1 suppliers will get the global ability to succeed in the market place, we can demand a greater pace. The growth of the demand for Automotive Tier 1 will be massive. There are collaboration opportunities in this area with the pace of development increasing, with recent examples of Maruti Suzuki joining VW in India, as VW is unable to do well in the Indian market. TATA linked hands with FIAT, VW and merged SKODA activities in the consolidation process. In such a dynamic condition, there are many options for firms to be bought over, or mergers and acquisitions will occur. It is very unlikely that this highly capital-intensive business would draw new entrants. The requisite investments in this room are huge, amounting to a few thousand crores.

1.20. **Indian Auto industry is at the junction** – In the past 70 years, the Indian Auto Industry has grown over the period. As fossil resources are being exhausted globally at a phenomenal pace, this field poses several obstacles today. India is 7-10 years behind the US and Europe in terms of technology, but if we equate fuel usage, India is at par with every other nation in the world. It is because the Indian reliance on crude oil is very high, and all the requisite attempts must be taken to minimize fuel consumption. India's mass population requires an only simple mode of travel; they require a 4-wheel car and basic driving facilities. Sales of the base edition of every vehicle are also very large relative to the completely loaded top-end version. The government, on the other side, will eventually determine the direction of mass transit, where the car sector will have a very significant part to play. Sharing mobility was born, and it became extremely common. In the future, this could have a positive or negative effect. Because you may drive the automobile of your choosing without necessarily buying it, the practice will shift and individuals will stop owning vehicles.

There are many challenges faced by the vehicle owner that may deter him from buying an automobile, such as parking room, maintenance costs, city traffic congestion, increasing work market instability. Work requiring ongoing place transition. It would be worth watching how the market responds to these challenges with these variables that play against purchasing a vehicle.

1.21. **Major Trends in the India Auto space –**

The following are some of the big developments seen in the Indian automobile industry.

1.21.1. **Increase in sales and distribution network** – Growing the supply and delivery network allows to hit distant regions to boost vehicle sales. Several occasions, when the requisite stuff is accessible close you. We prefer to purchase them. In reality, rural sales are picking up because of the scope of the distribution network.

1.21.2.   **New market exploration** – For sustainable development, continuous discovery of the new market place is key. The Indian OEM and Global OEMS have also perfected this art. Benchmarking examples such as Hyundai and Maruti Suzuki are increasingly used as an export center for India. Bajaj auto exports from India to all African and Asian countries as well. This intervention of all the auto majors tends to de-risk the uncertainty of the markets and bring the business the requisite stability.

1.21.3.   **Partnerships at OEM and Tier 1** – The increased demand for technological enhancements at Tier 1 manufacturers is a primary explanation for these forms of collaborations. The alliances are driven by mutual capital and cost-down constraints for OEMS. TATA takes care of the delivery of automobiles and after-sales operation for FIAT cars in India are the strongest examples. To build different kinds of cars, Volkswagen and Maruti agreed to join hands. OEM is now establishing a relationship by giving committed manufacturers a 100 percent stake of the venture. To provide greater supply chain synergies and new product growth, they tend to allow them the necessary room in the vendor parks.

1.21.4.   **Infotainment and electronics** – The vehicle's electronics and infotainment models are gaining prominence. Each new vehicle comes with multiple infotainment options, with GPS by design. Each new vehicle comes with different options. Haptic sensory choices are often common, and several personalization-related functions are common. A typical function is a reverse and front camera. A recent trend, which is becoming popular, is connected vehicles. Now the volume has risen to above 30 percent of the overall cost of output, the electronics content in the car was to the tune of 2-3 percent.

1.21.5.   **Social media platform importance** – Social networking outlets in the automotive marketing room are gaining in prominence. Social networking platforms such as Facebook, linked in, Twitter, what's app, numerous websites play a very significant role in shaping sentiment and popularizing fresh launch. To advertise their goods, even car firms utilize social networking platforms. Instead of print media, the young generation is seeing mostly on social media, thus the key to being present on the social media site.

1.21.6.   **Multi Brand Auto stations** – When purchasing the car buyers, it does not matter to travel to separate showrooms, but if it is far from the place of stay, it is hard to hit the service station when giving the car for operation. Therefore, the success of multi-brand service stations is gaining. These service stations are expected to have technical personnel who would have the expertise to do the service on most of the common vehicles. Because each vehicle has various systems to run, it often has different systems to manage.

1.21.7. **Financing Business developed by OEMS** – To get support for the cars they make, OEMS are changing numerous tactics. 99% of vehicle buyers in today's scenario buy automobiles with a lease or financing. Instead of offering the customer an initial discount, auto dealers now prefer to lower the interest rates on car loans several times and change the price that way. With own automotive finance, both carmakers are willing to be responsive to the demands of the consumer and shift with time. The versatility in delivering loans at cheaper interest rates to borrowers allows closing the sale on the spot.

1.21.8. **Used cars market** - In terms of running the vehicle, many new aspirants for the car can buy the car, although often the initial expense of buying the car is a challenge, so many people tend to deal in the secondary car sales market. This segment provides several alternatives to own huge luxury brands at cheaper rates, now the OEMS have already joined this area for a few days, providing many choices to own a vehicle at lower prices. In addition, the warranty is often issued for these cars by refurbishing the car engine and overall appearances, so that ownership costs are restricted.

1.21.9. **Genuine spare parts** – The marketing of authentic replacement parts is a strong pattern. It helps to improve the longevity of the vehicle with proper automotive maintenance. The car owner is therefore confident of the proper care and durability of the automobile by utilizing genuine replacement parts, too. The same tier one manufacturers that supply OEM parts for vehicle assembly hold some of their manufacturing to satisfy spares specifications.

1.21.10. **Light weighting and fuel efficiency** – This is the greatest pattern found in today's automobile sector. This pattern is very common in India because its reliance on crude oil is very strong and any fuel savings would result in forex savings. Even, with the latest pollution regulations, the weight of cars is so critical that it would end up saving large sums of money by growing the heavy metal content in the catalytic converters. The usage of lightweight and alloy metals helps to minimize weight in cars. Both car manufactures are mandated by the new standards to declare the vehicle mileage per liter of fuel in actual operating condition.

1.21.11. **Smaller Engines more mileage** –Many of the developments in the automobile sector in India are associated with the cost of ownership and initial purchasing prices. Smaller engines aid with greater mileage, but in terms of pickup, one has to compromise on the efficiency of the car at the same time. India has to strive harder to strike the correct mix between this and that. Every year, India sells around 4 million cars out of which 80 percent of automobiles have engine size from 1 liter to 1.5 liters. Lower car engine size offers better mileage, so it is used largely unlike the US, where 3 liters to 5-litre engines are more common. Cost affects much of India's purchasing decisions.

1.21.12. **Business cycles of Economy and Auto industry impact** – Economic cycles have a greater influence on the automotive industry's business cycles. Such periods describe the intake in the market place of different segments. The cash flow and mindset of the consumers shift a great deal owing to the economic cycles. The selling of the car sector goes on the highest during the high tides of the economic cycle and it is on the lowest side during the low tide. Because of these detrimental periods, the sectors mainly impacted are passenger vehicles and construction vehicle industries. Earlier, the frequency of economic cycles was 5-7 years, now the contraction and height of the economy are occurring quite regularly, as though many world economies have little space for more expansion. Any markets worldwide are saturated. The financial and vehicle sales periods are shown to be interdependent.

1.21.13. **Non-auto Business expansion** -Automotive tier 1 supplier aims to shield their company from economic business cycles by joining a non-automotive space. This sort of diversification would give them an advantage in the long term to thrive. The cost of doing business would be prevalent and the maintenance of business would increase. All of these firms are heading to the e-space to broaden their network and sell through the chaos. The white goods or appliances field maybe these non-auto rooms. It allows industries to minimize reliance on the car sector while holding the market base broader. Provided that their output scales are fine.

1.21.14. **Local sourcing and cost reduction** – Cost reduction is the key justification for all the OEMS who have invested in India through the FDI method to invest in India. India provides the world's lowest cost of skilled labor, so the cost of producing several components is substantially lower in India than in any other region. This is the primary explanation of why India is rapidly becoming the most desirable destination for low-cost component procurement for most MNC players. To keep them successful, the OEM is often needed to give the Tier 1 suppliers the required technology. Even then, it also helps in the long term. This has contributed to ACMA (Association of Manufacturers of Automobile Components) participants increasing faster in space than the OEMS.

1.21.15. **Foreign OEMs investing in India manufacturing** – Foreign OEMS also opened their operations in India, such as FIAT, VW Nissan and SAIC. This is done to take advantage of the low labor cost available in India, as stated early on, because of its strategic position and low available skilled labor, India is often viewed as an export manufacturing location. India's captive demand is still tremendous and India can sustain development momentum in vehicle sales through several recession cycles. This is the product of the Indian population's rising disposable income. In addition, the truth of existence is that the ratio of cars per 1,000 people is less than 40, but as economic growth rises, the scope to expand the car population is very strong.

1.21.16. **Multi plant locations for auto manufacturers** – Car transportation costs are very large, car manufacturing is often based on getting better supplies in the vicinity, and OEMS prefer to take advantage of the country's tax regimes, if any state offers tax incentives for a few years Auto majors tend to bring new plants in that field, it helps to take the tax advantage and also decrease the logistics cost as its very high in the population.

1.21.17. **Green Vehicle manufacturing and light weighting** – In the car sector, these words are mostly used for a few days. In-car production, every inch or every gram of content used must primarily conform to lightweight or green manufacturing. Manufacturers have begun to inquire regarding the state of products at the end of existence and what their influence on earth would be. To have minimum earth impact, any substance used in automobile production must conform to green manufacturing requirements. The total life of the car is deemed5 years, in which the customer changes the vehicle and wishes to go for a new vehicle. For this moment, it is important to dismiss the old one and it must not have any detrimental impact on the ecosystem. To reduce the engine load and to allow the car fuel effective, light weighting goes a long way. Various lightweight structures and high strength stainless steel have been utilized to render the car fuel effective for automotive manufactures. To lower the weight of the car, reduction of weight and development of green automobiles can assist with long sustenance in all human society. Various forms of innovative products used in automobile production provide numerous new market and job prospects for many companies involved in the automotive manufacturing phase.

1.21.18. **Differentiating customer experience** –Competition development has forced both OEM distribution, communications and after-service departments to plan for the differentiated consumer experience. From the purchasing process of the car, buyers at each stage must feel valuable before they intend to resell the vehicle again to buy a new vehicle. As he will later become a repeat client to the business, OEMS are trying to make any touchpoint to the customer as a delightful experience. It would assist with the client's long-term customer partnership. The client can also stay linked with the OEM in turn.

1.21.19. **Infotainment and Navigation** – Electronic devices in cars are the highest investment of any car producer. Earlier, the budget on electronics was around 10% of the vehicle's overall expense, now it is over 30% as a whole. Owing to the different electronic controls placed on contemporary vehicle systems, this has arisen; also, the infotainment and navigation systems allow a huge difference in the whole dynamics. With the shift in the speed of life and tons of travel undertaken by any human. Many drivers in the city wind up spending 3-4 hours in the car per day. It indicates that while 25% of the productive time is spent in the vehicle, certain parts of it would be more relaxed, entertaining and smoother. Excellent navigation devices and touch screen LED systems have made it easier to live in a vehicle.

1.21.20. **Improving the performance** - The automotive industry has now realized that major cities will have development limits, so they will have to switch to Tier 1 and Tier 2 cities for growth. Therefore, models explicitly for Tier 2 and Tier 3 cities are being created. They are now aggressively seeking alliances in these smaller cities to extend their distribution and support network. Significant development can only come from these cities in the future. Once the automobile industry focuses on the semi-urban and non-urban class of individuals, it can increase its efficiency and have better distribution and risk.

1.21.21. **Geographical presence and export Market** – The typical US and European economies are witnessing sluggish growth, so automobile industries are looking outside these countries for sustainability to continue the growth narrative. Many Indian firms are pursuing development in South Africa, the CIS and Russia for expansion. To boost expansion, India is also being established as a production hub for export. Indian farmers, currently based on Nepal, Sri Lanka and Bangladesh, are looking for development outside these countries. If the foundation for expansion is larger, the growth momentum will not be viable for car industries to proceed. The most ambitious undertaking, NATRIP-The National Automobile Testing and Research Infrastructure Project, has also been undertaken by the Government of India. This central and state government program, along with the support of the automotive industry, would help to establish the requisite testing facilities for the automotive industry to expand and develop new products appropriate for the new world order. This active involvement of government departments reflects the government's trust in the automobile market.

1.22. Key players and expansion plans.

- To extend its footprint in India, SAIC engines from China have taken over the GM facility in India, FIAT has extended into the current engine production line at the Ranjangaon facility.
- Mahindra has invested in the additional paint shop and production line in Chakan, Isuzu has opened its greenfield plant in Sri city AP Most of the automobile giants have opened a new plant in Gujrat to take advantage of government expenditure on automotive infrastructure. Cummins is investing heavily in the plant near Pune in Phaltan to expand to suit the rising population.
- Foton engines have gained large land of approx. 400 acres to open a Green Field facility to develop all automobile varieties in India

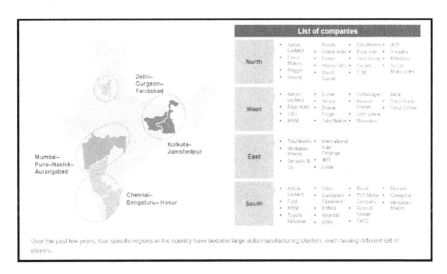

Chart 6.10 – Key players and spread of Auto Industry in India

Source – IBEF Auto industry update June 2020

Automotive industry in India is spread primarily in the states of Maharashtra, Karnataka, Tamilnadu, Delhi NCR, West Bengal and new area of Gujrat. The wide spread of the industry is helping in wide spread of employment generation also helping in balanced regional growth.

1.23. **Nationwide Industry footprint** - The automotive industry has a presence felt across the country, as seen in the above map. In the west part of India, followed by Delhi NCR and Tamilnadu, this industry and its Tier 1 suppliers are largely present. In the three states, as clearly seen in the photo, the industry has a substantial presence. Maharashtra, Delhi NCR, and Tamilnadu are these three states. In other regions, such as Jharkhand and Karnataka, it has some existence. Gujarat, where the government has built big infrastructure to suit the automobile industry, is the latest developing automotive center. Low cost, decent infrastructure, nearby Kandla seaport for exports, qualified labor supply and industry-friendly state policies have rendered this state a very desirable investment destination. To take advantage of the scenario, several existing corporations like TATA/Maruti/Honda have already set up their plants in the province.

1.24. **India investments** – Due to the lower labor cost of production in India, several automobile firms are investing in India. The output cost in India is approx. 20-25 percent less than the European average. This gives a tremendous competitive edge to the companies working in this space. Therefore, they have a well-defined plan for handling India's export center and holding its viability intact. Due to the volume of output, the cost of different raw materials is also reasonably economical in India.

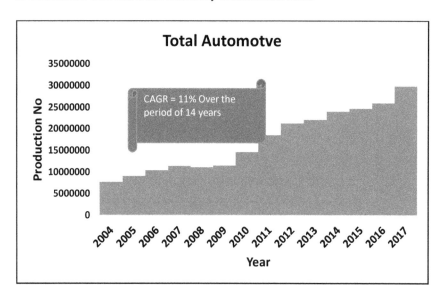

Chart 6.11 – consolidated growth of Auto industry from 2004 to 2017

Source – SIAM Database 2018

2007 and 2009 was the period during which, auto industry in India experienced a dip due to slow down in the economic activity, this is one of the indicator of linkage between the economy and auto industry.

Chapter 2 - Research methodology & Review of the literature.

Research methodology followed for this subject was unique in nature. Primary and secondary data was collected and correlation was established using various statistical techniques.

2.1. Introduction

- Automotive Industry in India consisting of Commercial vehicle, Passenger vehicle, three wheelers, two wheelers, Tractors and off road or construction vehicles. The industry is further classified by usage, fuel used, power and number of wheels used to drive the same. The global ranking of Indian automotive industry in terms of vehicles produced is first Rank for tractors and three wheelers, 2nd Rank for 2 wheelers, 5th Rank for commercial vehicles and 7th Rank for passenger vehicles. Each vehicle manufactures used 30000 to 40000 parts; hence, the effect of every single vehicle manufactured is multiplying on wealth generation and employment generation. From 2004 to 2017, the industry has grown 11% CAGR. Multi plant location has helped in geographical development and regional balance in industrial development and wide spread urbanization.

- This industry could be defined during the license Raj , and post liberalization era from 1991 onwards after the Manmohan Singh Government introduced the bill to open up the economy to FDI

- This industry is very promising in terms of employment generation & contribution to the Industrial growth

- This study will cover various aspects of this industry, various segments of the industry, their growth patterns and interdependency on the economic factors.

- Capital-intensive Industry, High Employment Generation- 2.5 crores population employed as per 2016 data by Automotive and Tier 1 industries.

- Size -73 Billion USD, 6 % Contribution to GDP, 22% share in manufacturing GDP. Generating direct employment to 13 million people. Automotive Industry is growing @ 5.9% CAGR since last 5 years.

2.2. Need of the Study

There is 3 fold need to do this study as follows

2.2.1. Population - As per the World Bank report 2017, India has second highest population growth in the world, In 1951 India had a population of 37.63 million with the

yearly growth of 1.61% year on year. In 1974, the population was 60.88 Million with the highest growth rate of 2.36%. In 2017, the population reached 133.87 million however, the growth rate decreased to 1.07%. Such a large population needs job for survival and wealth generation. It is understood based on various studies that automotive industry due to its cascading effect creates large amounts of jobs, which are key for massive population of India.\

2.2.2.   **Mobility needs for Atmanirbhar Bharat** – India imports 80 % of its crude requirement hence we need to spend huge amount of our FOREX reserves for the same. To have good balance between the imports and exports, India needs industries, which are capable of exports earning the required forex. Out of total usage of crude oil in India, it has only 18% of the domestic production, balance 82% is import. As per the data from petroleum ministry in 2017, India used around 198 MN Tons of crude oil.

2.2.3.   **Alternative Fuel** – As per drive from Government of India. There is a need to reduce dependency on fuel, 80% of the fuel imported is used for automotive applications. Hence the study will help focus on sectors with in automotive industry for usage of alternate fuel to some extent.

2.3.   Relevance & importance of Study

- Automobile is the one of the major factors for goods & people movement. It affects day-to-day life of every Indian citizen. Study of intercity & Intra city movement of goods & people will help us get more knowledge on this industry. There are six sub segments of the automotive industry as explained above; those will also be studied in detail.
- Geographical spread of this industry also helps in wide spread industrial growth and helps in balanced urban development

2.4.   Limitation of Study

- The Automotive industry study done is limited India demography any changes in the global level may impact the industry.
- Fuel cost increase beyond certain limits may impact the growth of industry.
- Economic factors may reduce the buying power of consumers and under such situations, the demand and supply situations may change.
- Heavy automation in the automotive industry may influence the job creation, which is highly unlikely in the country like India.

2.5. Objectives of Study

- To study the growth pattern of the automotive industry in India since 2004 to 2017.
- To understand the relation between the Economic Growth & Automotive industry growth pattern.
- To understand the challenges faced by this industry & provide suggestion to overcome the challenges.
- Compare the vision plan & study the challenges faced by the industry to meet vision plan.

2.6. Justification of Objectives

2.6.1. Period Justification 2004 to 2017 – The period taken for study is most recent period and during this time, the economy has taken two dips. This ups and down of the economy will likely give the real picture of the relationship with automotive industry.

2.6.2. Interdependency on the economy – As stated many times in this thesis, there is a strong interdependency of economic factors and automotive industry. Once we are able to understand the relationship, it becomes easy to influence the impacting factors and have the required effect.

2.6.3. Challenges – Once we are able to resolve and work around the challenges faced by this industry, one can focus well on the growth.

2.6.4. Vision plan – Government of India have worked out on the Vision plan for automotive industry in India called as AMP 2026 (Automotive mission plan 2026), the challenges faced and vision plan need to complement each other for fueling the growth.

2.7. Assumptions

- Government policies for automotive industry will remain attractive.
- No major change in the tax structure for automotive industry.
- Government will continue spend on infrastructure like previous trends.

2.8. Statement of the problem.

- **What are the factors responsible for growth of this industry?**

This study will help in getting more details on the Macro & micro factors responsible for the growth of automotive Industry in India. This industry is well organized in India similar to that of the global standards. There are known factors, which can largely influence this industry like Road infrastructure, economic growth, GDP, Industrial growth.

- **What are the challenges of this industry?**

  This study will also focus on the challenges faced during the period of study along with the problems, which may be faced in the future. Taking a complete view of the situation during the study, we will try to reach the logical resolution.

2.9. Statement of Hypothesis

- The growth of Automotive Industry is directly co- related with the economic growth of India- Ha
- The growth of Automotive Industry is directly not co- related with the economic growth of India - H0

2.10. Scope of study

Scope of this study is to understand the interdependency of various economic factors and their impact on automotive industry only. It may not be practical to take all the economic factors for study at a time. Hence, we have selected factors, which are key to the automotive industry like fuel prices, GDP, Population etc.

2.11. Universe and sample size

- Globally Automotive industry is highly organized and monthly /yearly manufacturing data per automotive manufacturer is easily available from authorized resources. In India SIAM (Society of Indian Automotive Manufacturers) and ACMA (Automotive Components manufacturers association of India) are the two representative bodies having 100% membership of all the manufacturers of this sector. They publish monthly data since last 15 years. The trend in share of business among the industry players is consistent for many years.

- The total Two-wheeler manufacturers are 12 , for Three-wheeler 7 manufacturers , passenger vehicle is manufactured by 15 players , Commercial vehicle have 10 manufacturers , farm equipment has 13 manufactures and last but not the least is construction equipment's are manufactured by 10 manufacturers

2.12. Justification of the sample size

- Total segments – There are total 6 segments in the automotive industry namely Two wheeler (2W) , Three wheeler (3W) , Passenger vehicles (PV) , Commercial vehicles (CV), Farm equipment's(Tractor) and Off road (construction equipment)

- First 4 segments namely 2W/3W/PC/CV contribute for more than 97% of the vehicles manufactured in India as per the production data of 2004 to 2017 the trend continues as per the study done (Pie chart presented in this chapter is indicative) , hence interviewers were selected from these 4 automotive manufacturing segments

- Top 7 manufacturers were identified from each of the segments using pareto analysis accounting for more than 85% of the individual segment production (Pareto analysis in shown in this chapter).

- Random sampling – Random sampling criteria was applied to select the respondents with min of 5 years of experience in the given field so as to have authenticity and weightage to the response.

- Out of 256 total sample universe size , 157 responded positively covering more than 61% of the sample size and 85% of vehicle population of entire segment total.

- In order to understand how each of the automotive company works. Let us understand the various department functional in each of the company. Below is the list of key departments who are custodian of the data required for our study

- Marketing Managers – Information related with Automotive market

- Sales Managers – Information related to yearly or monthly sales

- Product Managers – Information related to vehicle as product

- Segment Managers – Looking after typical segment of vehicles

List of All the automotive industry manufacturers as below , Out of all these manufacturers the major segments which contribute for 97% + production are 2W/3W/PV/CV . The farm equipment industry and construction equipment industry contributes very less. The data for 13 years from 2004 to 2017 was studied and same trend was found hence it made more sense to take interviews of people working in the top 4 segments 2W/3W/PV/CV.

Year	PV	CV	3W	2W	Tractor	Off road	Grand Total
2004	989560	550080	356223	5622741	179000	12000	7709604

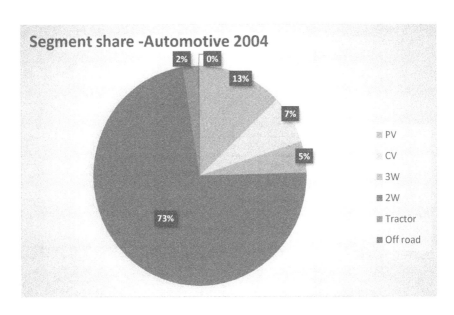

Chart 6.11-A- Automotive **industry segment share 2004**

Year	PV	CV	3W	2W	Tractor	Off road	Grand Total
2017	4010373	894551	1021911	23147057	691361	84500	29849753

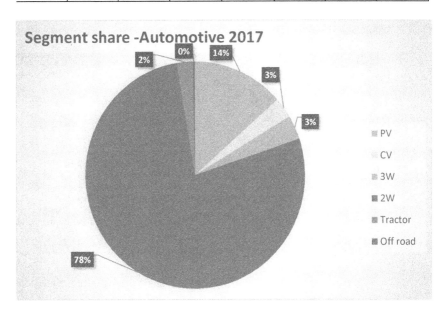

Chart 6.11-B - Automotive **industry segment share 2017**

Below is the list of all the manufacturers in the given segment. This data is available on public domain and all the manufacturers are members of authorized body of auto manufacturers called SIAM (Society of Indian automotive manufacturers)

Automotive sub segment	Total players
Two wheeler	12
Three wheeler	7
Passenger vehicle	15
Commercial vehicle	10
Farm equipment's	13
Construction equipment	10

PV-15 Manufacturers	CV - 10 Manufacturers	2W- 12 Manufacturers
Maruti Suzuki India Ltd	Tata Motors Ltd	Hero MotoCorp Ltd
Hyundai Motor India Ltd	Mahindra & Mahindra Ltd	Honda Motorcycle & Scooter
Mahindra & Mahindra Ltd	Ashok Leyland Ltd	Bajaj Auto Ltd
Renault India Pvt Ltd	VECVs - Eicher	TVS Motor Company Ltd
Tata Motors Ltd	Force Motors Ltd	India Yamaha Motor Pvt Ltd
Honda Cars India Ltd	SML Isuzu Ltd	Royal Enfield (Unit of Eicher Ltd)
Toyota Kirloskar Motor Pvt Ltd	Piaggio Vehicles Pvt Ltd	Suzuki Motorcycle India Pvt Ltd
Ford India Pvt Ltd	VECVs - Volvo	Mahindra Two Wheelers Ltd
Volkswagen India Pvt Ltd	AMW Motors Ltd	Piaggio Vehicles Pvt Ltd
Nissan Motor India Pvt Ltd	Isuzu Motors India Pvt Ltd	H-D Motor Company India Pvt Ltd
General Motors India Pvt Ltd		India Kawasaki MotorsPrivate Ltd
SkodaAuto India Pvt Ltd		Triumph Motorcycles (India) Pvt Ltd
FIAT INDIA AUTOMOBILES		
Force Motors Ltd		
Isuzu Motors India Pvt Ltd		

3W- 7 Manufacturers	Tractor-13 Manufacture	Off road (const)- 10 Manufacturers
Bajaj Auto Ltd	Mahindra	L&T Construction Equipment
Piaggio Vehicles Pvt Ltd	Sonalika	Volvo Construction Equipment India
Mahindra & Mahindra Ltd	TAFE	Hyundai Construction Equipment
Atul Auto Limited	Escorts	Mahindra Construction Equipments
TVS Motor Company Ltd	John Deere	Caterpillar
Scooters India Ltd	Eicher	Komatsu India Private Limite
Force Motots	CNH	ACE Construction Equipment
	Kubota	GAMZEN Private Limited
	V.S.T	Bull Machines Pvt Ltd
	Force	BEML LIMITED
	Captain	
	Indo Farm	
	Other	

Chart 6.11-C – Top manufacturers of automotive space

To further, justify the sample size. We have done pareto analysis for all the top 4 segments. The data for 10 years period was collected and average of the same was considered to identify top 7 players from the list based on their % market share.

Passenger vehicle Pareto

PV Manufacturers	2007 to 2017	Average 10 years	% share	Top 7
Maruti Suzuki India Ltd Total	13089044	1308904	40.71%	1
Hyundai Motor India Ltd Total	6482446	648245	20.16%	2
Tata Motors Ltd Total	2663661	266366	8.29%	3
Mahindra & Mahindra Ltd Total	2355941	235594	7.33%	4
Ford India Pvt Ltd Total	1382120	138212	4.30%	5
Toyota Kirloskar Motor Pvt Ltd Total	1340419	134042	4.17%	6
Honda Cars India Ltd Total	1180030	118003	3.67%	7
Nissan Motor India Pvt Ltd Total	1054472	105447	3.28%	
General Motors India Pvt Ltd Total	850740	85074	2.65%	
Volkswagen India Pvt Ltd Total	746704	74670	2.32%	
Renault India Pvt Ltd Total	485715	48572	1.51%	
SkodaAuto India Pvt Ltd Total	205683	20568	0.64%	
FIAT INDIA AUTOMOBILES	119681	11968	0.37%	
Force Motors Ltd Total	55141	5514	0.17%	
Hindustan Motors Ltd Total	45510	4551	0.14%	
BMW India Pvt Ltd Total	23154	2315	0.07%	
Mercedes-Benz India Pvt Ltd Total	21761	2176	0.07%	
FCA India Automobiles Pvt Ltd Total	18988	1899	0.06%	
Hindustan Motors Ltd Total	17869	1787	0.06%	
Isuzu Motors India Pvt Ltd Total	10889	1089	0.03%	
Ashok Leyland Ltd	1231	123	0.00%	
Tata-JLR* Total	420	42	0.00%	
Mahindra Electric Mobility Ltd Total	0	0	0.00%	
Grand Total	32150388	3215039	100.00%	

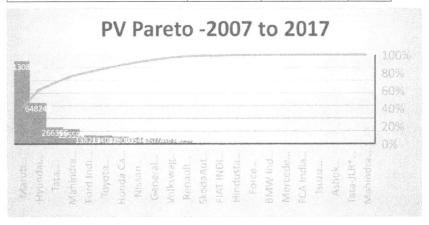

Chart 6.11-D – Passenger vehicle Pareto

The above Pareto done for passenger vehicle industry clearly indicate that top 7 manufacturers are Maruti Suzuki , Hyundai , Tata Motors , Mahindra , Ford , Toyota and Honda. Looking at the table its clear that top 7 manufacturers hold more than 88% market share in the passenger vehicle industry.

Commercial vehicles Pareto

Commercial Vehicles (CVs)	Total 2007 to 2017	Average for 10 years	% share	Top 7
Tata Motors Ltd Total	4071453	407145	26.21%	1
Mahindra & Mahindra Ltd** Total	1587110	158711	10.22%	2
Ashok Leyland Ltd Total	1133863	113386	7.30%	3
VECVs - Eicher Total	448720	44872	2.89%	4
Force Motors Ltd Total	202672	20267	1.30%	5
SML Isuzu Ltd Total	102576	10258	0.66%	6
Piaggio Vehicles Pvt Ltd Total	71573	7157	0.46%	7
AMW Motors Ltd Total	41554	4155	0.27%	
Swaraj Mazda Ltd Total	36938	3694	0.24%	
Mahindra Trucks and Buses Ltd Total	34693	3469	0.22%	
Maruti Suzuki India Ltd Total	10323	1032	0.07%	
VECVs - Volvo Total	9316	932	0.06%	
Tatra Vectra Motors Ltd Total	5315	532	0.03%	
Isuzu Motors India Pvt Ltd Total	4231	423	0.03%	
Volvo Buses India Pvt. Ltd. Total	3376	338	0.02%	
Hindustan Motors Ltd Total	1298	130	0.01%	
Mercedes-Benz India Pvt Ltd Total	968	97	0.01%	
Daimler India Commercial Vehicles	172	17	0.00%	
JBM Auto Ltd Total	7	1	0.00%	
Grand Total	15532647	1553265	100.00%	

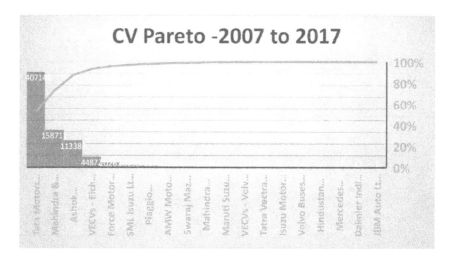

Chart 6.11-E – Commercial vehicle Pareto

The top 7 players in commercial vehicle industry hold more than 99% of the market share. They are namely Tata Motors ,Mahindra , Ashok Leyland , Volvo Eicher , Force motors , SML , and Piaggio. Single largest share holder for this segment in Tata Motors.

3W Pareto

3W Manufacturers	Total 2007 to 2017	Average for 10 years	% share	Top 7
Bajaj Auto Ltd Total	4812973	481297	56.67%	1
Piaggio Vehicles Pvt Ltd Total	2020261	202026	23.79%	2
Mahindra & Mahindra Ltd Total	609646	60965	7.18%	3
TVS Motor Company Ltd Total	587011	58701	6.91%	4
Atul Auto Limited Total	308732	30873	3.63%	5
Scooters India Ltd Total	129547	12955	1.53%	6
Force Motors Ltd Total	25498	2550	0.30%	7
Mahindra Electric Mobility Ltd Total	0	0	0.00%	
Total Three Wheelers	8493668	849367	100.00%	

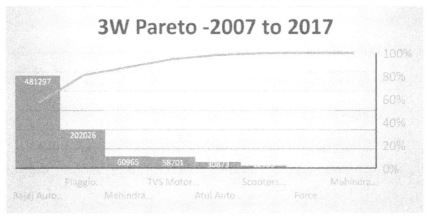

Chart 6.11-F – Three Wheeler vehicle Pareto

The top 7 Players hold more than 99% market share. They are namely Bajaj auto , Piaggio , Mahindra , TVS , Atul Auto , Scooters India and Force Motors

2W Pareto

2W Manufacturer	Total 2007 to 2017	Average for 10 years	% share	Top 7
Hero MotoCorp Ltd	56153208	5615321	34.07%	1
Bajaj Auto Ltd	33878733	3387873	20.55%	2
Honda Motorcycle & Scooter	32320883	3232088	19.61%	3
TVS Motor Company Ltd	22901039	2290104	13.89%	4
Hero MotoCorp Ltd	5830547	583055	3.54%	5
India Yamaha Motor Pvt Ltd	4367370	436737	2.65%	6
Royal Enfield (Unit of Eicher Ltd)	2741488	274149	1.66%	7
Suzuki Motorcycle India Pvt Ltd	2507082	250708	1.52%	
India Yamaha Motor Pvt Ltd	1634412	163441	0.99%	
Suzuki Motorcycle India Pvt Ltd	910507	91051	0.55%	
Mahindra Two Wheelers Ltd	1133501	113350	0.69%	
Piaggio Vehicles Pvt Ltd	228589	22859	0.14%	
Bajaj Auto Ltd	45258	4526	0.03%	
Kinetic Motor Company Ltd*	45116	4512	0.03%	
Electrotherm (India) Ltd	42508	4251	0.03%	
H-D Motor Company India Pvt Ltd	41178	4118	0.02%	
Majestic Auto Ltd	15717	1572	0.01%	
Kinetic Motor Company Ltd*	15090	1509	0.01%	
TVS Motor Company Ltd	8160	816	0.00%	
Kinetic Motor Company Ltd*	5746	575	0.00%	
India Kawasaki MotorsPrivate Ltd	2849	285	0.00%	
Triumph Motorcycles (India) Pvt Ltd	2549	255	0.00%	
LML Limited	0	0	0.00%	
UM Lohia Two Wheelers Pvt Ltd	0	0	0.00%	
Grand	164831530	16483153	100.00%	

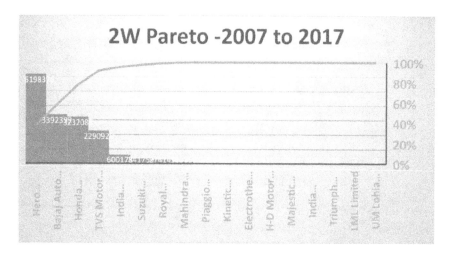

Chart 6.11-G – Two wheeler vehicle Pareto

Its clearly visible that top 7 , 2W manufacturers hold more than 95% market share of the 2W Industry, They are namely Hero Motocorp , Bajaj , Honda , TVS , Yamaha India , Suzuki , Royal Enfield.

Looking at the top 7 manufacturers from each of the key segments, we have covered more than 80% of the vehicles being manufactured in India. Every automotive company have a typical frontline and support structure to execute the business. The respondents selected were from the specific departments, which have the required information as below

Category	2W	3W	PV	CV	Total sample Universe	Sample size	% of sample universe
Marketing Managers	8	10	12	10	40	24	61.00
Sales managers	12	15	12	9	48	28	58.33
Product Managers	13	11	13	11	48	35	72.92
Segment Managers	7	8	8	9	32	19	59.38
Key account Managers	7	12	11	9	39	22	56.41
Production planning	4	8	6	6	24	14	58.33
Automotive Tier 1	6	7	7	5	25	15	60.00
Total	64	64	64	64	256	157	61.48

Out of the total sampling universe size of 256 as defined as above, 157 responded. The sample universe was 256 in our case; it means that 61.48% of the total sample size responded to the questionnaire. The respondents were selected very carefully based on their total industry experience in the field. As per the analysis given in the chapter 4 , 37% of the respondents had experience between 15-25years , 28% had experience more than 25 years, 27% had experience of 5-15 years.

2.13. Methods of data collection

- **Primary Data** – For every sub segment of automotive industry, top seven players were identified based on their production data, which represents 80% of the production volume for specific segment. Data collection was done using Video conferencing, Physical interviews, and requesting to fill in Google forms. Total of 157 people responded.

- **Secondary Data** – As this industry in organized one can have a very good quality of authentic data, which can be used, some of the well-known sources are SIAM journal, ACMA Journal s, various magazines, and CMIE reports. Government & Automotive association sites

2.14. Research Design

- The data from 2004 to 2017 for automotive production and various economic factors were gathered to understand the correlation from secondary resources. In addition, an exhaustive questionnaire was designed to collect the primary data and opinions from the industry experts of top five automotive companies from each of the sub segment.

- The result for primary data and secondary data were tabulated and compared using T test, trend analysis and Pearson correlation test to understand the strong point of co relation

2.15. Study of Literature

In order to gather the data required to do the research and get trends from the industry various forms of literatures were used which are in Book form, online form, internet sites, Old research from other universities are used as reference, details of the same as below.

2.15.1. Printed form of Books
Ramesh Singh /Indian Economy/2016 /Mc Graw Hill Education

The book published in 2016 by author Ramesh Singh gives overview of the India Economy. It touches upon each aspect of Indian economy and gives details on the way it functions. The book was published by McGraw Hill publication. This book nicely explains the definition National income, which is related to GDP of the country, methods of GDP calculation and its dependency of various factors. It also throws some light on industrial and agricultural sectors of the economy. One chapter is dedicated on the aspects related planning. The five-year planning cycles of India are replaced by NITI ayog. Author has also commented on the interdependency of infrastructure development and its positive impact on the economy as whole. He has given excellent examples of economic reforms, which Indian economy had to undergo since 1983 by PV Narsimharao government. The process of globalization is explained well. Cyclic nature of any business is well explained in the chapter7; it is applicable to the automotive industry also. We see a clear trend in the same as commercial vehicle industry faces this cycle every 3-4 years. During the early days of economic reforms, the cycle was coming after 6-7 years but in the modern times, this cycle is coming early in 3-4 years. The service sector has experienced major growth and highest employment generation in the past years, chapter 10 explains on the importance of service sector.

2.15.2.   C. Jeevanandam /Foreign Exchange/2009/ Sultan Chand & Sons

This book explains entire concept of foreign exchange system working and its impact on imports and exports. It explains on various foreign exchange contracts meanings in real world and mode of operation. The actual working of foreign exchange system is nicely explained in this book. This book also given idea on actual working of foreign exchange market and international financial system. The concepts explained in the book as well applicable to the automotive industry at large as India's fuel dependency is very high on imports. Many auto components are also. Working of forward rate contracts and raising funds thru the financial markets is discussed in length in part IV of the book

2.15.3. Francis Cherunilam/International Economics/2008/Tata McGraw Hill Publication

The author has made excellent effort in explaining the way international economic influences every one life. The balance of payment, interdependency of trade, demand supply concepts are explained well. There is a chapter on trade strategy explaining various international trade strategies in place. International business runs on various cooperation agreements between nations. All these regional co-operations and their impact on trade are explained well. Working of IMF is explained in lesson 22; trade policy of India is explained in chapter 31 along with the export sector problems explained well in chapter 34. Due to heavy import of crude oil and comparatively lesser exports, our economy is always a deficit economy. India's efforts on export promotion and reducing trade deficit are well appreciated.

2.15.4. Paul Samuelson and William Nordhaus /Economics /2010/ McGraw Hill, INC

One of the most referred book in the economics subjects for clearing all the concepts related to economics. The basic concepts of economics explained in part one as very useful for the understanding of this subject and applying the same to the subject of study. This chapter explains the problems of modern economy and concept of demand and supply. Applications of demand and supply are explained well in part 2. Production and business organizations are well-explained in part twochapter6; this becomes basis of manufacture or buy. Problems related to imperfect competition, monopoly, oligopoly are explained in chapter 10.Income distribution, regional developments and its impacts on economic development of the nation is discussed. The author has explain the relationship between business cycles and unemployment in chapter 29.

2.15.5. On line form of literature (.Pdf)

India - Motorcycle Manufacturing/Leading companies / REFERENCE CODE:MLIP1713-0005/Aug 2015 Published by Market line www.marketlineinfo.com

This is interesting report on the motorcycle industry in India. It given information in brief on their business profile, last 5 years financial results and production trends. It has covered all the major players in the same such as Bajaj auto Ltd, Hero moto cop, Honda motorcycle, and TVS group. It also discusses on their future strategies for growth

2.15.6. Indian Two-Wheeler Industry/ICRA research services /April 2016 , Published on www.ICRAINDIA.com

This report comments on the current state of the 2W industry, its leading players, short term and long term strategies. Sector outlook for the period. Has discussed in brief on leading 2W players like Bajaj,TVS, Honda and Royal Enfield Motors.

2.15.7. World Motorcycles/ Fredoniagroup /Oct 2016, Published on www.freedoniafocus.com

This published report given details about the total market of the motorcycles as per definition of North American motorcycle classifications. It takes in to account the Motorcycle manufacturers across the globe. Briefly touches upon their performance for last five years and their performance forecast for next 5 years. It also gives some focus on the various segments like Mopeds and scooters. And subsectors like electric driven vehicles in this space

2.15.8. Two and Three wheelers in India / June 2009, Published by Innovative Transport Solutions (I Trans) Pvt. Ltd., TBIU, IIT Delhi, New Delhi.

This report published online gives a complete picture on the two and three wheelers running on the Indian roads their population in the years 2005 to 2009. The driving forces behind this industry and the class of people buying these vehicles based on the need. It also discusses the advantages, which are provided by this class of transport against the use of any other public or privet transport. It also studies on the international trends for such class of vehicles. The study of 3W population on the city level helps in understanding the density of these vehicles in each city. Production trends for that period studied well in details in the report. It also put some efforts in study of traffic conditions and each category vehicle population for the period.

2.15.9. Report on Two wheeler industry /MotilalOswal / Dec 2013

The report available in the Pdf form gives complete visibility for the period of 2008 to 2013 on the scooters and motorcycle market in India. It gives reasons and strategies adapted by the 2W manufacturers during launch of each of the product. This gives the required reasons for fall of scooters market in early year of 2000, coming back of the segment of scooters in 2013 due to public demand. The balance sheet statement study, volumes study and strategy study has helped in overall understanding of the market for 2W in India.

2.15.10. Trans Steller journal publication Aug 2013 / FDI in 2W industry in India / Avinash Sharma / Institute of Business management – Mathura

This paper published in the journal helps in understanding the foreign direct investments (FDI) in India in the 2W manufacturing sector. Benefits of the FDI for the country's economy growth and regional growth. It also discusses the demerits of FDI in India. A brief classification of 2W industry and their types are explained.

2.15.11. The Indian Automotive industry /Evolving Dynamics / 2010 report / published by KPMG

This report gives some very different dynamics of Indian Automotive industry comparing the same with other markets of the world. It compares the same in terms of vehicles population per 1000 people. The report also discusses the dynamics on per capita income and car prices across the globe. It has also put some light on the age of population in India indicating the potential to grow for the automobile buyers. The report also tries to explain the milestones India achieved in last few years for developing green vehicles to support growing affordable needs of India. Despite of all the of all the odds in India, It still has need to grow for luxury vehicles.

2.15.12. Electric Two-Wheelers in India and Vietnam Market Analysis and Environmental Impacts/ Asian Development Bank / ISBN 978-971-561-873-1/ Publication 2009

This report published by Asian development Bank gives insights on the electrical 2W industry. Its understanding and comparison with the traditional 2W industry in terms of cost of ownership cost of buying and cost of maintenance. It compares the vehicle population of these vehicles in the city of Ahmedabad. Based on the report it is very clear that the electrical vehicles are much more beneficial to use that the traditional vehicles.

2.15.13. India Two Wheeler Sector/Credit Suisse/29 Aug 2012

This report given complete idea on India 2W exports to all across the world. Its competitive edge against Chinese and all other players in African market. Country level analysis for each market segment is part of this report for 2W industry. The Latin American market is most attractive among the lot. Analysis is done in terms of value and volume both.

2.15.14. CRISIL report on automotive industry / May 2013

This report covers the complete automotive industry, all the 4 segments of automotive industry that are twowheeler,threewheeler,four wheeler and Commercial vehicles. This report studies the last 5 years performance of the entire automotive industry. It studies the rise in state level income, which supports the growth of 2W industry. The increase in the spend on the rural road infrastructure gives the required boost for 2W sales. Also studies the export trends and comparison of sales to previous year's sales.

2.15.15. AUTO FUEL VISION AND POLICY 2025/ Government of India /May 2014

This is the comprehensive document, which covers the fuel standards for India. It compares the previous standards to these standards in terms of change. This report published by Government of India supports the new emission norms fuel where the Sulphur level is going down. It studies all the segments of automotive industry. Various fuel used as Gasoline, Diesel, CNG and LPG are covered well for the study. This fuel policy published is applicable until the year 2025; a new policy will cover the fuel space after this policy.

2.15.16. Automotive markets and opportunities /IBEF /2008

This report gives the complete overview of the automotive industry in India in 2008. It has also given details on automotive clusters formation in India and its impact on the regional development. The automotive cluster formation have helped in development spread across India. It has also studied the partnership formed in India from various MNC companies to do business in India. Looking at the economic factors and indicators, the growth potential of the industry can be projected.

2.15.17. Eicher investor's presentations /Feb 2016

This presentation prepared for the investors of Eicher motors gives details on commercial vehicles. Eicher investor's presentation gives details on the various products manufactured by company like trucks,buses, Bikes and off road vehicles in the collaboration with Polaris.

2.15.18. Annual reports of SIAM (from 1999 to 2019)

Every year The Society of Indian Automotive manufacturers do publish yearly report for the performance of automotive industry in India for the previous year. All these 20 reports published give complete idea on the sector level performance every year along with exports of the vehicles. It represents the automotive industry on various problems faced by the industry. These reports gives complete information on the performance, statistics and issues related to all segments of automotive industry in India.

2.15.19. State wise annual tractor sale report / Tractors manufacturers association /2017

Tractors manufacturers association in New Delhi have published the data on the tractor manufacturing in the country from FY 2000 to FY 2016. This has helped in understanding the overall growth of Tractor industry in India, which is part of the automotive industry in India

2.15.20. Escorts investor presentation /Nov 2017

The investor presentation of Escorts group gives compete idea on growth of tractor industry in India for last 10 years , it also gives idea on the agricultural reforms in India , the level of mechanization in India for the farm equipment's. As Escorts is also construction machinery manufacturer, it gives the idea on volumes and growth of construction industry in India.

2.15.21. Indian Passenger Vehicle Industry/ NMIMS JOURNAL OF ECONOMICS AND PUBLIC POLICY Volume II • Issue 1 • April 2017/ Author - KARUNAKAR B.

This research report gives idea on the Passenger vehicle classification in the Indian automotive industry. Classification in done in terms of the length of the vehicles and type of vehicle. It has also doe pareto analysis to identify the top fine manufacturer in each of the segment for further studies. Within the passenger vehicle industries it studies, further in sub segments like hatch back, SUV and sedan.

2.15.22. World Diesel Engines /Freedonia report /April 2014

This report published online by Freedonia helps in understand the trends in Diesel engines across the globe. One may want to understand that 100% trucks, Buses and SUV in India run the diesel fuel; even the tractors are run on the diesel engines. Our study of automotive industry of India is largely dependent on these sub segments and hence the inputs from this report are valuable for the study.

2.15.23. Construction equipment's /IBEF /Jan 2017 / www.ibef.org

This report on the construction equipment industry in India gives understanding from 2007 to 2016. It also studies on the interdependency of the infrastructure spend by government and its impact on sales of the construction equipment's. With clarity on growth, drives for this industry once can make out on pivotal points for further strategy for this industry. It has also studied on the sub segment of this industry based on applications. Major players in the segments are identified with their market share for further studies. Government spend on the infrastructure projects as a share of GDP is well explained in the report.

2.15.24. Global commercial vehicle market outlook /Nov 2014 / Power systems research

This report gives the performance of the global commercial vehicle industry since 2004 to 2013 and the future forecast for this industry. It has also put some light on the truck market dynamics by gross weight. It also gives the dynamics on various engine manufacturers across the globe and their market share and leadership data. It has also given some inputs based on region across the world. It gives the required detail on the engines manufactured by Indian manufacturer like VECV, Ashok Leyland and TATA Cummins for commercial vehicles market.

2.15.25. Indian auto component industry performance review FY 18/ ACMA report /www.acma.in

This report gives entire insight of the Indian automotive component industry from year 2012 to 2018. The report has complete information on the imports, exports from all countries of this industry. ACMA is authorized body of Indian Auto components manufacturers Association recognized by Government of India. This report also gives some insights on auto component level understanding of the matter. It also given information on India Automotive industry.

2.15.26. Automotive Mission plan 2026/ AMP 2026 /Gov. of India.

This report is published by Government of India considering the growth potential of the automotive industry. Government sees this industry as growth driven industry and has max potential to generate employment. It gives details on various schemes launched for automotive industry. Clearly indicating the vision government has for this industry moving forward in next 10 years from 2016. It also covers the aspect of developing alternate fuel technologies to address the fuel needs of India, also to reduce the fuel dependency on crude oil and minimize forex impact.

2.15.27. Role of Automobile Industry in Employment Generation in India: An Analysis of TATA Motors and Mahindra & Mahindra/NEW MAN INTERNATIONAL JOURNAL OF MULTIDISCIPLINARY STUDIES (ISSN: 2348-1390)/ Santosh Kumar Maurya UGC- NET/JRF Research Scholar, Department of Management Studies Nehru Gram Bharati University, Allahabad.

This journal touches the aspect of employment generation by TATA Motor and Mahindra and Mahindra

2.15.28. Automobiles: The economic outlook and employment situation/ PWC report /August 2013.

This online-published report gives complete outlook of the employment generation and importance of automotive industry for doing the same across regions of the world. It gives details of automotive industry contribution to the global economy as a whole.

Chapter 3 - Profile of Indian Auto Industry

3.1. Asia Motor Works (AMW) –

Asia Motor Works is one of the leading manufacturers of commercial vehicles located in Bhuj, Gujrat District, India. They produce HCV for India's expanding economy (heavy commercial vehicles). Their area of practice is Tipper and building machinery. They were formerly known as Asia Motor Works, and now they are known as AMW Ltd. The AMW product selection includes the whole HCV segment applications, beginning with long-haul shipping, application of the petroleum industry, applications of the building industry and applications of General Freight. For defense uses, the development facilities of AMW are distributed across 2 million sq. In Gujrat state, they invested in approx. Rest 5000 Crores on production lines at Bhuj. AMW manufactures tippers, trailers and total assembly of the body.

AMW exports vehicles from the Gujarat facility to Bangladesh, Nepal, Bhutan and Myanmar. They are a licensed business under TS 16949. In the past, they have won many awards from reputed organizations. In the test facility at AMW, every vehicle produced here is tested. They have a state of the art paint shop and assembly lines for the body store. They have a total of eight assembly facilities, including one in the UAE, another JV with Nissan in Japan to produce LCV, as well as a JV with John Deere to make construction machinery. They are one of India's fastest rising companies.

3.2. Atul Auto Ltd (AAL) -

Atul Auto Ltd is India's leading 3W manufacturer headquartered in Rajkot, with a wide product portfolio of 45 models in the 3W segment. It has both good carrier and cargo carrier models and is one of India's fastest Three-Wheeler manufactures. It has brands that are famous on the market, including Shakti, Smart, Gem and Gemini. Items of different payload capacities from 350 to 500 Kgs have been introduced. With local R&D, it has created the commodity. The automobile line that comprises the chassis shop, the paint shop and the production line has been finished. It continues to boost organizational success through creativity and enhancements at the local level. It has a total production capacity of 48,000 units, and 60,000 units in Ahmedabad are being installed with additional capacity. In 2017, Atul Auto had a revenue of 477 crores and a net profit of 37.32 crores.

3.3. Bajaj Auto Ltd -

Bajaj Auto Ltd, with its headquarters in Pune, is the world's largest 2W maker and the third largest motorcycle manufacturer in India. In 1945, it was created. Bajaj Auto is India's biggest exporter of 2W and 3W wheelers. It has factories in Aurangabad and Chakan. To produce state-of-the-art goods, the company has invested in R&D with the latest equipment at its Akurdi Pune site. In FY 2018, Bajaj auto reached the top range of INR 24700 crores, which is the highest in history for the firm. Through fresh releases to Malesia and the Philippines, business shipments rose to 1.39 million motorcycles. Bajaj also offered around 3.69 lakhs of strong 3WH on the domestic market at all times. Benefit after-tax saw a rise to Rs 4068 Crores of 6.3 per cent. In the Indian market, the business has already released a tiny 4W version named CUTE, which could substitute the comparatively unsafe Common Car, which is accessible by design. It has also planned to join the market of scooters that they left a few years earlier, seeing the poor demand in the scooter segment.

3.4. BMW –

BMW is an MNC based in the EU that has built a footprint in India. The group mostly operates three brands: BMW, Rolls Royse and Micro. All three labels are renowned for their luxury and durability. This business is also recognized for its developments in the introduction of electric vehicles and the EV space for new models. Activities in India include the manufacture of luxury motorcycles and financial services. The BMW group's overall expenditure in India is approx. 4900 crores. It has its headquarters in Gurgaon, a processing facility in Chennai, and a warehousing center in Mumbai. It also has a Gurgaon training facility. At its Chennai works, India subsidiary of BMW manufactures eight versions of the BMW I Series BMW 3 Series Grand Turismo. About the BMW 3 Series. The BMW 5, the BMW XI, the BMW X3, the BMW 7 and the BMW X5 Series.

Vehicle financing, insurance finance and commercial finance were dealt with by BMW financial services. It also has an IPO foreign procurement office located in India, which leverages the power of India's product producers and allows the components accessible to BMW internationally at competitive rates.

3.5. Daimler India commercial vehicles (DICV) – DAIMLER

The 100 per cent affiliate of Daimler AG Germany is Daimler India. That, in passenger cars, is the world champion. The company has a separate brand name Bharat Benz for India. It also makes buses for the Indian market and chassis for sale to other nations. It has a state of the art Greenfield facility near Chennai at Oragadam. It has already contributed approx. INR 6000 crores in the overall facility to build India's manufacturing base. It manufactures cars, spares and engines for all three brands, Mercedes Benz, Bharat Benz and FUSO, under one roof. It has a portion of the retailer and an in-house R&D center to promote the entire growth and distribution of the commodity. Also in India in 2018, the business has already accomplished its split.

3.6. Fiat Chrysler Automobiles (FCA) -

FCA is the world's seventh-largest car producer. It manufactures and sells automobiles and lights commercial vehicles around the globe, including India. For cars like Abarth, Alfa Romeo, Chrysler, Dodge, Fiat, Jeep, Lancia, Ram, FCA holds a number of the most expensive products. It is also present in the Car Part Manufacturing field on behalf of Magneti Marelli and Teksid. It is portrayed in the manufacturing sector by Comau Brand and in the after-sales service brand by Mopar. It is manufactured in 40 countries and distributed in more than 150 countries. All the labels are produced in India at the FIAT plant in Ranjangaon. It has already contributed approx. 280 M USD at the factory.

3.7. Force Motors Ltd -

Force Motors is a leader in the auto industry in India. Mr. Abhay Firodia, interested in the manufacture of LCV, recreational vehicles and engines, introduced it. It was classified previously as Bajaj Tempo Ltd. This business has numerous well-known brands such as matador, Minidor, traveller, Trax, etc. that are common in the Indian automotive industry. They are also interested in the manufacture of tractors. Force engines have technological ties to the ZF community, Daimler, MAN and Bosch. In the Indian car sector, this keeps them updated on the technology front. Business revenue for the 2018 FY was listed as

365210 lakhs with PAT at 14718 lakhs registered. Force motors deliver 3800 units each month, which also involves small commercial and utility vehicles, all added together. The organization faces some headwinds at the center of lead times for the production of new goods and the marketplace acceptability of these items.

3.8. <u>Ford Motors Pvt. Ltd -</u>

Ford Motors, the world's leader in US MNC car production, has invested USD 2 trillion so far in India in the Chennai integrated manufacturing facility, led by Sanand in Gujrat. In 1995, it joined the Indian market. Ford has a production potential of 610000 generators and 440000 automobiles placed together by both factories. Ford has branches in Chennai, Coimbatore and Sanand. Ford's overall workforce strength is approx. 11000. It clocked the turnover of the 22,000 crores goods generated by Ford are the customers' safest and well welcomed.

3.9. <u>Harley Davidson India -</u>

Harley, well recognized for its niche design and market image, is the famous adventure bike from the US. In 2009, it entered India as a wholly owned subsidiary, the first dealership was named in North and the production line began in Bawal Rajasthan in 2011. Both Harley Davidson distributors are the company's primary distributors and, as per the global policy of corporations, do not negotiate with any other 2W brand. Approx. Sale. 150 units of all the bikes placed together in India, which is fitting for the price tag it bears every bike from two lakhs onwards. The bikes also have a higher CC range of up to 2000 cc and more than 350. The biking enthusiast usually uses them for adventure purposes. They recently confirmed exit from India's manufacturing plant in 2020.

3.10. <u>Hero MotoCorp Ltd -</u>

Hero moto corp. Ltd is the biggest India-based 2W producer in the country. It was formerly referred to as Hero Honda Motors Ltd when it had a JV with Japanese Honda motorcycles. This firm was established after Honda separated from Hero. It attained the status as the world's largest 2W producer in 2001 and, since then, it has held this commendable position in the world. It operates from four production plants, namely Gurgaon, Dharuhera in the state of Haryana, Haridwar, and the fourth plant in Neemrana in Rajasthan. Jaipur, Rajasthan, has a state-of-the-art R&D hub. It has a distribution plant in Columbia as well. From 2007 to 2018, Hero moto corps' revenue rose from 37 lakh units to 75 lakh units. The turnover clocked 33398 crores from 12565 crores as well. From 1282 crores, PAT rose to 3697 crores. Their products are well received and admired by customers as well.

3.11. <u>Hindustan Motors Limited (HM)</u> -

In 1942, Mr. BM Birla founded Hindustan Motors at Okha in Gujrat, which then began with another plant in Kolkata in 1948, from which it ran for a long time. Due to numerous problems, this brand was sold to Peugeot in 2014; all of HM's main products were made from this factory, such as Ambassador, Contessa, etc. In Kolkata, the business is not operating anymore. The organization has been reliant on numerous government initiatives and their funding for the procurement of automobiles since its creation. After the growth of Maruti Suzuki, it was never managed as a competitive enterprise and could not withstand the market, so the Chennai plant assemblies of Mitsubishi and Isuzu engines collapsed.

3.12. <u>Honda Cars India Ltd., (HCIL)</u> -

Honda, because of its consistency and high product quality standards, is the most respected company in the world. In 1997, Honda became part of India. It has plants in 2 locations in India, one in UP in greater Noida and the other in Rajasthan in Tapukara. The production capability of both sites is 240000 units each year. In India, the company produces the most common models: CRV, City, Jazz, Brio, Amaze, etc. The ideal combination between fuel economy and engine strength is internationally recognized by Honda. Honda has created the world's first hydrogen fuel cell vehicle that only releases water vapor. It clocked INR 17000 crores topline, and in 2017, the breakeven was reached.

3.13. <u>Honda Motorcycle & Scooter India Pvt. Ltd. (HMSI)-</u>

The Honda motorcycle and scooter is a 100% owned subsidiary of the Japanese automotive company Honda. As far as volumes of 2W are concerned, HMSI is the number 2 company in India. It currently has 23 million consumers in India, with India holding a 26 per cent market share. It is the number 1 producer of scooters in India with the most famous Honda Activa model. It has a capacity of 16-lac 2W Manesar plant, 12 lakhs at Tapukara plant and a new plant recently established in Narsapura in Karnataka has an installed capacity of 18 lakhs 2W per year. It has more than 4500 outlets for the selling of its products. Honda is actively interested in India's healthy driving awareness activities and has invested in training schools to do the same. In the financial year ending in 2018, its gross sales surpassed INR 26800 crores.

3.14. <u>Hyundai Motor India Limited (HMIL)</u> -

Hyundai Motor India Limited (HMIL) is Hyundai Motor Corporation HMC-wholly Korea's owned subsidiary. After Maruti Suzuki, it is the second-largest automobile maker in India. It is also the biggest Indian exporter of vehicles. It treats India as the platform for all the countries in Europe and Africa to export their vehicles. The advantages of innovation in the best industrial methods in India and the potential to export from India can be leveraged by Hyundai. It has a state-of-the-art development facility in Chennai. For passenger vehicles, it was the biggest exporter from India, exporting from India to more than 85 countries. It has a global R&D hub in Hyderabad and can provide its customers in India with cutting-edge technical expertise. The topline of INR 36000 crores from Indian activities was achieved in the financial year ended in March 2018.

3.15. <u>India Kawasaki Motors Pvt. Ltd (IKM)</u> - **Kawasaki**

India In 2010, Kawasaki Motors Pvt Ltd formed its wholly owned subsidiary of Kawasaki Heavy Industries Japan in India. Its Indian headquarters are located in Pune. It is mainly involved in the manufacture of CKD motorcycles from its manufacturing site in Pune. In March 2017, their manufacturing plant in Pune was built. From its Chakan farm, IKM produces all versions of the Ninja variant. With 30 engineers working on creating new motorcycles, it also has an R&D centre built at the same plant.

3.16. Yamaha Motor (IYM) -

India Yamaha Motors (IYM) is a wholly owned subsidiary of the Japanese Yamaha Motor Company, which produces motorcycles and scooters in India. It established a JV in India for motorcycle manufacturing in 1985 and became a wholly owned subsidiary of Japan's Yamaha motor company in 2001. In India, IYM has three manufacturing facilities, namely in Surajpur (Uttar Pradesh), Faridabad (Haryana) and Kanchipuram (Tamil Nadu). It caters to domestic and overseas Indian markets. With integrated sales and marketing operations, it has state of the art R&D in India. In the financial year ended in 2018, it produced over 8 lakhs of 2W.

3.17. Isuzu Motors Limited -

Isuzu Motors Ltd is a Japan-based MNC engaged in the production of automotive pick-up derivatives. It is active throughout the world in light, medium and heavy vehicle manufacturing. In more than 25 countries, it has manufacturing operations and sells vehicles in more than 100 countries worldwide. More than six lakh units are produced all over the globe. Isuzu engines India Privet Ltd started operations as a wholly owned subsidiary in India in Chennai, India. It has a contract manufacturing agreement with Hindustan Chennai engines to manufacturing all of India's top leading models. In 107 acres, it stared at its new state of the art facility India at Sri City in Andhra Pradesh. At that facility, its leading models D max and MU Pick up are currently being manufactured. To support new products for India and also for exports, it plans to use this facility. Its products are premium SUV ranges, priced at over 25 lakhs. They are selling approx. More than 6000 vehicles in India also export vehicles to Nepal and Bhutan, which are mountain terrine countries, per year.

3.18. JCBL Limited -

JCBL was established in 1989 as a high-quality bus bodybuilder based in northern India. It builds buses and load carriers based on the leading manufacturers of automotive mobile chassis. It has ties with TATA, Mahindra, SML Isuzu, etc. to create bus bodies based on their manufactured commercial vehicles. The customised changes have been made following customer requirements in the design over the last 25 years. It also has links with state transport companies as well. It rolls out 5,000 buses per year from the plant on Delhi Chandigarh Highway, based out of Lalru. It has invested in R&D to develop newer concepts in the construction of buses and load body space. At its factory in the North, it also makes armored vehicles.

3.19. Mahindra & Mahindra Ltd. (M&M) -

Mahindra and Mahindra Ltd is the leading players in the off-road and SUV sectors. It is also a world leader in tractors and one of India's oldest players in the tractor segment. There are many plants in India, namely Kandivali, Nasik, Chakan, Rudrapur, which has a research and development centre in Chennai's Mahindra Research Valley. It develops all kinds of new vehicles from the Chennai site. With Ford from the US and SsangYong from Korea, the JV has recently been formed for the SUV segment and to manufacture the brands in India. In commercial vehicles and the 2W segment, it is also present. The Mahindra Group also manufactures yachts for hi-end clients in Mumbai. XUV 5OO, XUV 3OO, TUV, Xylo, Scorpio, Bolero, in the pickup segment it launched Jeeto and Maximo, are also present in 3W space with the brand Alpha, other well-known brands of Mahindra. The company also exports worldwide and has an active presence in South East Asia, SAARC countries, Latin America and Africa. It has a production capacity of 0.75 M vehicles in total. The Mahindra group is a $20 billion group overall and is growing at a rapid pace. They fabricate approx. All types put together 4.5 lakhs of vehicles per year.

3.20. Maruti Suzuki India Limited (MSIL) -

Maruti Suzuki India Ltd (MSIL) is India's leading producer of automobiles in the passenger car sector with a market share of approx. 50 per cent of the Indian passenger car segment produces nearly 4 million passenger cars each year, of which approximately 4 million are manufactured annually. Maruti Suzuki manufactures 2 million cars. It is a JV company for the Indian auto industry between the Suzuki motor company in Japan and the Government of India to produce the most affordable cars. MSIL's post-entry into Indian auto space vehicles became affordable for the public. The date today is approx. For every car user, 20 car models are user-friendly with 150 + variants to make.

Alto, Wagon R, Ertiga, Baleno, Ciaz, S cross, Gypsy etc. are some of the most common models. It has also recently entered the pick-up segment. The Green Initiative is supported by MSIL and most of its variants are available in CNG as an alternative fuel, which is

India's most affordable fuel. It has 2 production facilities in the state of Haryana, namely Manesar and Gurgaon. In the new Sanand automotive hub, the latest production facility is being installed. In Rohtak, there is a state of the art R&D centre. MSIL also exports cars from India to Latin American and African countries and from India to Europe.

Mercedes-Benz

3.21. <u>Mercedes-Benz India Pvt. Ltd (MBIL) -</u>

In 1994, MBIL was set up in India. It has a corporate office and a plant in the Maharashtra industrial area of Chakan. It is a wholly-owned subsidiary of the German Daimler Group. MBIL produces all passenger cars and buses from their Chakan facility and all commercial vehicles are manufactured under the company name DICV (Daimler India Commercial Vehicles) at the state-of-the-art Greenfield facility in Chennai. They have already invested 4,000 crores + in the manufacturing facility in India. The Maybach S 500, S-Class, E-Class, C-Class, CLA and GLA sedans are manufactured by MBIL. GLE and the SUVs of the GL-Class at their Chakan plant. They have 81 outlets for sale throughout India. MBIL has sold approx. 15000 units in FY 2018, with a turnover of approximately 6000 crores.

3.22. <u>Nissan Motor India Pvt. Ltd -</u>

The wholly-owned company of Nissan Motors Japan is Nissan Motor India. It began working in India in 2005 and reached an arrangement with the Tamilnadu government. Together with its global partner Renault, the JV group began the manufacture of numerous passenger car automobiles. Knowing the value for money approach that works in India, the manufacture of the most inexpensive vehicles in India began.

It has some of India's most famous and inexpensive brands, including Micra, Go, Kicks, etc. All vehicles bring together 2 lakh units a year from its Chennai factory.

PIAGGIO

3.23. <u>Piaggio Vehicles Private Limited (PVPI) -</u>

It is 30% held by the Italian subsidiary of Piaggio Automobiles. It has a state of the art development facility at MIDC Baramati, near Pune. Scooters such as Vespa and Aprilia are made. In 1998, PVPL began its operations in India. Her most popular 3W edition, Ape, has already been released. Which gives many existing players in the Indian industry a tough time. It has a processing potential of over 3 lakhs 3W and approx. 80000 4W merchandise carrier. It also spent INR 200 crores in R&D and expansion of the current plant in India to build and assemble electric vehicles.

Recently, all BS6 models of cars have been introduced to conform to the new pollution requirements.

3.24. Royal Enfield Motors (REM) -

Since 1901, REM has been making motorcycles. Among the biking enthusiasts for Himalayan trips, it is the most popular. With its classic style and most efficient engines, it is the long-drive option of many. Depending on the selection of riders, it has bikes varying from 250 to 1000 CC. It has 16 shops owned by the business and 400 + dealerships. Exports to more than 50 nations, including the United States, the Middle East, and the South East. For riding enthusiasts who view this as a lifestyle, there are clubs throughout the major cities.

In 2018, REM clocked 2500 crores in turnover, delivering approx. six lakhs of motorcycles each year.

3.25. Scania Commercial Vehicle's -

The existence of Scania commercial vehicles in India in the Narsapura industrial area was founded in 2011. 125 years ago, it was created. The current potential for production each year is 2500 trucks and 1000 buses. The leader of ethanol-driven buses in India. The dealer and distributor network in India in the south and west has begun to be developed. In India, it is connected with L&T for mining machinery. In India, it supplies generators, Lorries and buses.

It gives its passengers a special experience with the most luxurious buses for long haul driving. Scania was born in Sweden. It clocked revenue of marginally over INR 600 crores and sold approx. 1300 Premium Performance Trucks and Buses.

3.26. SKODA Auto India -

Skoda is part of the Czech Republic and a company of the Volkswagen Group. It is located in the industrial region of Shendra in Aurangabad. It began working in India in 2001. Any of the big brands it works with are Swift, Octavia and superb brands that are popular and well received by Indian clients. Skoda has a broad variety of items to sell. In India, it has 67 distribution outlets and 74 support outlets. The turnover in 2018 reaches INR 4000 crores and output is approx. 1-lakh automobiles.

3.27. Suzuki Motorcycle India Private Limited (SMIPL) - $\$$SUZUKI

SMIPL is solely held by an affiliate of the Japanese Suzuki Motor Company. In India, SMIPL produces 2W and began operations in India with the launch of Zeus in 2006. Its theory continually believes in value for capital. Worldwide, Suzuki goods are well accepted. Slightly over five lakhs, No of the motorcycle was produced by Suzuki motorcycle and the turnover of INR 500 crores clocked.

3.28. Tata Motors Limited (TML) - TATA MOTORS

TML, India's largest commercial vehicle maker, is a leader in the Indian automobile sector, involved in the area of passenger vehicles and construction equipment, sales over 45 trillion. It works in South Korea, Europe, Thailand, and South Africa by itself or through other subsidiaries. JV has been established with the Fiat engines in India to produce and provide after-sales service. Ace, 407, 709, INDICA, which acquired the Jaguar land rover, are some of the pioneer versions of TATA engines. For building equipment, it has a JV with Hitachi.

In Pune and Ranjangaon, truck-manufacturing plants in Rudrapur, Jamshedpur, Lucknow, and TML have passenger vehicle manufacturing plants. Dharwad and Lucknow bus production plants with JV with Marcopolo Bus. TML sells its commodities to several nations around the globe. Turnover was little over three lakh crores and generated approx. Over six lakhs of vehicles and approx. More than eight lakh passenger buses.

3.29. Toyota Kirloskar Motor Ltd. (TKML) -

In 1997, TKML was created. Its parent company is Japan's Toyota Motor Corporation. To establish this venture, it established a JV with Kirloskar in India. It is considered that TKML vehicles are the best in India. Created by creative minds holding consumer protection as the highest priority. In 2000, its first launch in India was Qualis, which was a huge success. As the days fly by next year, it has never looked back from introducing new items. Some are named LIVA, INNOVA, ETIOS, CAMRY, etc. It has a development facility in the state of Karnataka, in the manufacturing city of Bidadi. Spread through 432 acres. It has an installed capacity of 310000 cars. In recent times, Fortuner is his most popular and liked model, and TKML manufactured more than 100,000 Fortuner per year. It has also built the vendor area such that all essential products are assembled close the assembly line and meet the demand for development if required. A turnover of INR 21000 crores was clocked. Number of vehicles totaling 1.5 lakhs in 2018 were manufactured and sold

3.30. Triumph Motorcycles India -

The famous British brand, established in the United Kingdom in 1902, is Triumph. The CKD assembly line at Manesar Haryana has 750 dealers worldwide. It has a presence in the US, UK, India, South Africa, Japan, Spain, Italy, Brazil and Indonesia, to name a handful, with more than 2000 staff worldwide. It established itself in India in 2013 as a wholly owned subsidiary. 15 versions are manufactured in India under five brand groups. In India, it has 12 operating dealers that are located in all parts of the country.

RAT-Riding association of triumph has begun to support the brand and sports riding. It also offers all the riding gear to do this as a hobby and marketing of the company. Approx. with the In India, it sold sports bikes units 1200 no's in India for sales exceeding INR 1000 crores.

3.31. TVS Motor Company -

The TVS Company in India is a 100-year-old group with a group turnover of over USD 7 trillion. The TVS motor company was founded in 1979 and is the leading 2W producer in

India. It has a talented team of over 7000 staff members. With production facilities at Mysuru in Karnataka, Nalagadh in Himachal and Hosur in Tamilnadu, it is the third largest 2W manufacturing firm in India. It also has overseas presence in Indonesia. It is the first Deming award by a 2W manufacturing firm. We, Apache, Scooty, etc., are the most popular TVS types. At its Hosur factory, it has also begun producing 3W.

With the service stations linked to it, TVS has a dealership network of more than 3500. TVS has generated approx. Several automobiles and clocked turnover of approx. INR 20000 crores. Domestic and foreign sector revenues of 3 million units.

3.32. <u>VE Commercial Vehicles Limited (VECV)</u> -

VECV is a joint venture company between VOLVO from Sweden and Eicher group from India to manufacture commercial vehicles. The company started operations in 2008 and has a production site in Indore's industrial area of Pithampur. It also assembles VOLVO engines and has a complete assembly design set up in the state of Madhya Pradesh. Among the large fleet owners produced by VECV approx., its models are recognized for value for money with low maintenance costs. It managed to achieve top line turnover of over Rs.10000crores.

3.33. <u>Volkswagen India Pvt. Ltd (VW)</u> - Volkswagen

VW is the world's number one maker of passenger vehicles. This place has been held for a long time. It has invested in the green field facility at Chakan, near Pune. In the year 2009, it spent INR 4000 crores for the same. Its group corporation, SKODA, is headquartered in the industrial region of Shendra in Aurangabad. The Polo, Vento and Passat are some of the famous models introduced by VW. Despite its initiatives in India and its global role as the number 1 producer of passenger cars, India has not been able to have much impact. The VW Group's overall market share in India could not reach 3 per cent. Compared to other peers, the higher safety requirements VW adopted for its automobiles made the vehicles pricey for India. Also, the maintenance cost is well above the industry peers.

It has produced 82 per cent localization and approx. exports to more than 32 countries from India's VW manufacturing facility. It managed to produce and sale Vehicles of 1.5 lakhs and INR 12000 crores as top line

3.34. Volvo -

Since 2001, Volvo has been working in India from its production facility near Bangalore. Just VOLVO in India is accessible when it comes to protection and comfort. Buses are very common in India as VOLVO first purchased the idea of public transport luxury in India. VOLVO also assembles trucks and tippers from its plant in Bangalore for the mining industry. There are more than 7,000 Volvo buses running on Indian routes. Links with several state transport firms have also been created. Volvo also manufactures multi-axle buses that allow the turning radius to be better controlled. Volvo achieved INR 5500 crores as top line with 4000 bus in a year

The Automotive industry profile clearly indicates that this industry in capital intensive and , large capital investment is considered as barrier for this industry , example VW had to invest Rs 4000 CRS and Daimler had to invest Rs 8000 CRS to put up a green field facility in India.

3.35. Automotive Segment Profile

In the study below, we have considered all the six segments(Two wheelers , three wheelers , passenger car , commercial vehicles , tractors and construction equipment's) of the Indian automotive industry and studied them in detail on about their production numbers from 2004 to 2017, challenges faced by them, factors influencing them at the segment level.

3.36. Two Wheelers in India

India is the largest two-wheeler sector in the world, led by China and Indonesia. The two-wheeler industry has seen steady growth over recent years mainly led by high urban and rural demand due to a healthy economic scenario. The growing population has also created the need for daily public transport facilities, thus pushing demand for low-cost and fuel-efficient two-wheelers. The 2W industry will commonly be categorized as bikes, scooters and mopeds (70 per cent of all TW sales).

Motorcycle sales in India have risen at double-digit rates in recent years and have recently reached 1 million vehicles a month. The annual sales of motorcycles appear to overtake the on-road passenger car fleet and fuel use with a five-fold rise.

Year	Production No
2004	5622741
2005	6529829
2006	7608697
2007	8436212
2008	8009292
2009	8395613
2010	10510336
2011	13349349
2012	15744156
2013	16883049
2014	18489311
2015	18830227
2016	19933739
2017	23147057

Indian two wheeler industry manufactured 5622741 number of the vehicles in 2004 year. IN the year 2017 it manufactured 23147057 vehicles. The compounded annual growth for this segment of industry was 11% spread over the period of 14 years

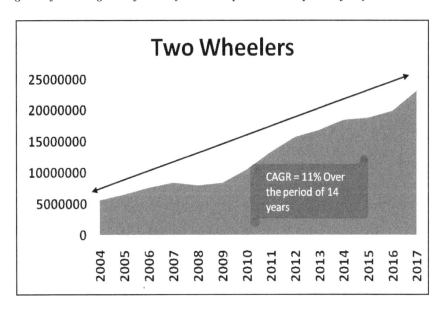

Chart 6.12- Two-wheeler Industry production

Source – MOSPI/SIAM

The two-wheeler output reported a marginal growth of 1.8% in 2015-16 and reached 18830227 units. During the year, the division generated modest revenue growth of 2.7%.

Though scooter sales increased 12.6 per cent, a decline in motorbike sales and mopeds has pulled the two-wheeler segment's overall sales rise. In 2016-17 (Apr-Jan), two-wheeler production rose 6.6 per cent a year after a flat pattern in the same timeframe last year. Over the same era, revenues in the two-wheel segment increased by 5.8% a year. In November and December 2016, two-wheeler drive sales decreased dramatically by 27.8% and 22.5%, respectively, behind the cash shortage of the government's demonetization drive. However, revenue grew by 29.7 per cent in January 2017 following the demonetization phase. In 2015-2016, the exports of two-wheelers accounted for approximately 15% of total sales of two-wheelers in 2015-2016, reflecting approximately 15% of total sales in the market. Africa and Latin America are the major export markets for the two-wheel segments. Although short-term demand is expected to remain under strain, demand is expected to steadily increase with steady oil prices and with players preparing a global footprint expansion.

Of all auto equipment groups, 2W is a high-volume segment of vehicles powered largely by the extent of available disposable income, which depends in turn on the condition of an economic turnaround, particularly in rural areas, which contributes close to 50% of the total 2W market. Given the above-average monsoon in 2016, the market for 2W segment is projected to keep increasing in both segments – scooters and motorcycles.

3.37. Types of Two Wheelers

There are three basic forms of two-wheelers on the Indian market: mopeds, bikes and scooters. There are two other types classified as "Scooterette," and the "Pass" category has practically vanished from the business. The key characteristics of these vehicles are listed below.

Mopeds: The bikes are normally powered by small single-cylinder air-cooled 2-hour gasoline motors with a displacement of less than 60 cc. They use a fixed belt or chain transmission, or a chain and belt transmission hybrid. Some versions use a two-speed transmission automatically variable to ensure a higher wheel torque at the start and low speeds and a lower cruise torque. Mopeds typically use bigger wheels than 14." These automobiles use low-cost cycle components for bars, braking, etc. The electricity used to regulate the horn and the lights are obtained from a magnet installed on a flywheel. Many mopeds do not have, or have, batteries of limited size. They have no self-starting arrangements and are equipped with pedals both for starting the engine and for standing. Mopeds are also the lack of a fuel tank in front of the rider, which provides an open space similar to the moped. This style of vehicle is still very common in many countries in

South-East Asia. It is not sold on the Indian market anymore. Motorcycles: Motorcycles do not require a comprehensive explanation since they are almost standardized in design. They are made of metal frames, use an integrated generator, clutch and transmission assembly and the final chain

Scientific assessment of the pollution and fuel usage capacity of transmission from the two and three wheels of India to the rear wheel. The normally fuel tank is positioned immediately opposite the passenger and above the motor. Motorcycles use 16" to 17" scale spokes. Virtually all Over a decade earlier, "scooters" regulated India's two-wheeler industry. Bajaj Auto Ltd. enjoyed a lion's share of the industry because of the powerful and stable success of the scooter. The scooter Bajaj was a variant of the famous one – that of the Italian scooter Piaggio. Bajaj manufactured these vehicles under Piaggio license. Following partial economic liberalization in the 1980s, big Japanese 2-wheelers Honda, Yamaha and Suzuki and Piaggio, of Italy (whose partnership had ended with Bajaj), formed joint-ventures to manufacture their state-of-the-art two-wheelers, most of which were small motorcycles. Honda also founded two separate firms, one of which was Kinetic Engineering, with its enormously successful scooter named „to be ready" powered by a 100cc 2-switch motor and a belt-driven variable transmission. The freshly renovated new Kinetic Honda dialect was famous primarily due to the state-of-the-art look, superior comfort, simple drive even for sari-clad women. Yamaha (Escorts) and Suzuki (TVS) also launched 100 cc 2-stroke motorcycles from their joint projects in India, which began to be increasingly ideal for the market, which until then had been more acquainted with the scooter.

Honda Towers' second venture with Hero Motors gave a fuel quality of under 100 cc 4 more than that of 2-strokes. Competitors had to introduce more fuel-efficient 4-stroke engines as a result of market success. Another significant aspect contributing to the implementation of 4-cycle engines was the adoption of more strict exhaust pollution requirements. While an oxidation catalytic converter had to be used to minimise large 2-stroke emissions of hydrocarbons, the four-stroke systems were able to satisfy the requirements by merely tuning and lean calibration. Bajaj Auto is the conventional four-stroke scooter manufacturer.

Technical assessment of pollution and fuel consumption capacity for reducing motorcycles produced under license from the Kawasaki Two and 3W in India. In contrast, the development of scooters has declined, because new models reflecting the state-of-the-art were launched into the industry. The next wave of economic liberalisation prompted

Honda to create its wholly-owned subsidiary. Because of its deal with Hero for manufacturers and distribution of motorcycles, Honda has joined the market with a 4-stroke scooter, while the market share of the 4-stroke motorcycles has been dramatically eroded. However, Honda's superior technologies helped re-establish the appeal of scooters with a phenomenal turnaround in the industry. The Honda scooter, due to the 4-valve engine, was inherently more fuel-efficient than the older 2-valve -engine ones. With the Hero Motors Party, Honda Alumni's second venture has improved fuel savings of 100 cc to 4 times better than 2-stroke powertrains. Sales success pushed opponents to unleash four-stroke motors with more power consumption. Another critical element in beginning 4-stroke motorcycles was the introduction of extremely stringent exhaust pollution regulations. Whilst a catalytic oxidation converter had to be used to mitigate the massive 2-stroke emissions of hydrocarbons to achieve the mass pollution specifications, fast tuning and slim calibration might meet the norm. Bajaj Auto is the traditional maker of four-stroke scooters. It should be noted, however, that relative shares of scooters and mopeds in the two-wheeler total market remained relatively low due to the scaling rate of motorcycle market development. The share of motorcycles has continued in the last five years and the share of scooters is increasing.

The three-vehicle types that within a few years starting from 2000, the growth rate of scooters and mopeds had been adverse. In future years, the growth rates of these two groups tend to have recovered and are now almost equal to vehicles, even though the former two are from a comparatively narrow baseline. Mopeds have a somewhat different past than scooters. Mopeds were initially launched by two producers in the early 1980s, mainly after the first wave of economic liberalisation. One was TVS Motors in Tamil Nadu state in the south of India and the other was Kinetic Engineering Ltd in the western state of Maharashtra. In the northern cities Majestic Auto, a part of the Hero party, based in northern India, also sold some numbers. Both these companies introduced local models which were mostly powered by small 50-60 cc 2-stroke engines and used fixed or variable transmission belt-powered. In the time when the only 2-wheeler alternative was the scooter, the mopeds were common. It seems that the launch of many other 2-wheelers, in particular, the fuel-efficient 4-hour motorbikes and the steady change of consumers' economic conditions have steadily diminished the market share of mopeds.

Currently, the largest and perhaps only maker of mopeds is TVS Motors and the demand appears to be limited largely to the southern countries. The moped models still seem to be experiencing little improvements and use the 2-hour motor. The reduction in the market share of mopeds was tried to compensate for the launch of the "scooterette" which appealed to a section due to its scooter-like appearance and its comfort and availability at a lower price. TVS is the largest scooterette maker in addition to mopeds.

3.38. <u>Technical Classification 2W</u>

To evaluate the market profiles for large requirements for two-wheelers sold in the region, a ranking established by the Society of Indian Automotive Manufacturers centered on wheel size and engine capacities has been implemented. Engine range, simple pricing points and certain features classify motorcycles into three groups. These groups may be classified as 'Entry-Level' or 'Commuter Regular,' 'Executive' or 'Commuter Deluxe' and 'Premium,' or 'Football' classes on the market. These words are loosely used in the industry and are not formally classified.

Motorcycles: It is seen that between 75 and 125 cc, the motorcycle segment has the greatest market share (58 per cent) of two-wheelers. The second highest market share is for engines with engine capacities from 125 cc to 250 cc (nearly 20 per cent). Scooters have the third-highest share of the industry (all engine capacities together) (around 15 per cent). Mopeds also have a relatively limited yet important 6 per cent market share.

3.39. <u>Overview of the Motorcycle Industry</u>

Motorcycle entry section

- The pattern in recent years for the market volume of motorcycles is in opposition to long-term consumption patterns
- The sub segment continues to expand, but is slower than the industry
- While the proportion of first-time buyers was decreased, segment volumes kept ground
- In the last two years, Hero MotoCorp further improved its role in the sub-segment

3. Executive segment of motorcycles

- Substitution market promoting growth in volume
- 100cc: In recent years, the sub-segment has had several different versions launched.
- 100cc: Rivalry is rising but Hero MotoCorp remains at the top
- 100cc: Bajaj Auto losses market share; an alternative approach is currently in operation
- Honda overtakes Hero MotoCorp and Bajaj Auto 125cc:
- 125cc: The sub-segment is more attractive than performance bikers for commuters

The premium segment of motorcycles

The >150cc category motorcycles are distinguished by a significant number of models even though the volume volumes of the sub-section are not adequate to sustain Bajaj Auto's leadership role in the sub-section by the Pulsar Bike series Hero MotoCorp slips from place 2 two years ago to the 4th position.

3.40. Major Manufacturers of Two Wheelers

There are presently six big manufacturers making two-wheelers in India. These involve, approximately in order of its share in the business, Hero Honda Motors Ltd. (HHML) (now Hero MotoCorp), Bajaj auto Ltd (BAL), TVS Motor Company Ltd. (TVS), Honda Motorcycle (HMSI), and Scooter India Pvt. Ltd. (M&M). HTML primarily develops bikes and fewer scooters. TVS sells a broad variety of bicycles, such as mopeds, motorcycles, and scooters. Until a few years back, it had a joint venture with Suzuki of Japan. Suzuki also operates a wholly-owned SMIL subsidiary including Yamaha (YMIL) and Honda (HMSI). Until recently, HMSI only produced scooters (through a continuing deal with Hero Honda) and now has on the market a variety of motorcycles. YMIL and SMIL primarily produce motorbikes, while SMIL still has a limited presence in the scooter market. Bajaj Auto was the leading scooter maker but has now discontinued the production of scooters and is now a large motorcycle manufacturer. It has also concluded a licensing agreement with Kawasaki of Japan for several high-end bikes, like the Ninja, in addition to other items of its brand.

In addition to these, several specialised markets such as Enfield India, Harley Davidson, Hyosung, Ducati and KTM are still involved in the Indian industry. BAL has a new share. Enfield India, one of the oldest motorcycle manufactures in India, has full manufacturing facilities. Others either import entirely assembled units or carry out the limited local assembly. The present study has not taken into consideration these specialised producers and their items because of their relatively small quantities and their very large prices outweigh those of medium-sized vehicles, which are mostly called recreational items.

The hero has the dominant share of almost 75% of this segment, led by the second by Bajaj Auto with a share of approximately 17%. On the other side, Bajaj Auto dominates the group 125-250 cc with a 45% share, while HMSI is second with a 23% share. Hero Honda has an estimated 13 per cent stake. Other manufacturers like Suzuki Motors, India Yamaha Motor and TVS Motors are very present in this segment of automobiles. Two-wheelers' average penetration in India is about 28% of all households. In towns, the penetration is in the range of 45%, whereas in rural areas, the penetration is just around 12% of households. The major push would come from the rural sector in the future.

Annual household income in the INR 300,000-500,000 range is 11 million urban households and 4.4 million rural households. The next segment comprises 25 million urban households and 23 million agricultural homes. At least a quarter (11-12 million) of these would shift into the two-wheeler procurement market during the next five-ten years.

Today, 72% of the bikes are in the entry segment, classified as 75 to 125 cc, and 27% in the executive segment (defined as 125-250 cc). In the luxury segment, only 1% of bikes are likely to continue to be a niche segment and their share is expected to rise beyond 2-2,5% during the next decade. However, it means that it would be a large and lucrative demand of around 200,000 to 250,000 units per year.

3.41. <u>Electric Two-Wheelers</u>

1. Transport. 2. Electric bikes. 3. Environmental effects. 4. India

E-scooters are two-wheel electric vehicles identical to scooters and motorcycles powered by petrol except that they run only on battery power. As an alternative to the petrol scooter and motorcycle, the e-scooter promises performance improvements and almost quiet elimination of air and noise pollution because of zero local tailpipe emissions. E-scooter has been common in China, but the regulations restricted it to low power (less than 500 W [W]), lightweight (less than 60 kg and low-speed (less than 40 km/h). These scooters do not have the required output to compete in other countries against fuel scooters and motorcycles. Given the wide domestic demand for smaller models, most Chinese e-bike manufacturers have little opportunity to build larger models for the export market only. As a result, current e-scooters are typically unsuitable for non-PRC industries. Any firms outside the PRC are designing larger e-scooters that are capable of competing against small-scale (<125 cc2) two-wheelers run on gasoline. However, the utility or environmental implications of such a change are unclear.

A summary of the history of the two-wheeler industry in India is helpfully divided into 10 blocks from the 1960s onwards, with each block tracing major changes in economic policy growth. In the first phase of 1960-1969, the development of the two-wheeler industry was encouraged through means such as encouraging external alliances and the gradual exclusion of non-manufacturing companies in the industry. During the era, 1970-1980 state regulations hit their height by the usage of the licensing scheme and some administrative actions. There were major changes in the world between 1981 and 1990. From 1991-1999, the next bloc saw changes gaining traction in different fields such as banking, commerce, revenue, industrial policy etc. In the present decade which began until 2000, the development of two wheels grew dramatically where demand for motorcycles increased and great demand also increased for super bicycles (more flexible and trendy motorcycles), leaving sales well behind of two other smaller wheels. Some of the key factors are the IT boom and the subsequent entrance of MNC and IT giants into the world, which has a big effect on the younger generation and also the numerous media for the supply and dissemination of knowledge not generated until a few years ago. Also, the production of the two-wheelers in India over the years Evolution Stage-I the auto industry was put on a pedestal in compliance with the 19 48 Industrial Policy Resolution in the 1948 Sixties and was thus supervised and governed by the government. The key idea was to facilitate production, in addition to discouraging imports of ready-to-use automobiles, car assembly companies were phased out by 1952 (Tariff Commission 1968) and only manufacturing companies approved their continuity. Automotive manufacturing needed the consent of authorized companies to open a factory, and the Government calculated the production ability of a corporation. Foreign partnerships were promoted during this time. Most businesses had some sort of partnership with international companies.

3.42. Evolution Stage 1-2W

In the 1970s cumulative growth for the two-wheeler industry during this time was strong (approximately 15 per cent annually), with the degree of regulation and control over the industry high. The first was the product of sharp increases in the price of oil in 1974 because two-wheelers were the favoured means of personal transportation due to superior fuel quality in contrast with four wheels. In the other side, regulatory measures like MRTP and FERA led to a regulated industry. The effect of MRTP was restricted since only big corporations like Bajaj Auto Ltd. had their growth rates curbed, since they were subject to this Act. FERA had a wider impact, though, as it a limited foreign investment in India. In the FERA motorcycle industry, technical deflation was not triggered, which contributed to new technologies nor businesses joining the sector, as this segment relied nearly exclusively on international technology partnerships. In the other side, the scooter and moped segment were technologically more autonomous and so new entries in the scooter and moped segments were available.

One of the factors for the launch of reforms in 1981 was the technical backwardness of the Indian two-wheeler industry during the 1980s. Both two-wheelers were permitted to operate together abroad up to an engine capacity of 100 cc. This led to a spate of new market entrants, the bulk of which joined the motorcycle industry, which brought new technologies that led to more productive manufacturing methods and goods. The selection of goods available has also expanded after approval for 'large banding' as part of the NEP in 1985 in the sector. This, combined with the announcement of the MES output for the two-wheel industry," provided companies with the flexibility to choose an optimal commodity and capacity combination that could help fit consumer demand into their production plan and thus increase their capacity usage and performance.

3.43. <u>Evolution Stage 2-2W</u>

During the 1990s, changes that started in the late 1970s witnessed their most critical transition in 1991 by way of economic liberalisation. The two-wheelers industry has been fully deregulated. Several changes were implemented in the field of trade to render Indian exports successful. In the 1990s, the two-wheel industry was defined by

3.43.1. A rise in the number of products on the market that rendered businesses successful based on product characteristics.

3.43.2. Increased sales in the motorcycle sector concerning the scooter segment which reverses the conventional trend.

From 2000 to date, the current decade saw the exponential growth in the purchasing and use of two-wheeler, particularly motorcycles. Besides, the emergence of companies linked to technology and technology in India and also BPO organisations which have seen a boom in jobs opportunities. Furthermore, the surge in jobs is the rise in wages and compensation of people who operate in these MNCs and major players. Also, women have started to gain higher-paying jobs, further boosting men's and women's spending strength. The media also played no small role in such influential transactions, offering detailed and thorough details about all potential goods including choices, specifications, pricing tactics, etc. All this material is accessible at a prospective consumer's hands or is available at their disposal. And if that is not enough, through their vigorous and enticing approaches, banks and financial institutions have rendered the purchase of consumer durables even at substantial rates simpler and instantly accessible. Credit cards and even debit cards made financial transfers so much smoother to offer convenient and long-term credit that, in essence, affects and allows purchasing choices easier. In reality, banks and financial institutions, especially private players, have been able to manipulate prospective buyers with enticing deals, which are not always cheap but which tempt customers to purchase decisions, often without thought or any awareness at all. (It's another thing if they are affordable in the long run).

Two-wheelers have always striven to provide innovative and improved features and have been able to keep ahead of rivalry that has rendered the customers' demands insatiable. Major players in the motorcycle industry have shrunk in enticing prospective customers with more and more developments so that they have been connected to financial institutions to lend buyers what they deem a zero-interest credit facility. The customers replied in no uncertain terms by withdrawing all the goodies these players have thrown to them so far that even a rise in fuel prices approximately one hundred per cent did not deter revenue from continuously rising. Motorcycle producers have improved the potential of cars to fight the fuel price rise and make automobiles more effective by consuming considerably less fuel and also by keeping to environmental requirements. All this has brought the concerned companies positive news and also the big consumer who initiates Publicity.

3.44. Driving forces -2W

The following are the industry drivers that affect demand and consumer expectations for two and three-wheelers.

The makers, finance authorities, regulators (the Ministry of the Environment and the Civil Society groups) and end consumers have four key powers in this field.

Manufacturers- They are major initial makers of machinery launching new versions and campaigning to help supply two-wheelers with facilities.

Financial Institutions- These businesses push the demand by providing low-interest loans that enable more citizens to buy two-wheelers.

Ministry of Environment Regulations and Civil Society Groups - There are no two-wheeler possession/sales laws in a community except for pollution legislation. India's pollution requirements are among the world's strictest. Consequently, the Ministry of the Environment, which sets pollution standards, and civic groups such as the Center for Science and Environment and other non-governmental organizations which lobby more rigorous standards often constitute the driving forces of industry.

End Users – Some real consumers currently use the vehicle and select the vehicles as choices, but often respond to the improvement in the price of the vehicle's best / worst quality.

3.45. Business Design-2W

In the present sense, there are early indicators of value output, powered by greater simplicity and unisexual nature, from motorcycles to automatic scooters in urban markets. Although HMSI has caught more of this value migration as far as it is the catalyst for this transition, Honda and TVS are well situated. Bajaj will miss out for now because of this exodus when it took the strategic stance of becoming the global motorcycle specialist

Japanese motorcycle shifting players the primary drivers were fuel economy, durability and suitability on bad roads, and conventional geared scooters were dominated by low expense, higher kilometers and less maintenance in competition with the bikes accessible locally by the mid-1990s. The arrival of Japanese players provided motorcycles with stability, longevity and fuel performance. In the 1990s, the transition from conventional geared scooters evolved at a rate that contributed to a rise in demand for better two-wheelers. Significant fuel price increases (in the late 1990s) resulted, attributable to their better performance, in a rapid and fast increase in motorbike share (scooter sales decreased annually by 30%-40% in the late 1990s, down 10-15% earlier). By the middle of 2000-geared scooters had been extinguished.

3.46. Why scooters had dominated pre-1990s

Lack of stable and fuel effective Motorcycles are usually more powerful and robust by design than scooters. Their ground clearance, solid springs and wider wheelbases are stronger. However, until the 1980s there was a shortage of durability and fuel quality in motorcycle brands. The Indian motorcycle industry only had three serious players – Bullet, Rajdoot and Jawa (Yezdi). Due to his solid suspension, Rajdoot was common in rural areas, while Bullet and Jawa were popular for their success in the urban markets. Although the models became common because of problems with mechanical durability and fuel quality, most consumers favoured the conventional geared scooters available. In the 1980s a shift in the Indian two-wheeled sector has occurred through joint projects with Indian partners, with the introduction of many Japanese players. They launched a range of 100cc motors with cutting edge technology, much more effective in fuel usage, more powerful and simpler to run. Hero Honda (now Hero MotoCorp; HMCL) has introduced four-stroke technology that is superior to Yamaha, Suzuki (through Bajaj) and Kawasaki two-stroke technology for fuel economy and durability. The change from geared scooters to motorcycles began in the 1990s. Motorcycles usually fitted best for bad roads, with their better clearance on earth, stronger suspension and wider wheelbase, were well performed in the comparatively weak village roads. Better technologies with fuel-efficient and more powerful engines: After the Japanese players join the industry and Hero Honda developed four-stroke technology, motors became more fuel-effective and fuel-efficient. Hero Honda fuel economy, design and strength ads Sharp rise in fuel prices intensified transition in the late 1990s In addition to improved looks, durability, reliability and fuel efficiency, the bikes increased the move away from standard geared scooters: The oil crisis in the late 1990s culminated in heavy rises in fuel prices. Their sales rose dramatically, as bikes became more fuel-efficient than conventional geared scooters. The price gap between bikes and geared scooters has narrowed with several motorcycle releases. This facilitated the buying of bikes. Powerful growth in the young (18-25 years old) customer demographic coupled with substantial rises in the available income contributed to a quantum leap in demand for the best two-wheelers – good-looking cars, higher strength and higher efficiency, but also fuel economy.

The key element in the change was the higher kilometers of four-stroke motorcycles. Scooters used two-hour technology at the period. They delivered 35-40km/h while Hero Honda delivered 60 km/h for four-hour 100cc motorcycles. Fuel prices grew dramatically in the late 1990s. With a fuel efficiency of 60kmpl motors was common and the proportion of four-stroke motors was tremendously increased over 1997-2001. Because of the wider wheels and longer wheelbase, bikes were even simpler. With the opening of the market in the early 1990s, commercial development and therefore travel requirements were growing. Motorcycles provided greater kilometers and comfort than scooters. While the prices of bikes (Inr30k v/s INR20k for scooters) were higher, customer funding hurried. In two-wheel financing then, Citibank was very violent. Following the general rise in wages, motorcycle demand was supported. The resurgence of scooters in the automatic sector Comfort, universal attractiveness and the need for economic growth as conventional geared scooters were sold less, the share of automatic scooters continued to rise, primarily driven by higher demand among working women, students (females) and elderly people. In the 2000s, the launch of Honda Activa gained acceptance among men due to characteristics including ease, convenience and universal use. In terms of performance, durability, and fuel efficiency, automatic scooters (especially those introduced by Honda) were far ahead of conventional geared scooters. There may be a further rise in the share of scooters on urban markets, powered by (a) additional demand from an expanded target population and (b) motorcycle users' replacement demand. Initially, urban women and students requested automatic scooters Ungeared scooters, mostly plastic body built (lightweight and smaller in size) engines with lower capacities (mostly sub-100cc), were also common among women. Usage by males was minimal, provided the small/feminine nature of plastic scooters. Companies sponsored automatic scooters by high-decibel endorsements based on women's empowerment. As economic growth grows and the inclusion of women in the workforce increases, the demand from female clients grew at a healthy pace until FY12. However, there is a strong shift towards large/unisex scooters after FY12. Acceptance among men has also accelerated development over the last four years, with 26 per cent CAGR volume for automated scooters. Big scooters (>100cc), with ~31% CAGR, developed faster. Much of this is motivated by increased adoption among men of automatic scooters. Reasons for the increasing success of automatic scooters include a substantial reduction in motorcycling output and efficiency: improvements in technology have greatly increased the output of modern scooters and are almost motorcycle speeds. Motorcycles also reduced the fuel efficiency difference versus motorcycles - 40-45 KM/LITER versus 60-65kmpl (35-40kmpl for geared scooters).

Universal appeal: Scooters, whether males or females, may be used as automatic transmission vehicles with self-start choice and consequent ease of driving.

Comfort and convenience: Automatic transmission scooters provide great comfort and convenience, particularly in urban conditions. Great primary family vehicle: High petrol costs and pollution render scooters handy for travel on a day-to-day basis, while motorcycles are used for on-time rides. Scooters are becoming popular with young people and business encounters suggest that scooters are gaining popularity among young people. Young college boys are purchasing products like Honda Dio and Yamaha Ray-Z. However, they are not yet appealing in contrast with cars, which are already a significant part of the industry. Attractiveness in young people will be the main point of inflexion. Sensing that, a host of male-specific items were introduced by double-wheeler players – Hero Master, Honda Aviator, Yamaha Ray Z and TVS Jupiter. With many recent launches centered on young people (young boys from 18-25 years), the acceptance of young people is also rising at a rapid rate, especially as the 'network' impact begins. HMCL focuses on positioning its Maestro scooters for young men as a 'smart' commodity.

Two-wheeler industry in India its development after the introduction of economic reforms and present scenario

The sense of independence and being one with Nature just emerges through a two-wheeler motor. Due to a compact, manageable scale, low maintenance and pricing and fast loan repayment, the Indians prefer two wheels. Indian streets are lined with people of all ages riding a two-wheeler. Motorized two wheels are used by the public as a status mark. So we'd see in India swanky four wheels jostling with our steed which is always reliable and healthy.

India is the world's second-largest manufacturer of two-wheelers. It is just in terms of the number of two-wheelers produced and domestic sales next to Japan and China. This differentiation was rendered for a broad range of factors such as the government of India's stringent policies on passenger vehicles, growing demand for personal transport, the inefficiency of public transport, etc. The Indian double wheel industry began in the early 1950s when the Indian Car Goods (API) started making scooters in India. Until 1958, API and Enfield were the only manufacturers. Since 1955 there has been a two-wheel industry in India that included segments such as scooters, bikes and mopeds. The rising sales volume in this industry at the time proved its high growth. Sales in 1971 were roughly 0.1 million units annually but grew to 3 million units annually in 1998. Similarly, during the intervening span, manufacturing capacities rose from an annual output of around 0.2 million units to more than 4 million units. This pattern continued to rise until the current year of 2006, with an additional 150% growth in this time.

The date below explicitly reveals that the two-wheel sector belongs to the vehicle industry, with the scooter industry being the biggest share. The chart nest, however, reveals the increasing significance of the scooter section, which is viewed as the family vehicle that holds more products in the front at the foot. Even the husband and wife can drive the modern scooter easily, both fashionable designs are also common amongst generation X.

Year	Total 2W	Scooter	Bike	Moped
2004	5622741	562274	4762462	298005
2005	6529829	718281	5471997	339551
2006	7608697	875000	6345653	388044
2007	8436212	1012345	7002056	421811
2008	8009292	1121301	6407434	480558
2009	8395613	1007474	6968359	419781
2010	10510336	1492468	8444004	573864
2011	13349349	1975704	10719527	654118
2012	15744156	2456088	12453627	834440
2013	16883049	3545440	12510339	827269
2014	18489311	4492903	13090432	905976
2015	18830227	5291294	12635082	903851
2016	19933739	6079790	12976864	877085
2017	23147057	7360764	14582646	1203647

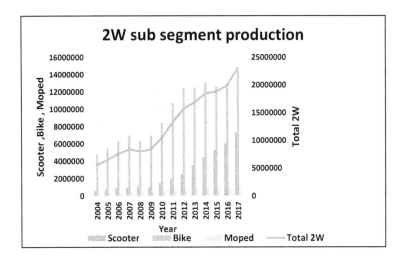

Chart 6.13- Graphical representation 2W segment,

Source IBEF automotive reports 2004 to 2018

During year 2013 to 2017 , It is seen that the scooter segment grew faster than that of Bike segment.

Growth Prospects and Key Drivers of the Indian Two Wheelers Industry

The rise of the Indian two-wheelers demonstrates the increasing demand for low-cost personal transport solutions among 300 million medium-sized Indians. Despite this remarkable rate of growth, the two-wheel penetration (two-wheelers per 1000 people) in India is still less than in other Asian states. This reality gives a chance for continuous demand development. In comparisons with Taiwan, Thailand, Malaysia, Vietnam, Indonesia and China, India has the lowest penetration for two-wheelers. In the current scenario, two-wheel industry development would be guided by a variety of factors:

3.47. A rise in India's Young Working Population

With per capita incomes growing, the Indian two-wheeler industry offers tremendous growth opportunities. This rise is important because 70% of the Indian population is below the age of 35 and 150 million will be introduced to the workforce in the next five years. The number of women in the urban population is also rising, contributing to the rise of gearless motors.

3.48. Rise of India's Rural Economy and Growth in Middle Income Households

The development prospects of the rural Indian economy provide the motorcycle industry in India with a big opportunity. The penetration of motorcycles among rural households with incomes above US$2,200 annually has now risen to more than 50%. The new two-wheel division, i.e. households in the US$2.200–12,000 range, is projected to rise by a CAGR of 10 per cent.

3.49. Greater Affordability of Vehicles

The rise in Indian two-wheeler sales was guided by an improvement in these vehicles' affordability. An overview of market patterns reveals that costs have stagnated more or less in the past. This was part of the commercial policy embraced by suppliers to achieve volume and to consciously lower costs. In the last five years, the running costs of leading producers have dropped by about 15%. With better funding, the willingness of the consumer to possess two wheels has increased.

3.50. Rapid Product Introduction and Shorter Product Life Cycle

In the last five years, the introduction of new models in the two-wheeler sector has seen a sharp rise. During this time, it is reported that approximately 50 new goods were started by producers to fill all price points and are aimed at different market segments.

3.51. Inadequate Public Transport Systems in most Urban Areas

The economic growth in the country and the growing migration into metropolitan areas have intensified the congestion of traffic in Indian cities and have intensified established infrastructure bottlenecks. Inadequate spatial development has culminated in transit networks not being compatible with the global boom and the rising urban population. This raised the reliance on personal modes of transport and gained from this infrastructure deficit on the two-wheelers industry.

3.52. Challenges faced by the industry

Given the good growth in the past and the high prospects in the future, several problems are confronting the two-wheelers industry.

3.53. Rising Customer Expectations

The rise of the Indian two-wheeler industry has introduced new customers into the sector. The Indian industry is projected to become more successful in the future. In the past, the broad variety of goods have often-increased consumers' standards about durability, design, efficiency and economy.

3.54. Environmental and Safety Concerns

The rise of the Indian two-wheeler industry has introduced new customers into the sector. The Indian industry is projected to become more successful in the future. In the past, the broad variety of goods have often-increased consumers' standards about durability, design, efficiency and economy.

3.55. Creation of Distribution Infrastructure

Leading corporations must ensure, on the one side, that they build sufficient infrastructures in terms of urban dealerships and gas stations and, on the other hand, their delivery system often stretches to rural areas.

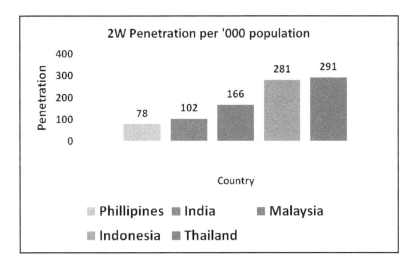

Chart 6.14- Global 2W industry penetration per 1000 person

Source – Hero MotoCorp investor presentation

The Hero moto corp. investor presentation indicates that Philippines have lowest level of 2W penetration @ 78 numbers of 2W /1000 Population, whereas India has 102 2W for the same density of population, highest density is with Thailand which is at 291 2w /1000 population

3.56. Lower penetration to improve growth

India has taken over China in 2W output in recent years as India takes over China. Compared to all other countries, however, penetration per 1000 citizens is much lower, so this factor will boost productivity since subsidies under MANAREGA would increase, many villagers would have the income to purchase 2W or bicycle graduate 2W.

3.57. Profile of Three-wheelers segment

Three-wheelers are a component of the country's automotive industries as they are one of India's most favorite means of transport in rural and urban areas. India is the world's largest producer and three-wheeler sector with industry volumes in 2015-2016 of approximately 943,533 units. Output decreased slightly by 1.6% in 2015-16 and reached 933,950 units in response to reduced demand from the main export markets. Exports rose by just 5% Y-Y, after growth of over 20% in the previous year. In 2016-2017 (Apr-January), total revenue decreased by approximately 15.9 per cent, owing to a significant decrease in exports over the period. Exports decreased 34 per cent over the span after cumulative causes, such as regulatory transportations in countries such as Sri Lanka (increase in import tariffs) and Bangladesh (three-wheelers not authorised to function on highways under new regulations), currency fluctuation, and a decline in export rewards. Demand for three-wheeler freight carriers remains under pressure in the domestic market as a consequence of the rivalry from small commercial vehicles (SCVs).

Sri Lanka, Bangladesh (in Southern Asia), Middle East and Africa make up around 90 per cent of the industry's exports. In recent years, however, Indian OEMs have also begun exploring relatively established ASEAN and Latin American markets. Bajaj Auto accounts for the largest export share of three-wheelers from India of 70 per cent, led by TVS engines of around 24 per cent. In providing point to point as well as feeder service in both urban and semi-urban areas, 3 wheelers play a crucial function.

3.58. Market Profile of Three Wheeler- Market Size

Year	Production
2004	356223
2005	374445

2006	434423
2007	556126
2008	500660
2009	497020
2010	619194
2011	799553
2012	839748
2013	830108
2014	949019
2015	934104
2016	783721
2017	1021911

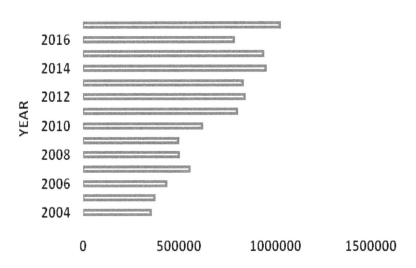

Chart 6.15- 3W industry production

Source – Team-BHP /SIAM 2019 reports

India manufactured 356223 numbers of 3W in 2004 and 1021911 in 2017.

Three-wheeled vehicles of different styles shape a very significant component of the Indian transport system. They operate as "Intermediate Public Transport (IPT)," in most cities either running as a flag-down taxi or on fixed roads such as omnibuses. Any of them often run from the city limits on ferry passengers to small towns and villages. Many of them are built as freight forwarders and act as intra-city freight vehicles. They are ideally equipped for moving comparatively low weights up to 500kg.

There are many explanations for why three-wheeled vehicles are common. Apart from the low initial and operational expense, the other key factor is the capacity to navigate the vehicle through tiny areas on the narrow streets, which are common of most towns and cities of the region. They have a tiny car park and are simple and affordable to manage. From the viewpoint of passengers, the service is versatile and affordable, cheaper than a four-wheeled cab but quicker and more reliable than an urban bus. Another motivating factor behind their growing success is the ability that they provide to many citizens to search for self-employment, not to mention the additional jobs generated by repair and maintenance. Per three-wheelers are expected to provide livelihoods for at least two families in India. In the last few years, the sales figures of three-wheelers (both types in total) have almost exceeded those of all other commercial vehicles. The above listed commercial vehicles comprise medium and heavy passengers and goods vehicles such as coaches, vans, light trucks, minibuses and others.

3.59. Types of Three Wheelers

In India, three-wheelers can be commonly separated into two types, passengers and freight carriers. Passenger carriers are of two types: one is the lightweight 4-person (three plus a driver) carrier, named the auto-rickshaw and the seven-person carrier (six plus a driver), which is also referred to as the "tempo." These two fundamental platforms often include the accompanying copies of products.

3.59.1. Passenger Careers - Three Wheelers

Auto Rickshaw The majority of three-wheeled vehicles in India are intended in addition to the driver for three passengers and are called rickshaws. In most major cities, these vehicles act as taxis for which the municipal authorities have authorised tariff meters. The auto-rickshaw is designed to reduce expense, weight and fuel consumption in the simplest possible way. Its architecture is known to be the strongest in terms of material input and operational performance for carrying out the expected mission at the lowest expense. The frame and body composed of pressed steel, each with a bench seat for the driver and the passengers. A cotton hood covers the inhabitants from rain and heat. A windshield covers the front, but normally the sides are free. The vehicle is driven just like a scooter by a handlebar. In the past years, the Rickshaw or the Tempo Six-Seat is another 3-wheeled vehicle that normally holds six people. These vehicles are operated by lightweight, single-cylinder diesel engines and are more or less like a small bus on fixed routes, also offering them the same competitive capacity. This vehicle comprises a tubular structure with a metal sheet built over it. This car often comes with a mesh hood and does not have doors on either the driver or the passenger cabin. It has two bench seats to each other for the drivers and one front bench seat for the driver and another rider. Government rules, however, do not allow a rider to use this seat and the vehicle remains named a six-seat rickshaw or tempo. This has a steering wheel such as in four-wheeled vehicles.

3.59.2. Commercial Vehicles-Three Wheelers

Over the years, the three-wheeler has become more common, which can be seen by the rise in annual output in the last 15 years, which has tripled in the last decade. The 3-wheel rate of growth has held pace with the quickly rising 2-wheel market, which has maintained 5 to 7% of the latter over the years. A significant number of 3-wheelers are shipped from India.

3.60. Major Manufacturers of Three Wheelers

There are seven big three-wheelers manufactures in India. Bajaj Auto is the leader and is certified to introduce in India the idea of 'auto-rickshaw.' Many other manufacturers have joined the industry and started selling a variety of three-wheeled vehicles like commercial vehicles and freight vehicles driven either by gasoline, gasoline, CNG or LPG. The key ones are Piaggio Pvt.Cars. Mahindra and Mahindra and Ltd. TVS Motors, which launched 4-seater auto rickshaw on selected markets, is the most recent entrant.

3.61. Fuels Used in Three Wheelers

Multiple three-wheelers are built and marketed at home and abroad which use petrol /Diesel or CNG as fuel. Some models can be worked on CNG or LPG. Until recently, the passenger auto-rickshaws of the group <four were almost entirely powered by oil engines. In this segment, the introduction of diesel-driven models has steadily shifted market shares that are now almost evenly split between diesel and gasoline. Many carriers of products are powered by diesel engines. The automobiles that are built to work on CNG or LPG are

mostly petrol models. Unlike in the passenger vehicle industry, these are not conversions of diesel motors.

Price Range -Typical on-road rates in India (including fees and taxes) range from INR 70,000/- for a 2-stroke petrol engine variant to over INR 1,00,000/- for a four-stroke engine.

3.62. Three-wheeler vs four Wheeler Taxi, India point of view

Greater usage of Rickshaw lowers parking space needs. A private car requires at least two car parks, one at home and one at its destination. Although a 3W requires just one parking space in the area, it eliminates the need for nine parking spaces at home and the destination as it performs 10 trips daily. A Rickshaw is a better fit for a car, carries the same population on average, and carries one-third of the car park and a half of the ground surface. All this lowers emission indirectly. Since Rickshaw has a tiny motor (175 cc vs 800 cc for automobiles), it contaminates per passenger considerably more than most vehicles. Its limited engine size achieves speeds of about 50 km/h, according to metropolitan speed limits. It also helps monitor other people's speeds. Due to lower speeds and lightweights, it is not easy for pedestrians and bikes to create serious collisions. Therefore, 3W use in urban areas of India should be promoted as far as possible. Some of the Indian cities lack the facilities needed to cope with mass transit, Rickshaw is the ideal alternative. Despite these realities, modern means of transport such as Uber and Ola have become simpler and quicker to transport the 3W space. This would eventually bring comparable advantages, as Automobile and Pubic transport are still being used relative to 3W, owing to the better living conditions in the area. However, the common mode of transport is still B and C class 3W.

The three-wheelers satisfy the transportation requirements of many that do not use private transport and are not supplied by the current public transport scheme. They represent the interests of a subset of society by serving as cost-effective taxis. They have fewer strength and higher kilometers than standard car taxis. The key guiding factors behind the 3W are politicians who determine different problems, such as the absolute permitted numbers in towns and fare policies, etc. Politicians in different Indian towns have a general propensity to phase out three wheels that they see as competition to public transit, pollution contaminants, sluggish and vulnerable. This informal alternate transport is not often accompanied by adequate evidence to refute these arguments. In comparison, the possibility that three-wheelers protect the travel of a certain portion of the populace (i.e. those who do not use private or current public transport) is often overlooked as legislation is developed. Government policies against two and three-wheelers India is a federal democracy, which implies that the central or national government is shared with the states for all their control on separate policy concerns. The central government usually establishes proposals on different topics; however, they are enacted by the States. Regulating a specific transport style by determining city boundaries, such as the introduction of helmet regulations or the control of pollution, is the duty of the state authority and results in various policies from state to state. The transport industry policies in India are conducted by two government ministries.

- Shipping, Public Transportation & Highways Ministry (MoSRT&H)
- Ministry of Urban Planning and Poverty Elimination (Urban).

No particular guidelines for two and three-wheelers are stated in the different policies of these ministries. Instead, legislative decisions seek to improve connectivity by promoting public transit and not encouraging the usage of private transport types. As two-wheelers are known as private cars, the policies are structured implicitly to prohibit the use of two-wheelers. No particular preference is stated in the private transport rules for a two-wheeler over a vehicle or car over a two-wheeler. In terms of road space, costs, versatility and release of greenhouse gases, two-wheelers have advantages. However, protection, pollution and equality of the two and three-wheelers problems must be discussed. In India, three-wheelers serve as intermediate public transport, the public transport feeder loop in major cities. They are the only transport accessible where public transport is inaccessible for those who do not own cars. An effective high-speed rapid transit system needs a strong three-wheelers network. The Ministry of Urban Development's policy recommendations however promotes mass transport though overlooked discussion of three-wheelers. The programs of other ministries, such as low-interest loans for the needy, allow individuals to purchase more than three-wheelers as work prospects.

Sr. No	City	3W Population 2005	Penetration per Lakh population
1	Gangtok	Nil	0
2	Shimla	Nil	0
3	Kanpur	5252	193
4	Kolkata	41946	285
5	Panji	293	302
6	Agra	4884	357
7	Pondichery	2017	397
8	Bhuvaneswar	3421	405
9	Jaipur	12513	467
10	Nagpur	10666	505
11	Guwahati	5567	525
12	Madurai	6361	537
13	Surat	19512	631
14	Trivendrum	7152	637
15	Chennai	45016	642
16	Bikaner	4125	645
17	Varanasi	12221	645
18	Kochi	12742	701
19	Ahmedabad	43865	739
20	Chandigarh	7256	751
21	Delhi	104747	756
22	Hyderabad	48898	766
23	Bhopal	11620	797
24	Hubli-dharwad	8407	868
25	Mumbai	156261	883
26	Patna	16302	888
27	Bangalore	77375	897
28	Amritsar	9903	913
29	Raipur	7478	1040
30	Pune	44590	1062

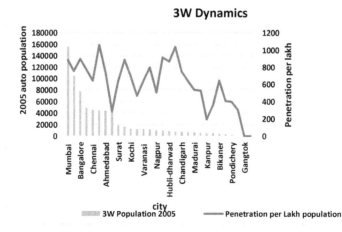

Chart 6.16- 3W city level penetration ,Source – RTO data

3W density per one lakh people is highest in the cities like Pune , Raipur and Amritsar to the tune of 1062 per lakh population in Pune and Cities like Gangtok and Shimla have no population of 3W , state policies largely decide on population of 3W in the given state.

The city-wise supply of 3W above data shows how the government seeks to make accessible the vehicle per lakh of the population with the city for fast transport. Lower the number of vehicles per lakh, greater is the chance of better business for the owner of the vehicle.

3.63. Three Wheeler Vehicles Exports from India

The three-wheelers segment reported the highest growth in automotive exports. In 2006-07, it rose to approximately 144,000 units at CAGR of 56.2% from 2001-02. Bajaj Auto is the biggest 3-wheel driver exporter with a 98% stake in 2006-07. 97% of the Bajaj Auto exports were in the three-wheeler's passenger edition, a fact that shows the need for low-cost public transport in the other developing countries. This pattern is also apparent in recent years.

3.64. Economically competitive transport infrastructure requirements

The fast growth achieved by the Indian economy has contributed to a growth in the production sector, in turn contributing to demand vehicles for products and services being transported across the world. India is switching to a hub and a spoke model in which the M&HCVs are used for travel between the cities (hubs) and the three-wheelers fulfil the need for last-mile transport connectivity. As a consequence, the market for the same is also growing.

Three-wheeler revenues are quite steady, or it saw progress a few years back, which is exactly why it still faces several challenges. For OLA and Uber urban transport, the riders choose to ride in the fully cramped vehicle as opposed to the Free Three-wheeler. Therefore, the three-wheelers are now more and more common in cities type B and c instead of cities class A. Thus, the growth for three-wheelers restricts itself, as the city expands, it tends to use four-wheelers rather than three.

3.65. Segment profile - Passenger Vehicles

The passenger car and utility industries in India include commercial vehicles and utility vehicles. In 2015-2016, passenger vehicle demand rose more than 6% since falling by

4.4% year-on-year in 2013-2014 and by about 4.3 per cent year-on-year in 2014-2015. In 2015-16, PV production surpassed 3,414,390 units. Total output increased by 9.6% Y-Y in 2016-17 (Apr-Jan), with the sharp rise of 32% in MUV production, although passenger car production increased only slightly over the span of approximately 4.8%. In December 2016,

Indian PV sales in 2015-2016 increased by about 6.9 per cent, as a result of a 12 per cent growth in sales of utility vehicles in 2015-2016. Meanwhile, the sales of passenger cars and transporters grew respectively by 5.7 per cent and 3.3 per cent throughout the year. High promotions and free offers by suppliers have powered development in domestic revenue. This along with the decrease in gasoline costs, product releases and interest rates culminated in a rise in Passenger Car sales. Nearly 90% of passenger cars are typically bought on financing. Financial availability and expenses are dependent on liquidity in the financial world, funding schemes and interest rates.

The PV industry is distinguished by comparatively low entry barriers and limited government regulatory intervention. The industry must however respect automotive pollution/emission regulations that appear to be more rigorous and require capital costs. The industry is important for the economy by supplying workers and usage of goods such as steel, aluminum, plastics, and tyres. Explicitly and indirectly. In prices of main inputs such as steel, aluminum and rubber, however, the industry has minimal influence, while it has strong negotiating leverage with product suppliers. The business is highly capital-intensive and it is important to create a strong distribution network to achieve substantial market share.

India exports nearly 20 per cent of its passenger vehicle sales. The USA, Western Europe, Japan and China are the largest passenger vehicle export markets. In 2015-2016 PV sales were reported with 3,443,901 units, 654,223 of which were exported.

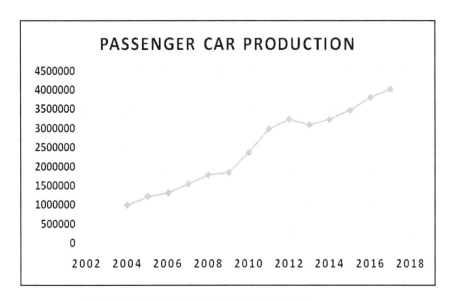

Year	Production
2004	989560
2005	1209876
2006	1309300
2007	1545223
2008	1777583
2009	1838593
2010	2357411
2011	2982772
2012	3231058
2013	3087973
2014	3221419
2015	3465045
2016	3801670
2017	4010373

Chart 6.17 - 4W industry production

Source – Team-BHP /SIAM 2019 reports

Passenger car segment manufactured 989560 vehicles in the year 2004 and in the year 2017 it manufactured 4010373 number

The passenger vehicle industry in India has risen from 3,087,973 vehicles in 2014 (FY 2014) to 3,221,419 (FY 2015) to 3,413,859 (FY 2016), up 5.97% from 4.3% last year. The increase in sales volumes was expressed in both types of passenger cars, largely due to lower fuel costs, better market feelings and lower interest rates. The rise was guided by economic recovery, a favourable general feeling in the nation and increased infrastructure spending. This is attributed to lower normal monsoons that influence the demand in rural India, despite the low agricultural feeling. Hatchback revenues were already down, but with new releases, the sedans started to rise considerably. The segment of utility vehicles has also shown development, primarily in soft-road UVs and multi-use vehicles. The passenger car industry has backward and forward ties to retail links, iron, copper, chemicals, paints, glass, appliances, capital, trucking, and storage forward links retail stores, credit and funding, logistics, ads, repair and servicing, service components, petroleum goods, gas stations, insurance.

3.66. Five Forces Analysis: Passenger vehicles

Five forces form competitiveness and assess the total viability of the business. Based on the finances, core competencies, market model and network, specific businesses will be exposed to differences in profitability over the industry average. A traditional automaker has a press office, body shop, paint shop, engine & transmission shop and assembly shop press shop: a digital operated production line turns sheet metal into high-dimensional detailed and clear body panels. Body Shop: It is a high-tech assembly line that manufactures full body panel shells. Automated robotic arms are used to maintain superior and reliable construction efficiency for complicated welding operations. Paint Shop: it allows us to have a broad variety of paints for consumer wants. Engine & Transmission Store: This is the shop where the heart of the vehicle is made, i.e. the engine and transmission. Assembly shop: here, both the motor and suspension components are installed into the vehicle, the electrical parts, the body parts etc. are checked in whole. This company consists of the Trim Line, Chassis Line, Final Line and the OK Line. The study of five powers is presented below.

3.67. Entry obstacles-

No business will come and start making vehicles. It is only foreign rivals with decades of international experience, size, technical specifications, management expertise and resources that have eroded Indian automobile corporations' market share. Globalization is an important trend in the domestic automotive industry. International auto manufacturers have gradually become simpler to access the domestic market by liberalised policies.

3.68. Competition -

The automotive sector is recognised as the Maruti Suzuki, Tata Motors, Mahindra & Mahindra, Hyundai, Toyota, Honda, Nissan, Ford, GM, Volkswagen, etc. (a market condition in which sellers are so few that the actions of any one of them will materially affect price). In general, highly competitive sectors have poor returns because competition costs are high. The auto companies recognise that price-based rivalry would not immediately contribute to market share gains but threatens profitability. They also traditionally tended to stop price-based rivalry. But the market has escalated more recently - rebates, preferred financing and long-term guarantees have helped draw buyers. Yet they also placed a strain on car sales' profit margins. Car firms upgrade their vehicles every year. It's part of regular activities, so there may be a concern if a corporation chooses to modify a car's configuration dramatically. These reforms may cause major delays and collisions, contributing to higher costs and slower growth in sales. While a modern idea can pay off considerably in the long term, it is still a risky plan. In India, there is strong competition from global brands (especially in the B segment), which represents a competitive supply of the same characteristics at a reduced price. There are frequent product advances and competitive frugal engineering. Foreign corporations have aggravated rivalry by modifying their standard designs and adjusting them to the needs of Indians.

3.69. Buyers' negotiation power –

Indian consumers have good negotiating power since they have an option of many other goods in the same price range from numerous manufacturers. In the other side, although buyers are very responsive to costs, they have little buying power and they never buy many vehicles. Increased gasoline costs decrease consumers' appetite for vehicles. Energy-efficient cars that offer value for money boost buyers' appetite. Government regulations also impact the automotive industry's production and supply the hand.

3.70. Bargaining Power of Suppliers–

Suppliers are divided. The majority of vendors depend on one or two automobile producers to buy the majority of their automotive goods. If an automotive company chooses to move manufacturers, the condition may be negative. As a consequence, vendors are highly sensitive to car manufacturers' requests and needs and have relatively limited control. The vendors have poor bargaining power since most automotive product makers are specialised in certain segments with just one consumer. In exchange, manufacturers depend on them. The life cycle of a car is very significant for parts suppliers. The more a car remains in service, the more new parts are required. However, modern parts last longer and are perfect for buyers but for parts suppliers, it is not so positive news. For example, as most car manufactures switch from rolling steel to stainless steel, the transition has increased the component life by many years.

3.71. **The threat of Substitutes-** The replacement for automobile transport is the possibility of people coming to their destinations by bus, train or aeroplane. The higher the expense of running a vehicle, the more inclined people are to search for alternate travel alternatives. Time, personal interest and convenience of the vehicle against the replacement often affect the evaluation of the danger faced by substitutes.

Sr No	Segment	Type	Length	Example
1	A1	Mini	Up to 3400 mm	Maruti 800 , Nano
2	A2	Compact	3401 to 4000 mm	Alto , Wagon R ,Palio , Indica
3	A3	Midsize	4001 to 4500 mm	City , SX4, Logan, Verna
4	A4	Executive	4501 to 4700 mm	Corolla,Civic,Octavia
5	A5	Premium	4701 to 5000 mm	Camry , E Class, Laura
6	A6	Luxury	Above 5000 mm	Mercedes S class,
7	B1	Van		Versa, Magic
8	B2	MUV/MPV		Innova , Sumo
9	SUV	CRV		Vitara

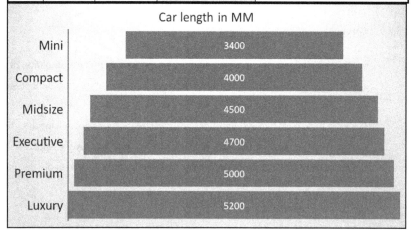

Chart 6.18- 4W industry Classification

Source – Maruti Suzuki, Investors presentation

3.72. 4w Industry classification-

Each type of car has a particular significance, below is the quick summary of each name for the end-user

3.72.1. **Vans :** Vans are used mostly for personal transportation. They normally have 1 or 1.5 sets, up to five to ten chairs, hardtops and prices up to 10 lakhs. One illustration is Maruti Suzuki's model Omni.

3.72.2. **Utility vehicles:** effective vehicles/sport utility vehicles are once again used for personal transport. For personal transport. They have two boxes, seats up to 5 or 10, 2x4 or 4x4 off-road and ladder on a frame in general. E.g. Toyota Innova, Safari Wind, etc. UV1: price up to INR. 15 lakhs < 4400 mm UV2: rates between INR. 15 and 25 lakhs the vehicle price depends upon the vehicle model, motor power and version.

3.72.3. **Trends :** Automobiles are highly reliant on market trends and tastes. Though automotive firms offer several cars to companies and car rental companies (fleet purchases), the main source of revenues is customer sales. The Indian automobile market is maturing and many new segments are developing and car manufactures are playing with it. The desires of an Indian car buyer vary from those of consumers in other areas of the world. Sedans and SUVs have usually deemed a luxury.

3.72.4. **Hatchbacks:**The Indian market is called the hatchback market. Compact cars are required today and even the Government has imposed legislation to encourage cars under four metres to be produced, as they attract lower duties and other taxes. Petroleum engines below 1.2 litres and diesel engines below 1500 cc also decreased excise duty. This leads to fuel consumption and also to emissions control. Since hatchbacks profit from sedans, more hatchbacks are sold in India. The India hatchback demand is roughly 50%, with about 26% heading to entry-level hatchbacks such as Hyundai Eon, Maruti Suzuki Alto, Maruti Suzuki Wagon R, 24% of luxury hatchbacks including Maruti Suzuki Swift, Hyundai i20, Nissan Micra and Fiat Punto Evo for 2015-16. The higher price gap between petrol and diesel cars in cars under INR 10 lakh is contributing to a greater pull for petrol cars. India is still predominantly a hatchback business, although in 2009 the proportion has dropped from 70% to 50%. Parking is a challenge with an increasing number of cars and bikes and a hatchback is an excellent option. With a lack of room even in the coming cities, there will be a higher demand for hatchbacks, especially those powered by petrol. Diesel would be the alternative for long-distance passengers.

3.73. Latest developments :

In the last few years, the pattern in purchasing has changed when sedans and SUVs with a range of fewer than 4 metres utilising the excise duty break. This has increased these latest segments' revenues. The Tata Indigo eCS originated with the compact sedan segment but Maruti Suzuki launched a sub-4-meter Swift DZire a few years back. This product has changed the game for the brand, and also Honda, Hyundai and Tata Motors have since entered the vehicle. In the category of SUV, the first mover in this segment is the Ford Ecosport, preceded by the Fiat Avventura. The hatchbacks like the Toyota Etios Cross and the Volkswagen Cross Polo are something of a cosmetic update.

3.74. Planned trends:

The utility category (including SUVs and MUVs) has roughly 26 per cent market share and the Sedans have 24 per cent. However, it was the case when Diesel rates were substantially less than petrol; now they are both priced in the same manner. Slowly again, the economy is moving towards petrol and demand for diesel cars will soon decline and some SUV market will be captured by sedans. Compact sedans and medium-sized sedans will soon see their sales, particularly for gasoline vehicles, rise. Also, premium hatchbacks, particularly petrol-powered vehicles, will rise in numbers. The domestic output of the passenger vehicle segment is seen below. In other categories, the overall market estimates comprise deliveries but exclude van purchases.

Car Segments	% share
Hatchback	50
SUV & MUV	26
Sedans	24

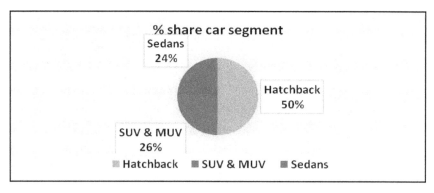

Chart 6.19- 4W segments

In the passenger car segment of automotive industry hatchback contribute for approx. 50% of the share ,Sedans which have boot space contribute 24% and SUV which is slightly premium segment contribute for 26% of share.

The above table reveals that India is still a small car market and is primarily guided by purchase costs and repair costs.

3.75. <u>Segment profile - Commercial Vehicles</u>

The Indian Commercial Vehicle (CV) industry comprises of MHCVs (trucks and buses) and light commercial vehicles (LCVs) for medium and large commercial vehicles (goods carrier and passenger vehicles). The market is categorized into light-duty trucks, medium-size vehicles and high-duty passenger vehicles depending on the heavyweight of the car. CVs are often graded based on engine power, energy, rated payload, compression ratio, overload extent, etc. In compliance with the Motor Vehicles Act – 1988, MHCVs surpass 7.5 tons. Vehicles focused on GVW are intermediate commercial vehicles, medium-sized commercial and heavy-duty vehicles. MHCV goods vehicles are primarily used for longer distances to bear higher loads. LCVs are primarily used to move travellers and commodities in towns with shorter distances. LCVs have a GVW of less than 7.5 tonnes. LCV products are further categorised as mini trucks (<=3.5 tons), pickups (<=3.5 tons) and high-end cars LCV goods vehicles (3.5 -7.5 tons).

Indian CV industry is controlled by-products carriers (roughly 88% of domestic CV revenues) and hence domestic sales are primarily based on economic activities, such as industrial and agricultural development. Additional factors that influence domestic commercial vehicle demand are:

1) GDP and macroeconomic stability of the world
2) Changes in freight movement in fuel and prices
3) The profitability of vehicle owners and public transit providers
4) Industrial Development Index
5) Credit availability and interest rates
6) Policies of government

Depressed economic growth during 2012-15 resulted in poor demand for freight; moreover, the profitability of transportation operators (TOs) was diminished by the spiraling fuel prices following partial deregulation of diesel. During the 2013-15 span, TOs restricted fleet adds due to low utilisation and lower profitability. In May 2014, a new government was established at the Center, followed by business sentiments. In 2015-16, revenue rose by 12 per cent. While the economy is not completely improving, progressive growth has been seen in the course of the year, supported by lower inflation and higher industries. Therefore, throughout 2014-15, transport operators resumed fleet acquisitions and in 2015-16, contributing to an increase in CV demand.

India exports about 10-15% of its commercial vehicle sales. China and the US became the main export markets for commercial vehicles. In 2015-2016, 787,393 units of CVs were recorded, 101,689 of them being exported. In 2016-2017, the country's exports to CVs stood at 91,250 units, around 14 per cent of total sales until January. However, the sales of commercial vehicles (CV) are forecast to rise slightly in 2016-2017. With CV manufacturers directed by the government to move from April 2020 to Bharat Stage (BS) VI emission levels, the sales of MHCV will decline in the span 2020-21. Because the BS-VI cars are comparatively cheaper, the fleet owners purchased more BS4 cars before the end of March 2020 to reduce unnecessary expenditure due to BS6.

Year	Production No
2004	550080
2005	707406
2006	782166
2007	539989
2008	484141
2009	466393
2010	721939
2011	881144
2012	832649
2013	699035
2014	698298
2015	786692
2016	810253
2017	894551

Commercial vehicle segment manufactured 5550080 numbers of vehicles in the year 2004 and it manufactured 894551 vehicles in the year 2017. However the nature of this industry is cyclic in nature and it's a real barometer of economy. when the industrial production was very low un like the other segments it had shown a dip in manufactured numbers in the year 2013 again at 699035

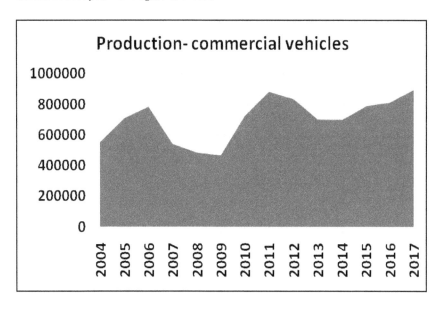

Chart 6.20- Commercial vehicles production statistics / Source –SIAM

3.76. <u>Exports of CVs from India</u>

Short automotive life cycles have driven businesses to bring contemporary goods to the Indian market as a consequence of faster substitution. The 14.1 per cent CAGR achieved between 2005-2006 and 2016-2017 by the domestic automotive industry rendered India one of the fastest-growing markets in the world. Successive administrations implemented stable economic strategies. The Indian government has maintained consistency in the country's reforms and initiatives, which led to overall economic development, including growth in the motor industry. Also, the Government has taken particular policy measures to raise local demand, such as reducing excise duty on smaller automobiles, etc. VAT introduction has rendered India one of the leading low-cost production outlets worldwide. India is projected to become the development centre for small cars. It has also been identified as a low-cost part source. Vehicles would also benefit a lot from the multinational outsourcing pattern to low-cost countries. Low-Cost Skilled Labor The rate of quality workers in India is among the lowest in the country. In terms of supply, India generates 400,000 engineering graduates annually and it is projected that approximately seven million qualified employees will join the workforce next year on average. Nine

Indian product manufacturers have already received the Deming Standard Award and the rest of the leading component manufacturers are accredited with ISO and QS.

Country	Ratio
China	1.17
Japan	1.1
USA	0.78
Germany	0.55
Russia	0.26
India	0.2

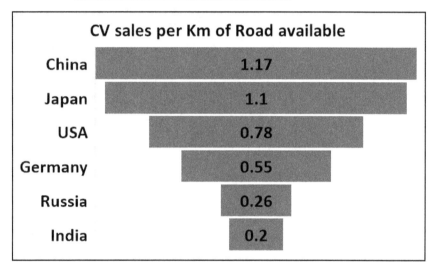

Chart 6.21 – Global Commercial vehicles penetration per Km

Source – OICA (International Organization of motor vehicles manufacturer)

The sales ratio of commercial vehicles to the road network of a nation demonstrates clearly that the scope for the growth of commercial vehicles is very large.

3.77. Growth in Industrial Production

In recent years, the Indian economy has expanded at 8.5% a year and has emerged as one of the fastest-growing economies in the world. In recent years, the manufacturing sector has expanded by 8-10% per annum. This has generated the need for goods transport and increased demand for CVs.

3.78. Enhanced access to low-cost financing

More than 90% of the CV transactions are on lease. In recent years, the availability of funding to CV buyers has increased. A vast number of financial firms have joined the CV market. This has made it far simpler for customers to access financing.

3.79. Path emergence as the main form of transport

The proportion of roads in India has been gradually growing and the percentage of railways has decreased. In the 1950s, the proportion of road transport in the total transport of goods was about 15%, now almost 60%. This is because of better road networks, decreased road and rail cost differentials and the benefits of last-mile access offered by the road.

3.80. Implementation of the Overloading Laws and others

The increased introduction of overload regulations has also led to a rise in the count of CVs on Indian highways. Furthermore, several countries have curtailed the use of old CVs, which has helped to raise demand in this segment for substitution.

3.81. Segment profile - Tractors and Off-Road vehicle industry

Tractors are known to be in the wider context member of the farm machinery category. Like an automobile, though, we treated it as part of the analysis. The Indian tractor industry is categorised into mini, medium and heavy tractors dependent on engine horsepower (HP). Tractors with engine capacity between 31 and 40 rule the tractor segment in India with sales of this size reaching 40 per cent. This is accompanied by the scale of the motor from '41-50' to 28 per cent in 2015-16. The market for large tractors has risen in recent years as a result of many changes. Most of the market comes from agriculture. Non-Agri production (infrastructure and construction) accounts for a smaller proportion of the overall output. In the last few years, Mahindra appears to be the market leader in the tractor industry with a position of over 37% in overall volumes. Another big tractor firm is Escorts Ltd. with a market share of about 10%. Other big firms in the Indian tractor sector are John Deere and TAFE. Following more than 11 per cent in 2015-16 (Apr-Jan), the output of tractors increased by over 15.8 per cent during the same span of 2016-17, thanks to improved farm feelings due to higher monsoon than anticipated, following a decline in min sale prices (MSPs) for different crops in 2015-16 (Apr-Jan).

The market for better farm sentiments and higher farming activities along with improved non-agricultural demand is projected to further boost over the last quarter of 2016-17.

The tractor industry has always been a barometer for India's rural economy. India's tractor industry is fairly young but has now been one-third the world's largest market, bar sub-20 HP belt-driven tractors used in China. China and the US are the other big tractor markets in the world.

Until 1960, the tractor's demand was completely fulfilled by imports. Indigenous tractor production started in 1961. India proceeded to import tractors to meet complete needs up to late 1970's and in the early 1980s had just crossed about 50,000 units, but today the Indian Tractor industry has risen to over 600,000 units. Since then, the Indian Tractor Industry has come a long way. Despite seasonal vagaries, volume development in the past 4 decades has demonstrated 7.5% CAGR tractor demand and consequently industry volumes.

During FY2016-17, the Indian tractor industry saw a positive growth pattern. Although domestic volumes rose by 18.2% between April 2016 and March 2017, exports stayed virtually flat. Standard monsoon was a big driver of development. It stimulated production and raised farmers' incomes, which ultimately helped raise tractor demand. Positional development has been seen in all major countries such as Maharashtra, Madhya Pradesh, Bihar, Karnataka, Gujarat, Andhra Pradesh and Uttar Pradesh.

Over the last three years, the southern region has continuously surpassed all other regions, with strong demand in Andhra Pradesh, Tamil Nadu and Telangana contributing to growth. Government support programs and stronger rural feelings helped hold the growth trend in these countries. In the current fiscal year, the eastern region continues to show a good volume growth, albeit on a low level, benefiting from numerous government interventions to improve agricultural mechanisation.

Demand in the central and western areas has recovered due to improving agricultural sentiments, based on projections of improved crop output and subsequent farm profits. The northern area is still lagging behind pan India's rise. The region's biggest tractor sector, Uttar Pradesh, has enjoyed healthy growth. As a consequence of poor transport and alternative demand, other main markets in Rajasthan and Punjab continue to battle.

Year	Tractor Production
2004	179000
2005	242000
2006	254000
2007	311000
2008	304000
2009	303000
2010	383000
2011	440331
2012	545109
2013	526912
2014	634151
2015	612994
2016	570791
2017	691361

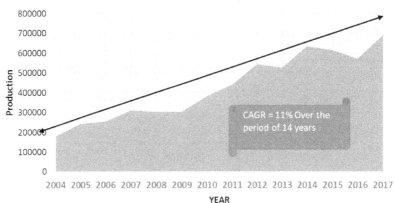

Chart 6.22- Tractor sales statistics, Source – Mahindra and Mahindra

India tractor industry manufactured 179000 tractors in the year 2004 and 691361 tractors in the year 2017. It has shown a CAGR growth of 11% over the period of 14 years from 2004 to 2017

State sales specifically show the areas that are at the forefront of agricultural production, as Maharashtra leads the industrial revolution, Punjab and Uttar Pradesh lead the green revolution.

State	2001	2002	2003	2004	2005	2006	2007	2008	2009	2010	2011	2012	2013	2014	2015	2016
Andhra	17520	12203	11263	10626	16615	22448	35613	43758	38417	34730	35173	53175	63275	74920	37028	30243
Assam	540	571	499	493	385	771	1120	1296	1588	3583	2430	2057	2099	2408	3557	5669
Bihar	17344	14028	13115	12235	14636	9946	11824	13104	17572	29050	26621	25981	28260	30187	36090	35402
Chhatisgad	0	4939	7129	6570	8790	10192	0	0	0	0	11134	9254	9221	12139	20011	16861
Gujrat	11546	13700	8434	10086	17078	23100	29651	25255	20179	24323	440911	41958	30765	44163	46411	39792
Haryana	16560	13697	11504	11688	12408	14709	20385	21627	22573	28671	28403	31533	23741	30599	30626	22685
Himachal	395	577	652	521	512	758	1117	891	907	1201	1404	1398	1255	1530	1519	1354
Jharkhand	0	2349	2961	2897	3643	5676	0	0	0	0	6524	6697	6756	8349	8169	8118
Jammu	850	1071	1271	1506	1135	1296	1178	1328	1115	1608	2128	2618	3577	3794	2601	2324
Karnataka	11261	8984	6512	8595	15560	25316	22455	17230	13835	23849	27244	29162	34861	37	33758	32804
Kerala	669	348	135	148	125	765	1848	493	374	582	671	631	570	385	268	332
Madhya Pradesh	21901	29818	24344	29568	33733	23828	19378	18242	24306	33342	48435	50597	70822	87831	63744	48375
Maharashtra	14420	8586	4867	7112	11545	17173	26070	29815	25610	34186	40951	56664	43245	46669	49839	42125
Odisa	4970	2622	3076	2933	4957	6683	7214	49193	5099	7909	12861	13277	15831	24277	10878	12668
Punjab	20879	19626	15484	13906	11715	12052	16201	18062	20027	28608	24122	26040	27900	35290	26074	17829
Rajasthan	14692	16228	10914	18241	23830	27949	34583	29456	25763	31822	53604	57191	44221	65405	64565	61193
Tamilnadu	9931	6053	4896	6487	12470	18294	21880	16894	14609	15768	20638	26298	18448	9865	8072	14667
Telangana	0	0	0	0	0	0	0	0	0	0	0	0	0	0	0	13153
Uttarakhand	0	1345	2861	2479	1869	2321	0	0	0	0	3893	5377	4600	4969	2205	2769
Uttarpradesh	65253	48165	39724	38842	46326	44307	48184	39682	51513	73686	76981	82613	84559	95653	92219	71527
West Bengal	3385	2510	2169	2001	3085	4337	5595	5354	6096	9186	13045	12187	12752	13756	12751	12934
Others	7449	7263	12798	12100	1340	24 18	1768	1522	1983	2315	1876	2172	876	1220	1078	945
Export	0	0	0	4567	20076	28097	33766	43553	41142	37622	62872	70772	62890	62677	75376	77485
Total	239565	214683	184608	203601	261833	300018	339830	376755	332708	422041	941921	607652	590524	656123	626839	571254

Chart 6.23- state-wise tractor sales

Source – MOSPI

OEMs	Market share 2018
Mahindra	40.2
TAFE	18.4
Escorts Ltd	11.8
Sonalika	12.2
Others	17.5
Total	100

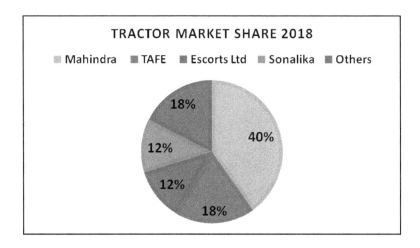

Chart 6.24- the share of Business (Tractors – India)

Source – Economic times Auto April 30 , 2019 update

Mahindra continues to be leader in the over market share of tractor with 40% share , TAFE and Escorts have market share of 18% each, Sonalika with 12 % and other small players contribute all put together 12% share

Mahindra and Mahindra remain at the forefront of tractors produced each year in India and the globe.

3.82. Segment profile - Off Road Vehicles

Year	Off road vehicles
2004	12000
2005	15000
2006	23000
2007	38000
2008	45500
2009	40500
2010	59700
2011	72200
2012	66400
2013	55900

Year	Off road vehicles
2014	60700
2015	68200
2016	76000
2017	84500
2018	97000

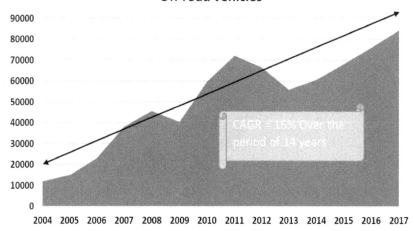

Off road vehicles

Chart 6.25 - Off-Road vehicles statistics

Source – JCB corporate presentation

Off road industry or popularly called as construction equipment segment manufactured 12000 vehicles in 2004 and 97000 vehicles in 2018. It clocked the growth of 16% over 14 years of period

Above figure demonstrates the production amount and development of off-road vehicles over the last 10 years. India wants massive investment in the automobile industry's construction equipment and off-road market. This sector is expected to expand as different proposals are announced by the new Indian PM Shri Narendra Modi. Few are homes for everyone, road network, major ports and national highway investments, Smart City plan. Just 24% of India's national highways have 4 roads, and the balance needs to be reached shortly. This would call for immense needs in the construction machinery market. This pattern is quite evident in the table above which discusses the rise in construction machinery over the past 10 years. Infrastructure growth is the section that requires 100% FDI to automatically function. In the past 3-4 years, many ventures announced by the government have attracted maximum FDI. This also lets India resolve trade imbalance crises with developed countries.

A well-developed infrastructure is the basis for growth in any country and paves the way for a better quality of life and a rapid increase in GDP, particularly for developing countries such as India. The Indian construction industry is recognised as the second-largest employer and contributor to economic development after agriculture. The building industry still accounts for the largest migration of FDI to the services sector and has more than 35 million national workers. The infrastructure sector accounts for 50 per cent of demand for construction activities in India, while the remainder comes from mining activities, residential and commercial production etc. It is projected that the Indian Construction Industry valuation reaches 126 billion dollars.

Five year plans	Spend plan in INR CR	Acual spend INR CR
1951-56	2069	1960
1956-57	4800	4673
1961-66	7500	8577
1969-74	15901	15779
1974-79	38853	39426
1980-85	97500	109292
1985-90	180000	218730
1992-97	434100	527012
1997-02	859200	705818
2002-07	1525639	1249322
2007-12	3644719	2862029
2012-17	8050124	Not Available

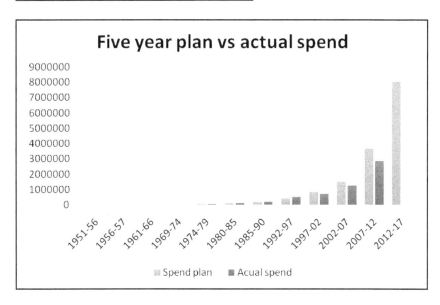

Chart 6.26 - Five-year plan spending

Source – MOSPI

Development in infrastructure is crucial to the industry's realization of its ability in India. The Government has committed nearly $1 trillion in capital spending in its 12th Five-Year Strategy, with 40% of the funds originating from the private sector. The Indian Government has strengthened FDI requirements for many sectors of infrastructure growth to encourage such investments. This is expected to stimulate demand for earthmoving and building machinery, and if the industry understands all its capacity, it might result in an industry worth $16 billion to $21 billion by 2021-22.

3.83. The 12th Five Year Plan

India's need to build infrastructure is also backed by government intentions as set out in the 12-Year Plan (FYP). The infrastructure is a crucial sector of the plan's budget, with an allocation of around $1 trillion (Rs.55 lakh crores). Five industries account for over 80% of the overall projected expenditure: energy, telecommunications, highways and bridges, irrigation and railway networks and public transportation systems.

Five year plans	Centre	State	Total
1951-56	1241	828	2069
1956-57	2559	2241	4800
1961-66	3600	3900	7500
1969-74	8870	7031	15901
1974-79	19954	18899	38853
1980-85	47250	50250	97500
1985-90	95534	84466	180000
1992-97	247865	186235	434100
1997-02	489361	369839	859200
2002-07	893183	632456	1525639
2007-12	2156572	1488147	3644719
2012-17	4333739	3716385	8050124

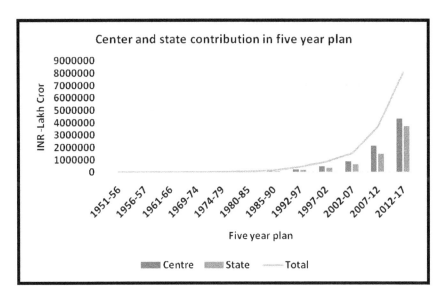

Chart 6.27- Five-year plan center vs state spending

Source – MOSPI

Indian road investments are set to leap overall, with the government preparing to expand on basic infrastructure plans expected to rise infrastructure expenses. Rs.8,8 lakh crores, 11th FYP, and Rs.26,8 lakh crores, 12th FYP, concentrated on four sectors: communication, power, road & bridge, and green energy. Investments were private.

3.84. Indian Urban Infrastructure

It is projected that US$ 650 billion is expected in urban infrastructure over the next 20 years. Almost 45 per cent of this is needed to build urban roads. The government has pursued various initiatives to improve urban infrastructure in the country and has invested approximately US$2 billion on the national urban regeneration mission Jawaharlal Nehru (JNNURM). It has also introduced the Small and Medium Towns Urban Infrastructure Planning Programme, which is investing US$1 billion to meet the infrastructure requirements of small towns and towns. There is also a renewed drive in this field into public-private partnerships (PPPs). Delhi – Mumbai Industrial Corridor (DMIC) is an ambitious infrastructure initiative that is conceptualised by the Japanese Government and seeks to transform modern industrial communities into "Smart Cities" and converge next-generation infrastructure technologies. Investment schemes worth US$ 200 trillion have already been authorised under the DMIC. DMIC performance contributed to several identical corridors such as the corridor in Bangalore Chennai, etc.

3.85. **Roads**

India has one of the world's biggest road networks, with just the USA and China behind. And to upgrade the road infrastructure of the nation. Under NHDP (National Highway Development Programme), so far, 33,500 km have been built or still have to be awarded a balance of 21,000 km. Comprehensive private sector commitments to the adoption of the NHDP are being exploited by contracting and public-private partnerships (PPP). The 12th FYP is predicting a more than 100% growth in projected expenditures in the 11th FYP, guided by higher objectives through national highways, state roads and rural roads. The FYP aims to cover over 13,000 km of modern national highways in remote areas and 1,58,000 km of new roads. As well as government expenditure, private funds rose from 5% in the 10th FYP to 20% in the 11th FYP, mostly due to factors such as 100% foreign external investments in road networks, 10- to 20-year tax cuts across concession times, and duty exemptions for road import equipment.

3.86. **Airports**

There are 454 airports in India, of which around 90 are commercially available and 16 globally designated. The busiest airports in India are Delhi and Mumbai with approximately 2.5 traffic times as the second busiest airport. This rise has placed immense strain on the country's established airport infrastructure. The Indian Government has estimated investments of about US$12 billion to help cope with additional demand in the next five years programme, and involvement by the private sector is likely to play a major role. The private sector is projected to contribute 75 per cent of the expenditure envisaged in the next five years programme.

3.87. **Railways**

Railways remain another significant priority for the growth of transport networks. During the 12th FYP, the government allocated approximately 5,19,000 crores for rail transport, of which approximately 95,000 INR. for expenditure in specialised freight corridors on the eastern and western routes. Before December 2013, 3,343 km of Modern Railway lines were created to provide a major boost to the infrastructure industries in the current five-year plan. The Dedicated Freight Corridor initiative is a big effort planned to draw private investment. Through the development of special freight lines, the project would decongest the roads between Delhi & Mumbai and Delhi & Kolkata at an approximate cost of US$ 6-7 billion.

3.88. Ports

The 12th FYP budgets Rs1.98.000 crores for ports, of which about 85% was charged by private players. As of December 2013, 217,5 million tonnes of potential handling capacity have been generated annually in our ports to improve infrastructure industries.

3.89. Indian Earthmoving & Machinery Industry

Infrastructure projects are the key factors of development for building machinery. Overall capital investments during the 12th Five-Year Plan (2012-17) represented around 10% of the Gross Domestic Product (GDP) relative to 7.6% in the previous Plan (2007-12).

Equipment type	% market share
Material processing equipment	6%
Material handling equipment	11%
Concrete equipment	15%
earth moving equipment	68%
Total	100%

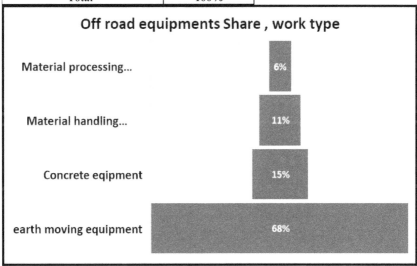

Chart 6.28- Market share of earthmoving equipment's

Source – JCB share holders PPT , 2017

In JCB shareholders PPT it is observed that 68% of the construction equipment manufactured are earth moving machines. This indicates that the basic need for infrastructure development is addressed by this specific equipment

3.90. Construction equipment market share by segment

The Indian construction equipment industry includes five major sectors: earthmoving equipment, road construction equipment, concrete equipment, handling equipment and processing equipment. Earthmoving machinery and road-building equipment constitute almost 70 per cent of the Indian demand for construction equipment. 65% of the earthmoving machinery and road building market is made up of Backhoe loaders. In the year 2002, backhoe chargers accounted for over 50% of earthmoving unit-based equipment revenues, led by rockers (about 23 per cent).

3.91. CE market contracted in 2018

Construction equipment's sales 2014 and 2018			
Type	2014	2018	% Change 2014-2018
Articulated Dump Trucks	10	10	0
Asphalt Finishers	750	1100	47
Backhoe Loaders	30000	38000	27
Compaction Equipment	2700	4500	67
Crawler Dozers	350	700	100
Crawler Excavators	11500	28000	143
Crawler Loaders	5	10	100
Mini Excavators	550	1200	118
Mobile Compressors	5000	7000	40
Mobile Cranes	6500	10000	54
Motor Graders	300	750	150
Rigid Dump Trucks	550	850	55
RTLTs	30	100	233
Skid-Steer Loaders	600	1000	67
Wheeled Excavators	10	10	0
Wheeled Loaders	1800	3500	94
Total Construction Equipment	60655	96730	59

During the study of construction equipment manufacturing data it is observed that as the infra spend from government increases this industry sales are going up. The trend was clearly seen from 2014 and 2018 data there was total rise of 59% in the production numbers during this period

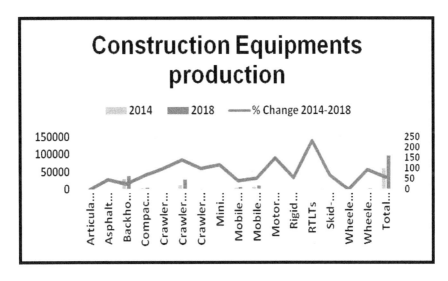

Chart 6.29 -Construction Equipment market in 2018,

Source – nbmcw.com

3.92. Financing and renting facilities in India

Much like any commodity involving high one-time capital costs, borrowing is a strong way to drive demand and to buy new consumers from the construction machinery industry. India's funding industry for earthmoving and building machinery was measured at INR 23,000 crores. Approximately 80 per cent of the machinery bought is funded. For manufactured machines, 90% of the equipment bought is sponsored much higher. The financing industry of the ECE is projected to expand by a compound annual growth pace of about 22 per cent over the next few years. The bulk of the finance is by loans, with leasing as a far second choice. Some 80% of the ECE consumers who want to fund are micro, small and medium-sized businesses. With ticket sizes ranging from Rs.20 lakh for an individual user's backhoe loader to Rs.20 crores for the procurement of bulk machinery by a construction corporation, the diversity of players supplying equipment funding has increased. Non-banking financial enterprises manage ECE finance between 75 and 80 percent. Financial intermediaries have a strong market share – over 80 per cent of all CE purchased in India is sponsored. The key purchasers of non-financed machinery comprise public and government companies. These are the percentage of expenditure in capital across industries but the penetration is far higher in CE alone. First Time Buyers (FTBs) lead the business with 60 per cent of the market share indicating a wide market with quick access to funding. Together, FTB and Mid (small retail buyers) shape the retail consumer category that is accountable for a big market.

Construction firms are exposed to considerable strain to slash capital spending and thus more and more machinery is leased on a monthly or hourly basis or as much of the content treated as necessary. Again, Indian rental penetration is still poor at about 7 to 8% relative to global levels of 50 to 80%. Construction equipment rental in India is still a highly fragmented industry but is projected to rise rapidly, likely above 30% a year in the mid-term. Several OEMs have already formed dedicated rental/leasing teams.

A robust rental market helps expenditure on project programs to be minimised by contracting equipment needs (including spare and service requirements) and improving equipment capability utilisation. Backhoe loaders, pick-nick car (PNC) cranes, baggers, motor graders, and vibratory compactors are the main equipment in Indian rental floors. The leasing and rental of machinery in India is less than Japan, the United States and China. The need for rental equipment would be expressed in high mid-term growth due to massive infrastructure spending. New players can also pursue possibilities in the area of machinery financing.

The limited participation of major integrated players reduces rental financing development. Because of today's limited business concentration and enormous development potential, increased access to finance would allow the sector to develop.

3.93. Key Challenges for Infrastructure and Construction Equipment Industry

Land procurement delays: development programs, land delays since projects being won could not purchase land until and until certain projects were launched. For e.g., the Trivandrum-Tamil Nadu boundary road project has had problems with land clearing, while the offer was awarded in 2010. Country-wide land acquisition laws have been universally applied, creating delays. Also, lenders are not likely to fund ventures until clearances are accessible and 100% access assured

Clearance delays: Forest and environmental delays also affect many development programs. Clearance procedures are also not used fairly, and multiple clearance justifications are given on numerous occasions. This not only impacts the pace of clearances but also often gives unsure messages to customers —, which also contributes to investment recovery. For e.g., the contractor for the 6-lane highway in Kishangarh-

Udaipur-Ahmedabad has closed the project, because environmental clearance has not succeeded. Similarly, the Chennai Port-Maduravoyal road project was undertaken without approval from the State Water Department. In addition to resolving infrastructure issues, the ECE industry will be based in three areas of the ECE environment to reach its maximum potential:

Financing

- Original equipment manufacturers (OEMs) provide restricted funding solutions in India and payment rates are mostly unfavourable to initial consumers. As a consequence, access to finance prohibits numerous potential consumers from shopping.

- Leasing is a reasonable choice for consumers who wish to limit their high capital expenses. However, Indian penetration is considerably smaller (7 per cent to 8 per cent) than in other wide ECE markets (65 per cent in the United States and 35 per cent in China).

- The secondary Indian equipment industry is underdeveloped.

- Recovery is an important problem for non-bank finance companies whose big ECE funding suppliers are not very tolerant of legislation related to defaults and bad debts.

Disclosure of qualified staff

1) If the ECE industry expands quickly, there would be a rise in the need for qualified operators and mechanics. The shortage of professional labour would possibly be a concern. Many government agencies, ECE firms and business organisations seek to address the problem of capability shortages, however, cooperation between them should be strengthened.

2) Many buyers of construction machinery are independent players who prefer instruction on the job for operators and mechanics and who do not want to spend a premium for professional employees.

3) Specialized classes in construction machinery service at industrial training institutes are not part of technical training since the large expense of equipment ensures that hands-on training is costly. ECE educational institutes operated by OEMs prove to be costly for groups with low wages.

4) There is a shortage of standardised national protection and efficiency standards. Execution on the ground is a concern because of the industry's fractured existence. (Around three-fourths of the business are independent entrepreneurs.)

Components

- OEM demand differs widely because of market volatility, rendering capability preparation challenging for suppliers of components.

- India is the sector where manufacturers of products prefer to concentrate on things at the bottom of the technical continuum while focusing on high-tech imports. Thus, there is a technological disparity at the producer end, where consumer requirement for improved accessibility and conformity in line with fuel efficiency regulations does not meet indigenous components manufactured.

- Suppliers are often limited for operating margins because the consumer is highly informed of price and value.

3.94. The Way Ahead: India will become the third largest building sector in the world by 2025

All indicators point to a nation that will be prudent to concentrate on infrastructure growth. And the demand for earthmoving and building machinery (ECE) would increase as it happens. The growth of a fleet size ECE is strongly linked to the growth of the building sector (infrastructure proxy), which has a strong coefficient of correlation (more than 0.99). Shortly, construction is expected to develop mainly in India as a result of transport infrastructures development (tracks, highways, airports, ports), urban infrastructure (mass transit networks, water and sanitation, urban buildings) and rural infrastructure (rural roads, irrigation, rural housing) – three primary sectors that drive ECE demand. With massive infrastructure spending and projected development in India, ECE's stock is expected to rise robustly in the foreseeable future.

3.95. OFF Road/Construction vehicles

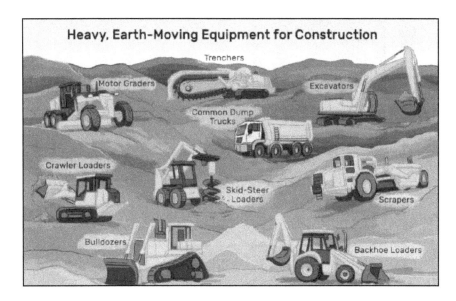

Chart 6.30 - Types of Off-Road Equipment's

Source – JCB corporate presentation

Different forms of road and building machinery have been utilised based on their usage and volume of operation. Engine graders are used for road levelling, soil displacement is used by excavators. Backhoe loaders. loaders. Are used for road creation. Dump trucks are used for the vast variety of dump motions.

Other Data resources relevant for the study

3.96 -Internet sites for secondary data source

3.96.1 www.mospi.nic.in

The ministry of statistics and program implementation is the internet site maintained and updated by Government of India in order to have public access of the information related to various aspects of economy. This site keeps track of various aspects related to Indian economy. This includes population, GDP growth rate, population related information etc.

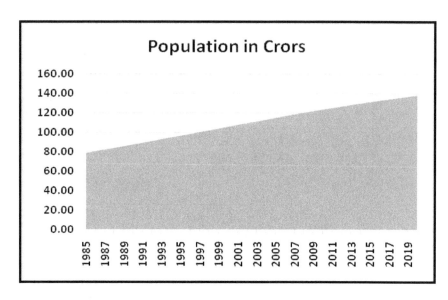

Chart 6.31 – India population1985-2019

Source- MOSPI

India population continues to grow @ 2% average, in the recent years it has shown reduction in growth rate of population

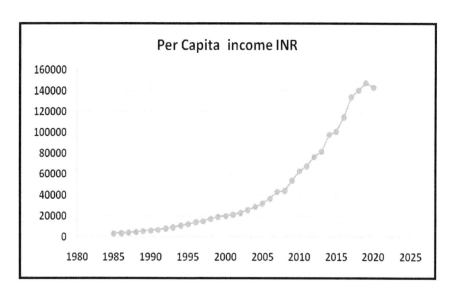

Chart 6.32 – Per capita income 1985-2020 India

Source - MOSPI

India has shown steady rise in per Capita income from Rs 4000 in 1985 to Rs 140 k in 2019

Per Capita Income – This is determined by dividing the GDP by the country's total population. It reflects a simple indication of people's discretionary income as per capita income rises, so does the disposable income. With the discretionary income growing, everybody chooses what to do with it after saving them money on essential food, clothes and housing. People look to meet their mobility needs the following graph reveals the spending expected by the Government of India for different sectors of expenditure

Steady rise in per capita income is good indicator of economic growth. The growth is sustained for more than 35 years. We can say that the growth isn't pseudo , and it's a real growth. Sustained growth helps in creating the required demand for all kinds of goods and creates pull in the economy

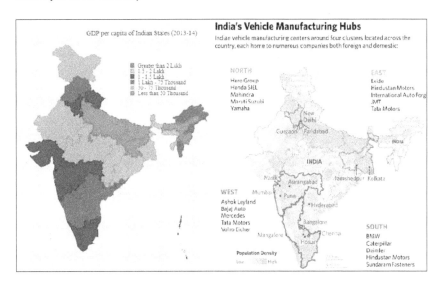

Chart 6.33- Average Per Capita income Vs Automotive Hubs -India

Source – MOSPI and Geographical study

Automotive industry spread is seen in Maharashtra , NCR region , Tamilnadu , Karnataka and near Jamshedpur , also the per capita income is higher in these regions compared to the national average .

GDP per Capita for India – The left diagram indicates a per capita income of the person state in India, much as a demographic is protected by the auto industry in India, specifically referring to the partnership between the Indian economy and the development of the auto industry in India. Gurgaon and Noida are expanding tremendously in the north, where most Japanese OEMs have set up their shops. West is historically renowned for being host to the homegrown automotive industry. South of India is traditionally renowned for its fusion of the Korean and Indian automotive industry where the main players include Hyundai, Ashok Leyland and TVs.

Cascading effect – It is interesting to note that the investment done by automotive giants in states of India which are Maharashtra , Karnataka , Tamilnadu ,West Bengal also the NCR region . These automotive companies do create automotive clusters for supply of critical automotive parts. Every company manufacturing automotive parts do create employment opportunity in some form , increasing the income for that region. This cascading effect moves across the boundaries of states as volume increases, example is Rajkot , Jaipur , many more cities in India which do not have automotive industry as base , however they have companies which manufacture the required parts for automotive industry and hence it is able to see the growth in disposable income. This income contributes to over all regional growth

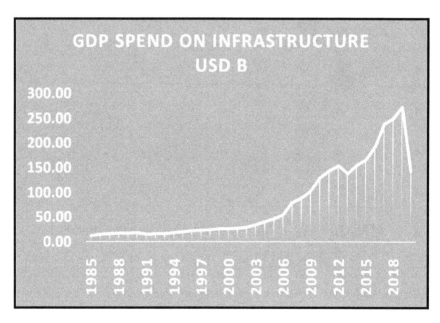

Chart 6.34 - Infrastructure spend-India 1985-2020

Source MOSPI and

https://www.researchgate.net/publication/23778624_Infrastructure_Development_in_India_An_Appraisal

Infrastructure spend of India was less than 20 USD Billion which substancially grew to 275 USD Billion and have shown some dip in 2019 -2020 due to economic slow down and Covid 19

Infrastructure spending - India's infrastructure spending continually contributes to prosperity, which helps to transfer capital and create wealth. Significant governmental interventions relating to airports, roads offer the money rotation the requisite traction.

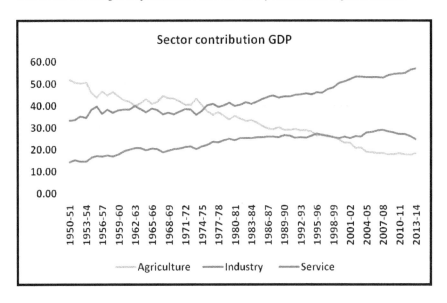

Chart 6.35 - Sector wise GDP contribution 1950-2014

Source – MOSPI / https://statisticstimes.com/economy/country/india-gdp-sectorwise

The agricultural dependency of Indian economy has moved from 50% to less than 20% over period 70 years from independence, at the same time the industrial segment have grown from 15% to 30% , and service sector from 30% to 55% during the same period

Sector data - As above seen in the sector contribution, the service sector contributes greatly, but the entire service sector is reliant on the manufacturing sector. There has been a gradual downturn in the agriculture market. Usually, this is what tends to happen in all developed countries, the development sector and the service industries.

3.96.2 https://dipp.gov.in

Departments of industrial promotion and internal trade is the department owned by Government of India. This give all the information related to industrial development and promotion. It has a special focus on make in India.

Every year, India generates more than 24 million automobiles and hires more than 72 million individuals in India. The underlying reasoning used for the estimation of jobs is that the automobile sector has a direct and indirect effect on the rate of work creation. Each vehicle rolls down direct or indirect employment as produced below, as below.

Vehicle category	Employee per vehicle manufactured
Passenger vehicle	6
Commercial vehicle	13
Three-wheeler	4
Two-wheeler	1
Tractor	13
Off Road vehicle	13

Chart 6.36 – Job creation logic by Automotive Industry

Source – Automotive sector report 2016, Dept. of heavy industries GOI

As per automotive sector report published in 2016, Government of India have confirmed the strong linkage between employment and manufacturing auto. Employment generated by manufacturing each PV is 6, CV-13,Three Wheel -4, Two wheel – 1, Tractor -13, and Off road – 13 persons

If the government relies, more on vehicle roll down, the generation of jobs would be automatic to that degree and the vehicle roll down needs to think more.

3.96.3 auto.economictimes.indiatimes.com

Economic times have special channel to focus on the automotive industry trends and latest happenings, it covers the same and keep giving latest updates on this channel

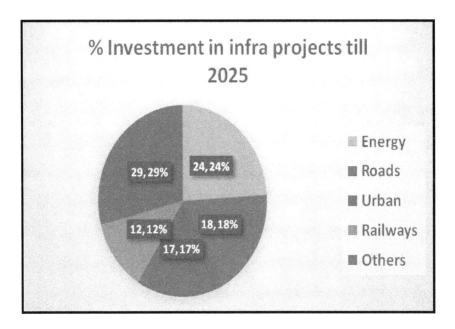

Chart 6.37 - Infrastructure investment spread -India

Source- Economic times, 20 March 2020

India spending on road infrastructure is 18% of GDP in from 2020 to 2025 , which is a good indicator as decided by government

The government invests the most on the mobility of all industries. India aims to have an economy of 5 trillion so that it could invest a great deal on infrastructure. Close cooperation between state and central governments is required. Such spending has long intervals for investor returns. In the current capitalist economies, however, development is characterized as infrastructure growth, mobility, GDP and PPP (Purchasing Power Parity). The spend from government is aimed towards growing the infrastructure. More and more investment in infrastructure projects will help have a good boost in automotive industry as well.

3.96.4 www.morth.nic.in

Ministry or road transport and highways keeps track of the road infrastructure development across India every year. This site maintained by the government gives complete statistics on Highways, rural roads, surfaced roads and PMY roads. This gives comprehensive data on year wise road development for last 50 years period

3.96.5 www.siam.in

Society of Indian Automotive Manufacturers (SIAM) is the central body, which is a representative body of all the automotive manufacturers in India. They keep track of all the production trends, export trend, domestic sales, various new models launched. SIAM also, SIAM also publishes the report of model wise data for the automotive industry in India.

Similar to SIAM there are other global organizations for every country, which provides the local manufacturing data for the automotive space

SAFE - Society for Automotive Fitness & Environment

OICA- Organization of Motor Vehicle Manufacturers

IMMA- International Motorcycle Manufacturers Association

VDA- German Association of the Automotive Industry

JAMA- Japan Automobile Manufacturers Association

SMMT- The Society of Motor Manufacturers and Traders

TAIA- The Thai Automotive Industry Association

MAA- Malaysian Automotive Association

GAIKINDO- Indonesian Automotive Industry Association

AAF- ASEAN Automotive Federation

To support the automobile industry in India and the automotive parts industry in India, SIAM and ACMA also organize regional exhibitions.

Two-wheelers	Commercial Vehicles	Passenger Vehicles

• Andhra Pradesh
  • Hero Motocrop
• Haryana
  • Hero Honda, Harley-
   Davidson, Honda. Suzuki
• Himachal Pradesh
  • TVS Motors
• Madhya Pradesh
  • M&M
• Rajasthan
  • Hero Motocorp, Honda
• Uttar Pradesh
  • India Yamaha Motor Pvt Ltd
• Uttarakhand
  • Hero Honda, Bajaj Auto
• Karnataka
  • TVS, Honda
• Tamil Nadu
  • TVS, Royal Enfield, Yamaha
• Maharashtra
  • Piaggio & C. Spa, Aprilia,
   Kinetic, Beneli, Kawasaki,
   KTM
	• Andhra Pradesh
	  • Isuzu Motors
	• Telangana
	  • M&M
	• Himachal Pradesh
	  • TAFE
	• Jharkhand
	  • Tata Motors
	• Madhya Pradesh
	  • Hindustan Motors, MAN
	   Force Trucks Pvt Ltd, TAFE
	• Punjab
	  • SML Isuzu
	• Rajasthan
	  • Ashok Leyland, TAFE
	• Uttar Pradesh
	  • Tata Motors
	• Uttarakhand
	  • Ashok Leyland, Tata Motors,
	   M&M
	• Karnataka
	  • Scania CV Ind Pvt Ltd, TAFE,
	   Tata Motors, Volvo
	• Tamil Nadu
	  • Ashok Leyland, BharatBenz,
	   Kamaz Vectra, TAFE, TVS,
	   Caterpillar Ind Pvt Ltd
	• West Bengal
	  • Hindustan Motors
	• Gujarat
	  • Asia Motor Works (AMW)
	• Maharashtra
	  • Ashok Leyland, Bajaj Auto,
	   Force Motors, Mahindra
	   Navistar, Premier
		• Andhra Pradesh
		  • Isuzu Motors
		• Haryana
		  • Maruti Suzuki
		• Himachal Pradesh
		  • International Cars & Motors
		   Ltd
		• Rajasthan
		  • Honda Cars India
		• Uttar Pradesh
		  • Honda Siel Cars India
		• Karnataka
		  • Mahindra REVA, Toyota
		   Kirloskar Motor Pvt Ltd
		• Tamil Nadu
		  • BMW, Ford, Hyundai,
		   Mitsubishi, Ranault, Nissan
		   Motors, Hindustan Motors
		• West Bengal
		  • Hindustan Motors
		• Gujarat
		  • GM, Tata Motors, Ford
		   (planned)
		• Maharashtra
		  • GM, Tata Motors, Fiat,
		   M&M, Mercedes-Benz,
		   Premier, Jaguar & Land
		   Rover, Audi, Skoda,
		   Volkwagen, M&M, Jeep

Chart 6.38- Auto industry plants- state level

Source – SIAM/Geographical study

The automotive industry spread is seen across India , but largely in the state of Maharashtra , NCR region Tamilnadu and Karnataka at large.

The figure above shows the spread of the Indian car industry across all the major Indian states. Most 2W manufacturers also produce 3W, so they are not separately categorized. This spread in the Indian population has a wide impact. This allows urbanisation to spread widely and development can be spread over India. Tractor industry spreads across parts of India as India is an agro-economy, which is also home to the world's largest producer of tractors in India. The building equipment industry is also located in northern and western India.

3.96.6 Automotive mission plan 2026, /www.dhi.nic.in

The Government of India made knowing the significance of the Indian auto industry and its importance to the Indian economy, a special initiative named the Automotive Mission Plan. We will study this strategy and highlight the relevance of the automotive sector to the Indian economy. Below are the numerous explanations why policymakers have suggested granting unique treatment to the automobile industry.

Wide impact across sectors – Owing to its scale and diverse products used, the automobile industry has a wide influence across markets. The metal industry is improved by the full metal framework, and all sorts of alloys used to support the metal industries other than the steel industry. The car industry requires plenty of adhesives, dye, pretreatment additives, and several types of chemicals. The artificial yarn industry is boosted by the different fabrics used in the manufacture of chairs. As all tires use only natural rubber as a part, the rubber industry depends largely on the auto industry.

The plastic manufacturing sector has the biggest edge. By utilizing full plastic interior parts, the car industry is seeking to accomplish weight loss. This gives the fuel efficiency and other elements of the vehicle architecture a significant benefit. This company utilizes all kinds of plastic such as LDPE, HDPE, NYLON, EPDM, etc. These are petroleum goods, offering the petroleum industry a breather as well.

Employment generation – As this business has a broad influence on the economy, it often provides tremendous opportunities for jobs. It creates jobs through sectors such as car production firms, Tier 1 companies providing automotive industry parts, tire industry, plastic components, press shops, manufacturing shops, etc. The same is also reliant on several service-related industries. As per the government proposal, in the next 10 years, 65 million jobs are expected to be created. It now has 29 million workers.

GDP contribution – The vehicle sector has crossed USD 93 trillion now. It contributes more than 49% of the country's manufacturing GDP, thereby adding more than 7% of the country's GDP. The above statistics illustrate the strong success of India's automotive industry and its contribution to economic development and wealth creation by countries.

Common objectives of Make in India and AMP 2026 – Popular Make in India and AMP 2026 targets-All of the India and AMP 2026 targets are compatible with each other as follows:

- Growth of the economy coupled with GDP
- Centers of regional development
- Generation of Jobs
- Fiscal gap elimination

- Render India the center of exports
- Making India a competitive manufacturing nation also boosts scientific science,
- Enhancement of Innovations

The early major service sector, as discussed, often relies on the automobile industry. They receive a massive amount of revenue from the automobile sector from their dealerships, manufacturers, gas stations, insurance brokers. There is a fair range of roadside garages above and above the approved service stations that survive on repair work in the automobile industry.

To accomplish this aim, AMP 2026 also aims to achieve a perfect compromise between personal mobility, public transit system and environmental balance. The main views taken into consideration during the AMP 2026 proposal are as follows.

1) Due to numerous manufacturing operations, the disposable income for the general population would rise, which will generate a need for two w industry for faster mobility. People are going to graduate from cycle in to 2W.
2) Urban mobility is powered by 4W and becomes a person's sign of rank and personality.
3) GDP development and overall progress in the trade and road and mining industries would provide the requisite boost for commercial vehicles.

3.96.7 www.acma.in

Automotive components manufacturer's association is apex body representing the auto component industry in India. It keep the track of various members, it represents the auto component industry from India globally, participates in various exhibitions for business growth. This body keeps track of all the import, export, employment generation done by auto component industry

Overview of the Indian Auto Part industry

As part of the literature analysis, the ACMA-Automotive Parts Manufacturing Association page summarizes the information below.

Auto component industry in India 2017-18

Turnover	Rs 3,45,635 crors/ USD 51.2 Billion
Contribution to GDP	2.3 %
Exports	Rs 90,571 crors / USD 13.5 Billion
Share in India export	4%
Auto Aftermarket Value	Rs 61,601 crors / USD 9.2 Billion
Employment	Direct 1.5 Million & Indirect 1.5 Million

Chart 6.39– Snapshot by Auto component industry

Source – ACMA (Auto components manufacturers association) 2017-2018 report

Auto component industry supports automotive industry for all the components required. As per Automotive components manufacturers association (ACMA), auto components industry turnover is 51.2 USD Billion, contribution to GDP is 2.3% creates approx. 3 million employment

The above chart makes it quite clear about the significance of the automotive aspect of the Indian economy. Looking at its contribution to GDP and exporting its study-focused worth. The bulk of automobile industries concentrate on the manufacture of genuine cars and essential parts. These Tier 1 factories produce most of the other components needed. They are usually situated in the vicinity of the key vehicle production site. It should be remembered that the speed at which cars are manufactured is incredible to research, for instance, a standard SUV or passenger car manufacturing plant produces one vehicle in 1 min. and a truck manufacturing plant produces a truck in 12-15 min. Every SUV or passenger car usually has somewhere between 25,000 and 40,000 pieces of spare parts when fully constructed forms a vehicle.

Looking at the above logic and automotive manufacturing pace, it is very critical for the auto assembly plant to have a Tier 1 industry close to the venue to preserve low-cost logistics.

Automotive components –

Auto component	Value (INR crors)	% share
Cooling System	10369	3
Engine components	89865	26
Suspension and Breaking	48389	14
Drive and steering	44933	13
Body ,chassis and BIW	58758	17
Electricals and Electronics	34564	10
Interior	41476	12
Consumable	17282	5
Total	345635	100

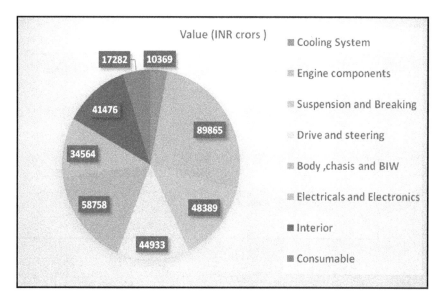

Chart 6.40 – Broad level component break up-Auto comp

Source – ACMA (Auto components manufacturers association) 2017-18

Auto component industry consist of many components, ACMA report of 2017-18 indicates that total contribution of automotive industry was 345635 Crors. Out of the total turnover of the auto component industry 26% was from the engine related components..17% was with body and chassis , 14 % was with suspension , 12 % contribution was from interior systems, cooling systems contributed lowest.

As mentioned before, as seen in the pie chart above, any vehicle running on the roads requires several components. There, by providing jobs in different markets, the automobile industry affects many industries throughout the regions. Often plastic components and rubber parts are used in interiors and much of the exterior and motor are metal parts. As customers offer electronics more and more meaning, both navigation and infotainment are becoming increasingly relevant.

Exports USD Million	FY 2017	FY 2018
Europe	3830	4660
North America	2830	3700
Asia	2940	3420
LatAm	480	770
Africa	670	690
CIS	140	210

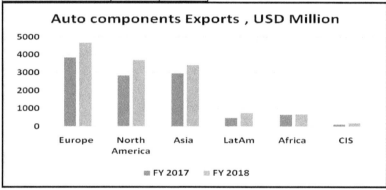

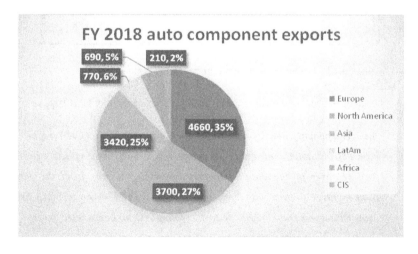

Chart 6.41 – Global Export statistics-Auto components

Source – ACMA (Auto components manufacturers association)

Indian auto component industry contributes a lot for exports as well, highest exports in 2017 were to Europe @ 3830 USD million and lowest were to CIS countries @140 USD million.

The graph above simply shows the tale of the world's automobile output figures. The largest density of car output is located in Europe and North America. India has the lowest production cost and the highest availability for this industry of the highly qualified labor needed. This unusual mix renders it a perfect location for all sorts of technologically innovative vehicle components to be made. India can exploit the company's strength and earn the Forex needed for the region. The production firm has already set up shops in India for several car products.

Auto component industry exports	USD Billion
2004	1.2
2005	1.5
2006	3.1
2007	3.8
2008	4
2009	3.4
2010	5.2
2011	6.8
2012	9.7
2013	10.3
2014	11.2
2015	10.9
2016	10.9
2017	13.5

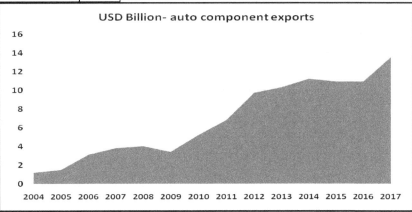

Chart 6.42 – Export revenue USDB –Auto Comp

Source – ACMA (Auto components manufacturers association)

Total exports in 2004 was 1.4 USD billion and that in 2017 were 13.5 USD Billion. In these 14 years the exports grew @ 20.11 % CAGR

This graphic depiction often shows the same value of the car product sector and the automotive industry, dominated by North America in Europe, dominated by Germany,

Auto component industry Imports	USD Billion
2004	1.3
2005	1.8
2006	2.3
2007	3.1
2008	4.8
2009	8.2
2010	8
2011	10.9
2012	13.7
2013	12.8
2014	13.5
2015	13.8
2016	13.5
2017	15.9

France and the United Kingdom in Asia, dominated by Japan, China, Thailand other than India, is almost equivalent in exports in America.

Country	USDB 2017	% share
China	4.29	27
Germany	2.23	14
Japan	1.75	11
S Korea	1.59	10
USA	1.11	7
Thailand	0.95	6
Italy	0.48	3
UK	0.32	2
Czech	0.32	2
France	0.32	2
Others	2.54	16
Total	15.9	100

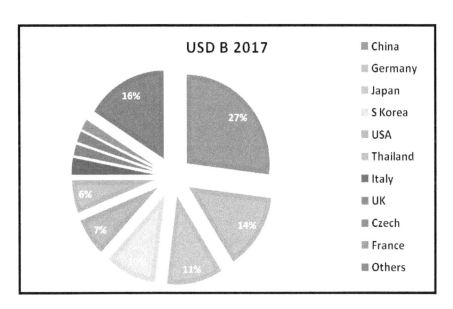

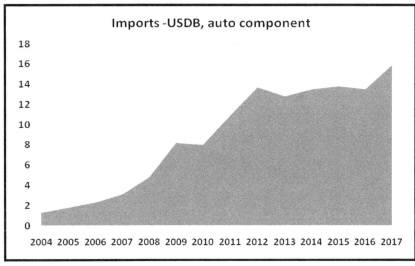

Auto components imports

Chart 6.43 – Auto component imports

Source – ACMA (Auto components manufacturers association) 2018 report

The import study for auto components indicate that in 2017 the highest import was from China @ 27 %, 4.29 USD Billion. Lowest imports were @2% recorded from UK/Czech/France with the value of 0.32 USD Billion. The auto component imports

were at 1.3 USD Billion in 2004 which increased to 15.09 USD Billion in 2017; effective CAGR growth was 19.13%

There are two major factors behind the imports of automobile parts, one being low on the prices compared to domestic production due to scale of manufacturing . China has a broad production scale for all automobile parts, thus the cost at which China produces these components can never be matched worldwide. The other element of the importation of car products is the fabrication of technical components, such as the development of exhaust pieces, engine parts, etc.

Most cost-driven components are imported into India, such as Thailand, China, Myanmar and Vietnam from different Asian countries. The Indian automobile industry depends primarily on Germany and North America for all the technology and engineering components involved.

3.96.8 https://population.un.org/

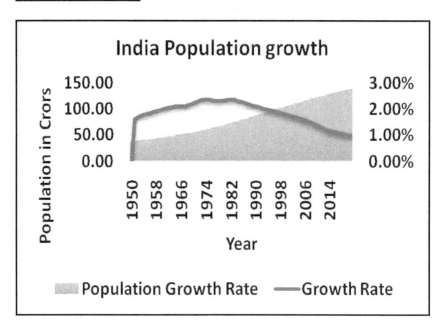

Chart 6.44– Population of India and growth rate 1950-2014

Source – World Bank /United Nations Population prospects report 2017 revision

India has second highest population growth in the world, In 1951 India had a population of 37.63 million with the yearly growth of 1.61% year on year. In 1974, the

population was 60.88 Million with the highest growth rate of 2.36%. In 2017, the population reached 133.87 million however, the growth rate decreased to 1.07%

Population – This is one of India's greatest assets in terms of captive consumption. India's economy may be insulated from several global slowdowns because its domestic demand is very high. India accounts for 17% of the world's population and thus regulates a significant part of demand. India's population rises by 1 per cent annually, and by 2030, India will rapidly take over China, becoming the world's most populist nation. More about roughly the energy and purchasing capacity of 50 per cent of the population of India is indicated by 48% of the population below the age of 30.

Top 50 countries ,world population

Chart 6.45 – Population density chart –world

China and India contribute for more that 50% of world population

Sr No	Country	Population in Crors
1	China	139.40
2	India	132.61
3	United States	33.26
4	Indonesia	26.70
5	Pakistan	23.35
6	Nigeria	21.40
7	Brazil	21.17
8	Bangladesh	16.27
9	Russia	14.17
10	Mexico	12.86
11	Japan	12.55
12	Philippines	10.92
13	Ethiopia	10.81
14	Egypt	10.41
15	Congo	10.18
16	Vietnam	9.87
17	Iran	8.49
18	Turkey	8.20
19	Germany	8.02
20	Thailand	6.90
21	France	6.78
22	United Kingdom	6.58
23	Italy	6.24
24	Tanzania	5.86
25	Burma	5.66
26	South Africa	5.65
27	Kenya	5.35
28	Korea, South	5.18
29	Spain	5.00
30	Colombia	4.91
31	Sudan	4.56
32	Argentina	4.55
33	Ukraine	4.39
34	Uganda	4.33
35	Algeria	4.30
36	Iraq	3.89
37	Poland	3.83
38	Canada	3.77
39	Afghanistan	3.66
40	Morocco	3.56
41	Saudi Arabia	3.42
42	Malaysia	3.27
43	Angola	3.25
44	Peru	3.19
45	Uzbekistan	3.06
46	Nepal	3.03
47	Mozambique	3.01
48	Yemen	2.99
49	Ghana	2.93
50	Venezuela	2.86

Countries with population more than 5 Crores (Top 29 countries)

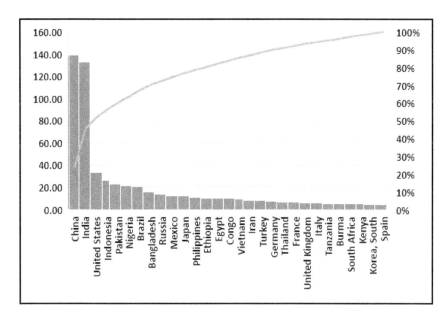

Chart 6.46 - India population share in world population (top 50)

Source – World Bank /United Nations Population prospects report 2017 revision

Top 6 countries in terms of population are china ,India , US , ,Indonesia , Pakistan, Nigeria. By all means these countries will act as engines for future growth.

Above chart is clear indicator of importance of India as far as population is concerned. Out of 7 Billion Global population India is approx. 1.4 billion, which accounts to 17.9% or almost 18 %. It means a lot to us; on one side, it puts the undue pressure on the natural resources at the same time due to higher captive consumption. The Indian Economy is independent of many external aspects, it is able to manage and grow on the internal consumption largely. During the recent recession cycles of Global economy, India was largely insulated from the ill effects of the same.

3.96.9 WORLD BANK DATA BASE - https://data.worldbank.org/country/IN -

Word Bank provides comprehensive data on the GDP and population for all the countries

	USDB	Unit	INR CRORS	Crores	INR
Year	GDP	FOREX rate	GDP	Population	Per Capita income INR
1985	238	12	293936	78	3747
1986	253	13	318718	80	3974
1987	284	13	367740	82	4486
1988	300	14	417113	84	4981
1989	300	16	487208	86	5696
1990	327	18	571568	87	6545
1991	275	23	624986	89	7012
1992	293	26	760130	91	8359
1993	284	30	866495	93	9343
1994	333	31	1044652	95	11047
1995	367	32	1188884	96	12334
1996	400	35	1416456	98	14419
1997	423	36	1536603	100	15352
1998	429	41	1769105	102	17353
1999	467	43	2010213	104	19365
2000	477	45	2142020	106	20273
2001	494	47	2330856	108	21682
2002	524	49	2546046	109	23287
2003	618	47	2880367	111	25914
2004	722	45	3270246	113	28950
2005	834	44	3678910	115	32057
2006	949	45	4300463	117	36898
2007	1239	41	5122025	118	43289
2008	1224	44	5326059	120	44359
2009	1365	48	6609756	122	54279
2010	1708	46	7812788	123	63298
2011	1823	47	8508174	125	68050
2012	1828	53	9766908	127	77161
2013	1857	57	10503465	128	82004
2014	2039	62	12709897	130	98100
2015	2104	63	13246306	131	101105
2016	2294	66	15246722	132	115112
2017	2653	68	17983060	134	134335
2018	2713	70	19016609	135	140589
2019	2869	70	20194398	137	147791
2020	2593	76	19802126	138	143493

Chart 6.47– 35 years data for the GDP of India 1985-2020

Source - World Bank

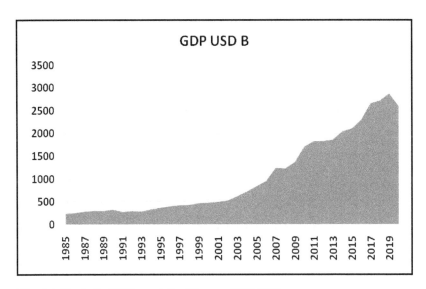

Chart 6.48 – India GDP graph for 35 years 1985-2020

Source - World Bank

India GDP in INR is largely dependent on conversion rate of USD to INR . It has shown phenomenal growth from 2003 till 2019 , growing from 618 USD Billion in year 2003 to USD Billion 2868 in year 2019

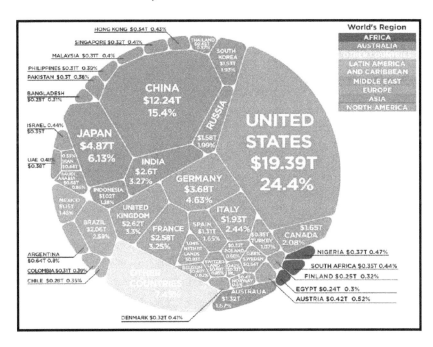

Chart 6.49- World GDP (Regional GDP)

Source – world economy report by how much .net 2018 /World Bank data

India carries close to 18% of the world's population, it still makes 3% of GDP, rendering it one of the world's most aspirational post-G8 economies.

3.96.10 India GDP – GDP is the final measurement in the defined period of all products and services generated by a government. India's GDP growth rate was considerably strong between 2001 and 2010 and has declined to some degree because of world economic cycles and the multinational influence and very high interdependence of most countries.

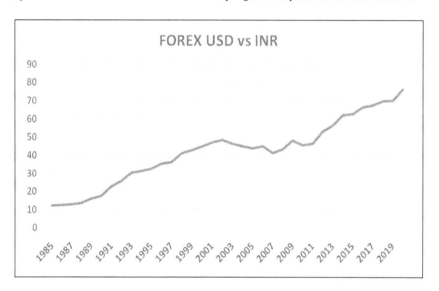

Chart 6.50 – USD to INR exchange rate from 1985 to 2019

Source – RBI data on Forex

India has experienced constant devaluation of its currency in line with most of the Asian currencies over a period of time

3.96.11 https://www.oica.net/- International Organization of Motor Vehicle Manufacturers

International Organization of Motor Vehicle Manufacturers , is the independent organisation keeping track of every nations automotive manufacturing. It also keeps track on various regulations related to automotive industry. It is a good reference for all statistical data for every nations automotive industry

According to the International Organization, India will only have 0.2 commercial vehicles per km of the route, relative to other developing countries such as the US and China that are 0.78 and 1.17 no per km or more.

Country	cv per Km
China	1.17
Japan	1.1
USA	0.78
Germany	0.55
Russia	0.26
India	0.2

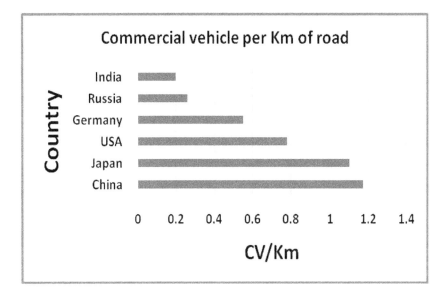

Chart 6.51- Global Commercial vehicles sales Vs Road network

Source – International Organization of Motor vehicles manufacturer

India has lowest density of commercial vehicles compared to any other country in the world. Having highest population to support it for further growth. India is correctly placed to encash this situation to grow further multifold in the space of commercial vehicles.

Commercial vehicles is considered as one of the major indicator of any economy. Once the population feels confident in economy , they start buying various materials which are in need , this gives pull for various commercial activities and goods and services needs to be transported. This needs commercial vehicles hence the sale of commercial is considered as one of the major indicator of growth in economy.

The international motor vehicle manufacturer's association, India, has the lowest penetration of commercial vehicles in comparable countries. If the overall road transport details are split by the road network, the Indian ratio is just 0.2 per cent. That ensures that the population of commercial vehicles can also rise quite strongly as the economic output increases.

Employment world Bank report ,2018

Year	Agricultural	Industry	services
2007	53.86	20.62	25.7
2008	53.16	20.72	26.13
2009	52.38	21.33	26.3
2010	51.52	21.81	26.68
2011	48.8	23.45	27.75
2012	47	24.36	28.54
2013	46.66	23.79	29.55
2014	45.52	23.94	30.54
2015	44.36	23.8	31.74
2016	43.44	23.72	32.84
2017	42.74	23.79	33.48

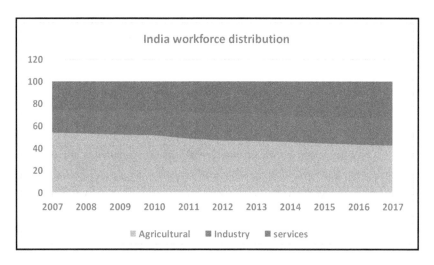

Chart 6.52 - Distribution of workforce per economic sector in percentage

The highest employment generation in India is from agricultural sector then service sector and around 20% is created by Industrial sector

According to World Bank details on India, approx. 25 per cent of the total jobs produced come from the business, the agricultures provide big jobs, but this sector also faces the instability of the monsoon, which gives the whole economy stability and helps improve the generation of the wealth.

3.96.12 https://mopng.gov.in/ (Ministry of petrolium and natural gas) -Study of Fuel Dynamics

Year	Petrol INR per Ltr	Diesel INR per Ltr	LPG INR per Ltr	CNG INR per kg
1989	8.5	3.5	0	0
1990	12.23	4.08	0	0
1991	14.62	5.05	0	0
1992	15.71	6.11	0	0
1993	15.5	6.5	0	0
1994	16.78	6.98	0	0
1995	18	8	0	0
1996	21.13	9.04	0	0
1997	22.84	10.34	0	0
1998	23.94	10	0	0
1999	23.8	9.94	0	0
2000	28.44	14.04	0	0
2001	25	15	0	0
2002	26.54	16.59	0	0
2003	32.49	21.12	0	0
2004	36	25	0	0
2005	40.49	28.45	0	0

Year	Petrol INR per Ltr	Diesel INR per Ltr	LPG INR per Ltr	CNG INR per kg
2006	47.51	32.47	0	0
2007	42.85	30.25	0	0
2008	45.56	31.8	0	0
2009	44.72	32.87	0	0
2010	47.93	38.1	30.51	0
2011	63.37	41.12	41.19	0
2012	73.18	40.91	47.92	0
2013	63.09	49.69	49.68	35.1
2014	71.51	57.28	36.94	35.2
2015	66.29	52.28	36.29	38
2016	63.02	51.67	32.29	39
2017	65.32	54.9	44.5	39
2018	78.43	69.31	48.47	40.61

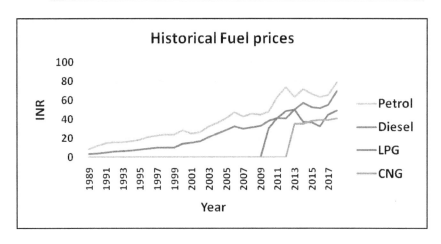

Chart 6.53 - Fuel price comparison from 1989 -2018

Source – Petroleum Ministry

The traditional fuels are petrol and Diesel , however during 2009 and 2012 new fuels were introduced to India namely LPG and CNG , CNG continues to be the most competitive fuel in the current times @ RS 56 per Kgs against Gasoline and Diesel which have crossed Rs. 100

From the above figure, it is clear that fuel prices have shown steady growth over the last 30 years. At the same time, the car industry has shown a pattern of growth. It can never be directly related to the growth of the automotive industry but. It may well be linked to economic activity. As economic activity improves, demand both for mobility and fuel consumption increases, which means growth in both the automotive industry and fuel prices.

Crude Oil	MN Ton
Domestic production	34.8
Import	159.4

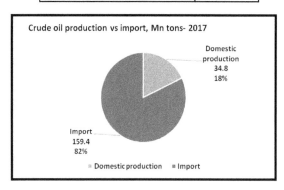

Chart 6.54 - Petroleum import and production 2017

Source – Ministry of petroleum

Out of total usage of crude oil in India it has only 18% of the domestic production, balance 82% is import

Year	Average
1987	19.2
1988	15.97
1989	19.64
1990	24.53
1991	21.54
1992	20.58
1993	18.43
1994	17.2
1995	18.43
1996	22.12
1997	20.61
1998	14.42
1999	19.35
2000	30.38
2001	25.98
2002	26.19
2003	31.08
2004	41.51
2005	56.64
2006	66.05
2007	72.34
2008	99.67
2009	61.95
2010	79.48
2011	94.88
2012	94.05
2013	97.98
2014	93.17
2015	48.66
2016	43.29
2017	50.8
2018	65.23
2019	56.99
2020	39.68

Domestic crude oil production is mainly driven by Cairn energy who is able to explore oil well in the Rajasthan area. Domestic crude is always beneficial for the Indian economy as it saves us from spending the forex reserves. Which can be used for some other purpose. The Pie chart is clear indicator of 82% of the total crude oil is imported by India.

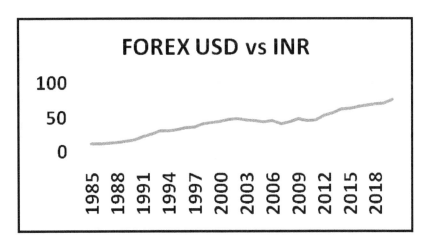

Chart 6.55 - Foreign exchange USD vs INR 1985 - 2019 ,Source – RBI

In 1985 1 USD was equal to Rs 10, Year 2018 saw the value going down to Rs78 , Now in 2021 its recovered at Rs 74

The current exchange rate is 1 USD = 75 INR , It means that over a period of time the Indian Rupee currency is devaluated against USD , we in India have to pay more for getting the fuel

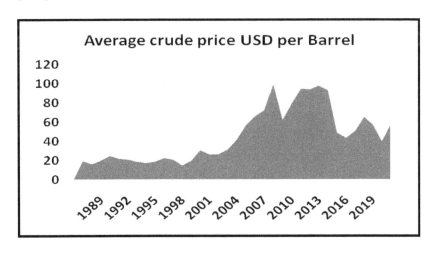

Chart 6.56 - Crude oil price study 1989-2021

Crude oil prices started from USD 20 per barrel in 1987 moved as high as USD 100 per barrel in 2013 , It came down to USD 40 during Covid times in 2020 due to low demand

3.96.13 Fuel price Impact OPEC data published / Petroleum Ministry (India) –

The fuel price is the highest running cost for vehicles and drop plays a vital role in the car owner's pocket. However, auto enthusiasts and buyers are worried each year about price growth for car fuel when India imports almost 80% of its fuel requirements in various countries, all of which are made in USD, with USD vs INR movement in the last 30 years, where USD moved from four INR per USD to 76 INR per USD. This is due to India's oil dependency on its neighbors. The global crude oil has shown enormous price volatility due to various policy reasons and supply issues. Crude oil has seen shifts from USD 20 to USD 143 per barrel. Despite this kind of volatility of forex / crude oil/fuel prices, there have been no negative long-term signs for the automotive industry in India. This shows clearly that the Indian car industry is captive and relies less on external factors in the long term.

	USDB	Unit	INR CRORS	Kms	Crors	INR	INR	No	No	No	No	No	No	No
Year	GDP-USDB	FOREX	GDP-INRCR	Road length	Population	Gasoline prices	Diesel prices	PV	CV	3W	2W	Tractor	Off road	Grand Total
2004	699.7	43.35	3033199.5	3621507	112.60	36.49	24.35	989560	550080	356223	5622741	179000	12000	7709604
2005	834	43.67	3642078	3809156	114.40	40.84	29.77	1209876	707406	374445	6529829	242000	15000	9078556
2006	949	44.6	4232540	3880651	116.20	46.76	33.65	1309300	782166	434423	7608697	254000	23000	10411586
2007	1239	43.12	5342568	4016401	118.00	46.41	32.85	1545223	539989	556126	8436212	311000	38000	11426550
2008	1224	40.03	4899672	4109592	119.70	48.65	34.04	1777583	484141	500660	8009292	304000	45500	11121176
2009	1365	50.57	6902805	4471509	121.40	43.37	32.76	1838593	466393	497020	8395613	303000	40500	11541119
2010	1708	44.82	7655256	4582439	123.10	50.98	38.51	2357411	721939	619194	10510336	383000	59700	14651580
2011	1836	44.53	8175708	4676838	124.70	61.47	40.01	2982772	881144	799553	13349349	440331	72200	18525349
2012	1832	50.87	8591600	4865394	126.30	68.97	43.47	3231058	832649	839748	15744156	545109	66400	21259120
2013	1862	54.28	9285000	5231922	127.90	72.68	52.03	3087973	699035	830108	16883049	526912	55900	22082977
2014	2039	60.01	12234000	5402485	129.40	73.7	66.79	3221419	698298	949019	18489311	634151	60700	24052898
2015	2058	62.29	12822200	5472144	130.90	66.5	56.85	3465045	786692	934104	18830227	612994	68200	24697262
2016	2265	66.25	15008400	5600000	132.40	66.7	54.1	3801670	810253	783721	19933739	570791	76000	25976174
2017	2697	64.86	17493700	5800000	133.90	73.24	60.47	4010373	894551	1021911	23147057	691361	84500	29849753

Chart 6.57- Automotive production and Economic factors comparison

Source – SIAM /World Bank / MOSPI

The complete comparison between the GDP , fuel prices , population , road infrastructure growth shows a strong co relation when studied for the data collected from 2004 to 2017

When we compile all data together for birds' eye view in the single table. It shows a clear picture of GDP/Forex/Road Length/Fuel prices / all automotive sectors are growing together with the Indian Economy. Even if the fuel price shows an increase in the trend, there has been no decline in automotive sales. This table shows a clear link between different sectors of the Indian economy and the automotive industry. With the growth of global industrial activity and supply situations in which fuel prices fluctuate, the same logic is applied to Indian automotive sales. The increasing economic activity gives people extra confidence and spends more on various things, which means that car sales will also rise. Similar logic also applies when economic activity decreases automotive sales as well as fuel prices. In the long term, however, the longer horizon car sales are independent of fuel prices. It should be noted that mobility is increasingly needed for faster economic growth, and automobile sales are the highest barometer for this.

3.96.14 www.morth.nic.in - Road transport yearbook 2016-17

Ministry or road transport and highways keeps track of the road infrastructure development across India every year. This site maintained by the government gives complete statistics on Highways , rural roads , surfaced roads and PMY roads. This gives comprehensive data on year wise road development for last 50 years period

Road infrastructure in India

India has only next to the United States, the second-largest infrastructure in the world. Total Indian road count is approximate, 5.8 Million km; more than 68% of the country's goods are transported by road. This links the movement of goods to the increase in the automotive industry. 90 per cent of passengers use the road infrastructure to travel every day from one destination to another. In fiscal 2019-20, the government expected the total expenditure for road infrastructure to be approximate. INR 83000 crores Government plans to also have many projects that are also being developed under the Public-Private Partnership (PPP) and that will generate the required jobs. As of 2017, the PPP initiative already identified 312 projects.

NHAI (India National Highway Authority is expected to have INR 1 lakh crores as revenue in the next five years. It is anticipated that by 2022, the Indian Government will complete 200,000 km of the National Highways.

Type	Km
State Highway	155222
National Highway	132500
Other roads	5207044

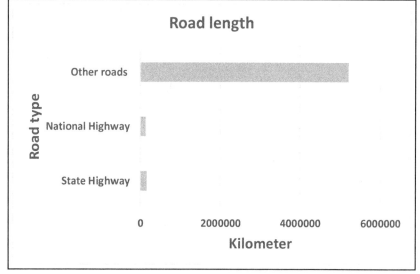

Chart 6.58 - Road length snapshot 2017

Source –MOSPI / Road transport yearbook 2016-17

The road length by end of FY 2019 was 155222 kilometres of state highways, 132500 kilometres of national highway, other roads contributed for 5207044 km.

The diagram above provides an idea of three road categories in India. National roads are usually center-led ventures that obtain maximum support from the center; they are strategic and are of national significance. National roads typically pass across multiple states. Maximum highway traffic on them linking multiple manufacturing and agricultural highways. National roads linking state capitals with the national capital are known. State roads in the state are developed that link all the state's major cities. Smaller roads link small towns

Growth in the industrial output – Industrial production growth guided by domestic use and demands for exports for quicker products and material transportation. Because factories are situated in the countries, roads must be constructed in areas to allow the transport of products and citizens.

Increase in the truck and Bus movement – The transportation of products requires more motor vehicles on the highways. Road infrastructure is a gateway to the transportation of commercial vehicles.

Farm produce movement – India is a country with a population of 130 crores. For the transfer of agricultural production for faster use until they expire also smaller roads are important. Smaller roads have an end-to-end communication for farm production, which is important for quicker output.

2W/3W.Passenger vehicle traffic – When individuals earn ample discretionary income, versatility is necessary for numerous purposes, including job commutation. Intra-city social movements, 3W are used as mass transit in many local towns as well.

India's automobile development has been great and has expanded on all fronts. This has contributed to the need for a fast turnaround on the road building. In brief, the rise in manufacturing production, the need for mobility has propelled growth in the automobile sector, while the growth in national road and road networks has been achieved.

Road Category	Road length	% share
National Highway	114158	1.94
State Highway	175036	2.97
District Road	586181	9.94
Rural Road	4166916	70.65
Urban Road	526483	8.93
Project Road	328897	5.58
Total	5897671	100

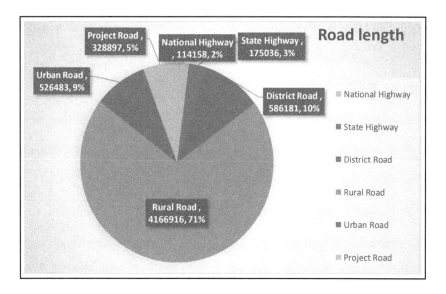

Chart 6.59 - Various road length -India 2017

Source – Road transport yearbook 2016-17

In the statistical report of 2016-17 published by Government of India it was seen that out of the complete length of highways around 2% are national highways , 3% belong to state highways , 10% were district roads and 70% of the roads belong to rural area.Total road length was 58 lakh KM.

The complete length of the road approximately 59-lakh km is classified into different road categories, national highway, provincial roads, urban roads and project roads. Each road role serves a different economic purpose and overall development. National and state roads are typically used for transportation of manufacturing production, and rural and urban roads are used mainly for agricultural transport.

Road type	1970-71	1980-81	1990-91	2000-01	2010-11	2013-14	2014-15	2015-16	2016-17
National	23838	31671	33650	57737	70934	91287	97991	101011	114158
State	56765	94359	127311	132100	163898	170818	167109	176166	175036
District	276833	421895	509435	736001	998895	1082267	1101178	561940	586181
Rural	354530	628865	1260430	1972016	2749804	3304328	3337255	3935337	4166916
Urban	72120	123120	186799	252001	411679	457467	467106	509730	526483
Project	130893	185511	209737	223665	281628	296319	301505	319109	328897
Total	914979	1485421	2327362	3373520	4676838	5402486	5472144	5603293	5897671

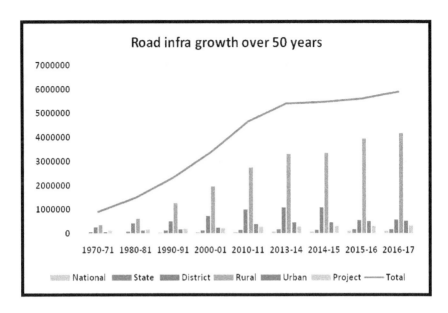

Chart 6.60- Road infra development over 50 years(1970-2017) -India

Source – MOSPI/ Road transport yearbook 2016-17

The data collected from 1970 to 201 shows growth in various type of road lengths. National highway length increased from 23838 km to 114158 km , state highway shown growth from 56765 km to 175036 km , district highway from 276833 km to 586181 km , rural from354530 km to 4166916 km , urban roads from 72120 km to 526483 km , project roads from 130893 km to 328897 km. Total road length adding all above move from 914979 km to 5897671 km

The diagram above on an improvement in road duration is self-explanatory and the increase in road development in the first 50 years after freedom is almost identical in the last 20 years. As industrialization is gathering pace in India, the desire for improved roads has largely been felt over the last 20 years, so the pace of new highway development has also risen significantly over the last 20 years. Initially, 50 years the road height and road width were narrower and thus it was feasible to construct a longer road. Modern days have seen the roads becoming 6-8 lanes but the period it takes for them is longer. They are, nevertheless, true motors for faster economic development.

If we take example of US economy we can understand that the road infrastructure development led to economic development in the state. Most of the countries in the world which are developed countries have much better infrastructure. Taking example from these countries if we follow the same path it will definitely help us in infrastructure development which is coupled with economic development.

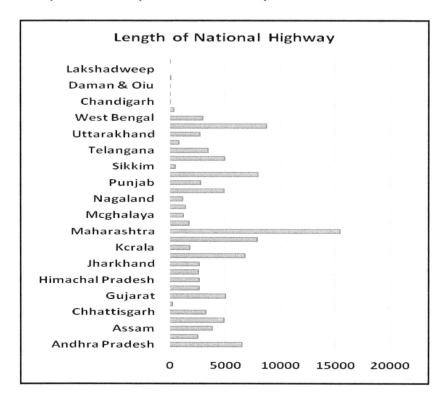

Industrial regions such as Maharashtra, Tamilnadu and Karnataka have demonstrated higher growth rates for modern highways in recent years. Increased industrial activity has fostered road development. It should also be remembered that certain areas of strategic impotence along the border also saw the development of highways.

Sl. No.	Name of State/ UT	Length of NH	%share of NH
1	Andhra Pradesh	6467	6
2	Arunachal Pradesh	2513	2
3	Assam	3844	3
4	Bihar	4839	4
5	Chhattisgarh	3232	3
6	Goa	263	0
7	Gujarat	5017	4
8	Haryana	2623	2
9	Himachal Pradesh	2643	2
10	Jammu & Kashmir	2601	2
11	Jharkhand	2654	2
12	Karnataka	6762	6
13	Kcrala	1811	2
14	Madhya Pradesh	7854	7
15	Maharashtra	15437	14
16	Manipur	1745	2
17	Mcghalaya	1203	1
18	Mizoram	1382	1
19	Nagaland	1173	1
20	Odisha	4838	4
21	Punjab	2769	2
22	Rajasthan	7906	7
23	Sikkim	463	0
24	Tamil Nadu	4946	4
25	Telangana	3455	3
26	Tripura	806	1
27	Uttarakhand	2713	2
28	Utta.r Pradesh	8712	8
29	West Bengal	2956	3
30	Andaman & Nicobar Island	330	0
31	Chandigarh	15	0
32	Dadar & Nagar Havcli	31	0
33	Daman & Oiu	22	0
34	Delhi	69	0
35	Lakshadweep	0	0
36	Puduchcrry	64	0
	Total	114158	100

Chart 6.61 - State-wise Road % share of National highway 2017

Source – MOSPI/ Road transport yearbook 2016-17

The sensible state allocation of the national roads demonstrates explicitly that more developed countries are successful at optimizing their share of the national roads. Maharashtra, Karnataka, Gujrat, West Bengal, Uttar Pradesh are the main states of nation. The automotive industry is a big incentive for money. It generates a large cluster next to any location where the automobile industry spends. There is a lot of movement of replacement parts and other parts. It requires fast movement of vehicles, as most cars are built on the just in time principle (JIT). Wide transport of persons and products needs large road networks, both throughout the region and in the Nations.

As the automobile industry in India is established in Maharashtra, Andhra Pradesh, Delhi, Rajasthan, Gujrat and Tamil Nadu as clusters, it has pulled a strategy to build the infrastructure essential to sustain the industry. The pull generated by the automotive industry demanded the construction of the requisite infrastructure.

3.96.15 https://worldroadstatistics.org/ -World road statistics

Country	Road length Km in '000	World ranking	Population 2016 in lakhs	Km per 1000 people
US	6646	1	3234	20.55
INDIA	5898	2	12102	4.87
CHINA	4696	3	13787	3.41
BRAZIL	1512	4	2077	7.28
RUSSIA	1499	5	1443	10.38
CANADA	1126	6	363	31.05
FRANCE	1088	7	669	16.27
AUSTRALIA	874	8	242	36.08
SPAIN	667	9	465	14.34
GERMANY	643	10	823	7.81
INDONESIA	538	11	2611	2.06
THAILAND	507	12	689	7.36
UK	422	13	656	6.43
POLAND	420	14	380	11.07
MEXICO	393	15	1275	3.08

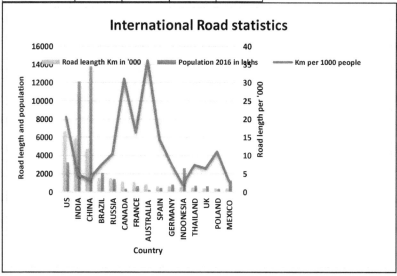

Chart 6.62 - International Road infrastructure 2018 per 1000 population

Source – World road statistics, 2018 published by International Road Federation Geneva

World road statistics clearly indicate that US , Canada and Australia have excellent road infrastructure which exceeds more than 20 kms per 1000 numbers of populations , however the developed countries indicate that the Km per 1000 population is much lower below 5 km /1000 population in case of India , china and Indonesia due to higher number of population. This indicates the scope of further development of infrastructure and growth

Based on the chart above, which shows how long the roads are globally comparable to India, we can easily understand that even though India stands 2 in terms of sheer road length, we take the ratio of the km/1000 accessible population, we can easily understand that India is experiencing a big development situation, the rate of construction of highways is enormous. Given the high population rate, we would require many facilities to accommodate this huge population.

Chapter-4   -   Data Analysis, Interpretation and Hypothesis Testing

4.1. Introduction

An investigation of economic growth and growth of automotive industry is the primary crux of the present research. It is well understood by the policy makers in automotive industry and development of any industry is the result of economic factors classified naturally into micro factors and macro factors. It doesn't required clarification to understand that industry level factors referred as micro factors and economy level factors are classified under macro factors. Though, primary focus has been given on the major factors, namely, road infrastructure, economic growth of the country, GDP, industrial growth and growth of automotive industry.

This entire exercise of the analysis of primary as well as secondary data has been centered towards understanding challenges faced by the automotive industry with intension to provide workable solutions and to understand growth pattern of the automotive industry in India from 2004 to 2017. These are basically the objectives of the present study. In this view of matter present study has been classified into three parts.

Accommodating above discussion, *PART-I*, of the present chapter provide quantified details in the tabular form for responses collected from working executives of automotive industry basically related to marketing and product development. Subsequently, in *PART-II* of the present chapter, an effort has been made to investigate growth pattern of automotive industry as comparative exploration with the Indian economy. Detailed discussion on the procedure, test statistics and interpretation of hypothesis has been presented with the help of *PART-III* of this chapter.

Automotive industry at a glance 2010 to 2020

Category	2010-11	2011-12	2012-13	2013-14	2014-15	2015-16	2016-17	2017-18	2018-19	2019-20
Passenger Vehicles	2982772	3146069	3231058	3087973	3221419	3465045	3801670	4020267	4028471	3434013
Commercial Vehicles	799553	879289	839748	830108	698298	786692	810253	895448	1112405	752022
Three Wheelers	760735	929136	832649	699035	949019	934104	783721	1022181	1268833	1133858
Two Wheelers	13349349	15427532	15744156	16883049	18489311	18830227	19933739	23154838	24499777	21036294
Grand Total	17892409	20382026	20647611	21500165	23358047	24016599	25330967	29094447	30914874	26362282

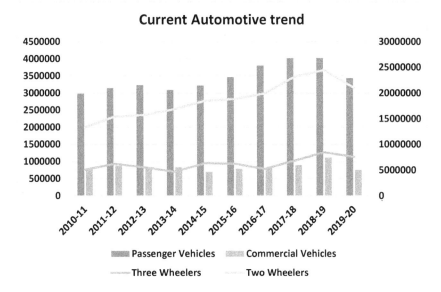

Chart No 6.63 -Production trend of automotive industry (SIAM data)2010-20
Source – SIAM

The four major pillars of automotive industry are 2W, 3W, 4W and CV (commercial vehicles), the ratio between them remains almost constant thru out the span of study. If we have to arrange them in large to small numbers just for the volumes produced, largest number will be 2W segment and smallest will be from commercial vehicles industry.

The above production table clearly indicates that 2w is the largest automotive segment in the automotive world, followed by Passenger vehicles, commercial vehicle and 3W respectively.

4.2. Automotive segment companies

As explained early automotive industry is highly capital incentive. Hence, the companies who will invest and start production will be limited to the capital available. Not everyone can afford to start the industry. India has only below number of total players in the market.

Table 4.1 - Automotive sub segments players Source

Automotive sub segment	Total players
Two wheeler	12
Three wheeler	7
Passenger vehicle	15
Commercial vehicle	10
Farm equipment's	13
Construction equipment	10

SIAM database, ACMA database, Team BHP,

The total Two wheeler manufacturers are 12 , for Three wheeler 7 manufacturers , passenger vehicle is manufactured by 15 players , Commercial vehicle have 10 manufacturers , farm equipment has 13 manufactures and last but not the least is construction equipment's are manufactured by 10 manufacturers

Based on the volumes published in the SIAM database or in their annual reports. Pareto analysis was done and top five manufacturers were selected from each of the category. This resulted in covering more than the 85% of the population of vehicles manufactured each of the year. The detailed pareto has been presented and justified in the beginning of chapter No 2 to justify the total sampling size

PART-I

4.3. Analysis of Challenges faced by Automotive Industry

This entire part has been based on the primary data collected purposefully for this present chapter. 157 respondents out of 256 responded to the which is approx. 62% of the total sample population. All the respondent have good amout of experience dealing with automotive industry , experience was the criteria applied while selecting the respondents. These 157 respondents belong to the top 7 manufacturers of each of the segment. This part of the chapter has been presented with help of three Sections. *In Section-(a)* demographic variables have been quantified, tabulated and presented.

Section-(a)

Demographic Information

With the help of *Table No. 4.1 A*, details of the respondents have been mentioned based on age and education. It would be seen from the table that, majority (more than 35 per cent) of the respondents belongs to age category of 40 to 50 years followed by age category 30-40 years of age accommodating approximately 30.57 per cent of total respondents. Clubbing two categories will result into total 65 per cent of respondents representing age group of 30 to 50 years.

Table No. 4.1 A - Distribution of Respondents according to Age and Education

Sr. No.	Education	Age of Respondents				
		20-30	30-40	40-50	50+	Grand Total
I	II	III	IV	V	VI	VI
1	Diploma	1	1			2
2	Graduation	8	32	34	23	97
3	Ph. D		1	3	2	6
4	Post- Graduation	7	14	19	12	52
	Grand Total	16	48	56	37	157

(Source: Field Investigation)

On the part of education of respondents, it would be seen from the table no. 4.1B that, almost 61 per cent of the respondents are graduated and 33 per cent are postgraduate. There are six respondents having doctoral degree 2 respondents are diploma holders.

Table No. 4.1 (B) - Distribution of Respondents according to Age and Education (Per cent)

Sr. No.	Education	Age of respondents				
		20-30	30-40	40-50	50+	Grand Total
I	II	III	IV	V	VI	VII
1	Diploma	0.64%	0.64%	0.00%	0.00%	1.27%
2	Graduation	5.10%	20.38%	21.66%	14.65%	61.78%
3	Ph. D	0.00%	0.64%	1.91%	1.27%	3.82%
4	Post- Graduation	4.46%	8.92%	12.10%	7.64%	33.12%
	Grand Total	10.19%	30.57%	35.67%	23.57%	100.00%

(Source: Field Investigation)

In this way, **Table no. 4.1A** provided details in number of respondents whereas, **Table No. 4.1B** provided same quantified data expressed in per cent. Ultimately, it is required to note here that, the respondents participated in the study are academically suitable in responding to the questions and also are well matured with the experience of automotive industry. The distribution of respondents have been efficiently presented with the help of **Chart No. 6.64**

Distribution of respondents as per age

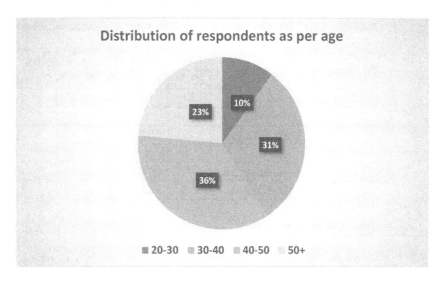

Chart No. 6.64 - Distribution of respondents as per age

Out of the 157 respondents 10% has age between 20-30 years , 31% had age between 30-40 years , 36% had age between 40-50 years and rest 23% had age 50+ years

The distribution of respondents again has been presented according to age and experience with the help of *Table No. 4.2* and *Table No. 4.2(A)* in terms of percent. It would be seen therefore from the tables that, more than 65 per cent of the respondents possess automotive industry experience of more than 15 years. This aspect has been efficiently depicted with graphical presentation using pie chart as most appropriate tool. In this view of matter, *Chart No. 6.65* has been provided below.

Table No. 4.2 Distribution of Respondents according to Age and Experience

Sr. No.	Experience in Industry	Age of respondents				
		20-30	30-40	40-50	50+	Grand Total
I	II	III	IV	V	VI	VII
1	0-5 years	10	1			11
2	15-25 years		14	43	1	58
3	25+ years			10	35	45
4	5-15 years	6	33	3	1	43
	Grand Total	16	48	56	37	157

(Source: Field Investigation)

Table No. 4.2(A) Distribution of Respondents according to Age and Experience (In percent)

Sr. No.	Experience in years	Age in Years				
		20-30	30-40	40-50	50+	Grand Total
I	II	III	IV	V	VI	VII
1	0-5 years	6.37%	0.64%	0.00%	0.00%	7.01%
2	15-25 years	0.00%	8.92%	27.39%	0.64%	36.94%
3	25+ years	0.00%	0.00%	6.37%	22.29%	28.66%
4	5-15 years	3.82%	21.02%	1.91%	0.64%	27.39%
	Grand Total	10.19%	30.57%	35.67%	23.57%	100.00%

(Source: Field Investigation)

Respondents had a good amount of experience which can be proved from the data that 37% of the respondents had experience between 15-25years , 28% had experience 25years +, 27% had experience of 5-15 years

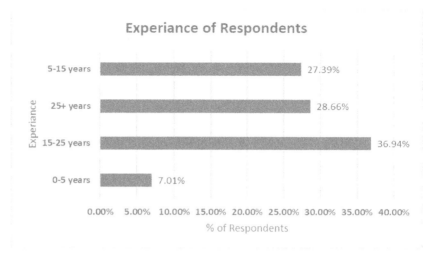

Chart No. 6.65 - Distribution of respondents as per experience

In the view of providing insights into the development of automotive sector along with economic development, experience of the respondents may provide validity for the responses. In the next section of the present chapter, an effort has been made to quantify responses for assessing factors responsible for growth of Indian Economy.

Section-(b)

4.4. <u>Factors for Growth of Indian Economy</u>

In this section of the part, assessment for economic growth of India has been made based on the opinions collected from the industry professionals. Basically, questions have been asked to quantify several factors and indicators responsible for economic growth of India.

With reference made to the ***Table No. 4.3 and Chart No. 6.66***, five indicators have been assessed to investigate whether they are responsible for economic growth of India. These indicators are; (i) agriculture income; (ii) foreign direct investment; (iii) index of industrial production; (iv) infrastructural development; and (v) per capita income. It would be seen therefore, from the table that, according to 42 per cent of respondents, per capita income is most relevant indicator of the economic growth followed by Index of Industrial Production (IIP) (rated by approximately 32 per cent of the respondents).

Table No. 4.3 - **Most relevant Indicator for economic growth**

Sr. No.	Indicators of economic growth	Experience of Respondents				
		0-5 years	15-25 years	25+ years	5-15 years	Grand Total
I	II	III	IV	V	VI	VII
1	Agriculture income	0.00%	3.18%	3.82%	3.18%	10.19%
2	Foreign direct investment	0.00%	1.91%	1.27%	1.27%	4.46%
3	Index of Industrial production (IIP)	3.82%	10.83%	9.55%	7.64%	31.85%
4	Infrastructure	1.91%	2.55%	3.18%	3.82%	11.46%
5	Per Capita income	1.27%	18.47%	10.83%	11.46%	42.04%
	Grand Total	7.01%	36.94%	28.66%	27.39%	100.00%

(Source: Field Investigation)

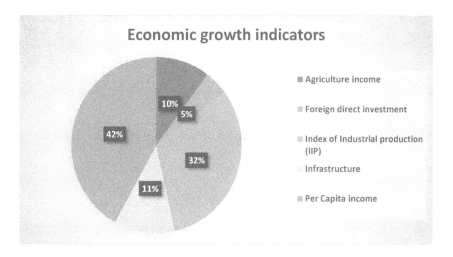

Chart No. 6.66 – Economic growth indicators

On the economic growth indicators, it was observed that 32% respondents indicated their choice as index of industrial production and 42% gave preference to per capita income.

Technically, it has to be anticipated here that, economic growth is the efficient utilization of all economic resources available with the particular country. Thus, every indicator mentioned above plays an essential role in understanding the overall growth of economy on various aspects.

The main concern of this research has been to investigate the possible impact of economic growth on automotive industry growth and vice versa. With this intension, question was asked to the respondents and tabulated results have been mentioned below with the help of *Table No. 4.4 and Chart No. 6.67.* It would be seen that, industrial production impacted on GDP growth as stated by more than 62 per cent of the respondents. As GDP is the indicator based on productions of services and goods in particular year. Also, the equal weightage has been given to all remaining factors as an impact of industrial production. The reason may be stated that, in a circular flow of economy, converting industrial production into purchasing power, disposable income may take time period varied in a nature considering efficiency of economic cycle.

Table No. 4.4 -Growth in industrial production and its impact

Sr. No.	Factors impacted	Experience of Respondents				
		0-5 years	15-25 years	25+ years	5-15 years	Grand Total
I	II	III	IV	V	VI	VII
1	Automobile sales	0.64%	4.46%	2.55%	2.55%	10.19%
2	Disposable income of people	1.91%	3.18%	2.55%	3.18%	10.83%
3	GDP growth	3.82%	24.20%	17.20%	17.20%	62.42%
4	Increase in purchasing power	0.00%	4.46%	5.73%	3.82%	14.01%
5	No impact	0.64%	0.64%	0.64%	0.64%	2.55%
	Grand Total	7.01%	36.94%	28.66%	27.39%	100.00%

(Source: Field Investigation)

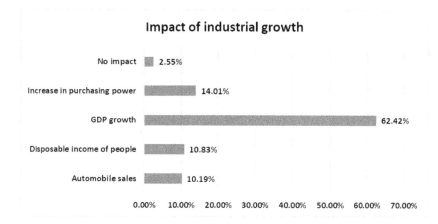

Chart No. 6.67 – Impact of industrial growth

During the field investigation for impacts of industrial growth , 62% indicated that GDP growth will be positively impacted , and 14% responded that the purchasing power of the population will go up

On the same line as discussed above, impact of increase in road infrastructure also has been assessed in the present study. In *Table No. 4.5 and Chart No. 6.68*, quantified responses were received and tabulated on this aspect. Five factors have been identified in this view of matter, namely; (a) catalyze GDP growth; (b) improve economic efficiency; (c) rise in Automobile sales; (d) rise in employment; (e) Rise in Industrial investment. Now, with reference to the **Table no. 4.5**, it would be seen that major impact of road infrastructure has been observed on improving economic efficiency (as stated by 39 per cent of the respondents). Also, secondary impact has been registered as per 28 per cent of the respondents on the factors called catalyzing GDP growth. Also, more than 16 per cent of the respondents have mentioned that, increase in road infrastructure is having impact on automobile sales in positive linear trend.

Table No. 4.5 -Impact of increase in road infrastructure

Sr. No	Impact factors	Experience of Respondents				
		0-5 years	15-25 years	25+ years	5-15 years	Grand Total
I	II	III	IV	V	VI	VII
1	Catalyze GDP growth	1.91%	10.19%	6.37%	9.55%	28.03%
2	Improve Economic efficiency	3.18%	12.74%	13.38%	10.19%	39.49%
3	Rise in Automobile sales	0.64%	9.55%	4.46%	1.91%	16.56%
4	Rise in employment	0.00%	1.91%	0.64%	0.64%	3.18%
5	Rise in Industrial investment	1.27%	2.55%	3.82%	5.10%	12.74%
	Grand Total	7.01%	36.94%	28.66%	27.39%	100.00%

(Source: Field Investigation)

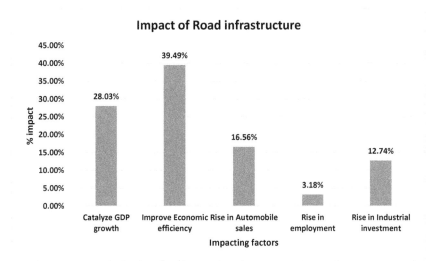

Chart No. 6.68 - Impact of Road infrastructure

Field investigation indicated that around 40% of respondents believe that road infrastructure will improve economic efficiency , while 28% feel that it will catalyze the economic growth 16% also felt that the automotive sales will rise due to rise in road infrastructure

In a summary of this section, it may be noted that, per capita income and index of industrial production are the key indicators of economic growth. Moreover, it also has to be noted that, growth in industrial production is having impact on GDP growth and simultaneously, impact of increase in road infrastructure may be seen on improving economic efficiency.

Section-(c)

4.5 Assessment of Automotive Industry

In this section, an effort has been made to investigate and quantify parameters of automotive industry. Primarily, opinions of the respondents have been asked on the aspect of factors responsible for growth of automobile industry. The responses on this aspect have been quantified, tabulated and presented with the help of *Table No. 4.6*. It is seen from the table that, rapid urbanization is the factor rated on higher side for being responsible to growth of automobile industry (rated by 37.58 per cent of the respondents). Further, factors such as disposable income and road infrastructure has been found approximately equal (more than 21 per cent of respondents) weightage on the aspect of growth of automobile industry). The least weightage has been found for overall industrial growth being responsible for growth of automobile industry.

Table No. 4.6-Factors responsible for growth of Automobile industry

Sr. No.	Factors	Experience of Respondents				
		0-5 years	15-25 years	25+ years	5-15 years	Grand Total
I	II	III	IV	V	VI	VII
1	Disposable income	1.27%	8.92%	3.82%	8.28%	22.29%
2	Industrial growth	1.27%	4.46%	4.46%	2.55%	12.74%
3	Intercity mobility needs	0.64%	2.55%	0.64%	1.91%	5.73%
4	Rapid Urbanization	3.18%	12.10%	12.74%	9.55%	37.58%
5	Road Infrastructure	0.64%	8.92%	7.01%	5.10%	21.66%
	Grand Total	7.01%	36.94%	28.66%	27.39%	100.00%

(Source: Field Investigation)

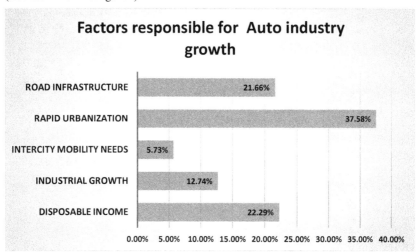

Chart No. 6.69 – Factors responsible for auto industry growth

Factors responsible for auto industry growth indicated that highest importance was given to rapid urbanization @ 37% . It can also be noted that 22% also felt that disposable income was important, 21% felt that road infrastructure played a role in this.

It is natural that, sales of the particular industry will have essential role in influencing growth of that industry. The same aspect has been quantified and presented with the help of *Table No. 4.7 and Chart No. 6.70*, below. In this view of matter, an investigation of five factors being responsible for sales of commercial vehicles has been investigated. These five factors are; (a) agriculture growth; (b) fuel price; (c) industrial growth; (d) road infrastructure; and (e) urbanization. Considering the tabulated results of this aspect, it is seen that, industrial growth is a factor responsible sale of commercial vehicles (as rated by 45 per cent of the respondents) followed by urbanization as stated by 22 per cent of the respondents. The sales of the automotive industry is particularly dependent on the purchasing power of the customer. This aspect has been investigated in further tables.

Table No. 4.7-**Factors affecting commercial vehicle sales**

Sr. No.	Factors	Experience of Respondents				
		0-5 years	15-25 years	25+ years	5-15 years	Grand Total
I	II	III	IV	V	VI	VII
1	Agriculture growth	0.64%	1.91%	3.18%	2.55%	8.28%
2	Fuel prices	0.00%	5.10%	1.91%	3.18%	10.19%
3	Industrial growth	2.55%	16.56%	14.65%	11.46%	45.22%
4	Road Infrastructure	0.00%	7.64%	3.18%	3.18%	14.01%
5	Urbanization	3.82%	5.73%	5.73%	7.01%	22.29%
	Grand Total	**7.01%**	**36.94%**	**28.66%**	**27.39%**	**100.00%**

(Source: Field Investigation)

FACTORS AFFECTING COMMERCIAL VEHICLE SALES

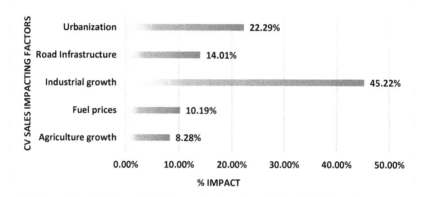

Chart No. 6.70 – Factors affecting commercial vehicle sales

(factors affecting commercial vehicle sales) – 45% felt that industrial growth , and 22% for urbanization and 14% gave their opinion on road infrastructure are the most influencing factors for commercial vehicle sales

Surprisingly, approximately 76 per cent of the respondents have stated that people who will end up buying 2W are with the income bracket of INR 10000 to INR 25000 per month. Looking at the urban class of the people and less penetrated market like India compared to similar ASIAN countries like china and Indonesia , we still have a large scope to have more two wheelers on the Road as people go high in the income bracket there are less chance they will buy 2W *(see Table No. 4.8 and Chart No 6.71*

Table No. 4.8 -Most relevant income Bracket for buying 2W

Sr. No.	Income Bracket INR	Experience of Respondents				
		0-5 years	15-25 years	25+ years	5-15 years	Grand Total
I	II	III	IV	V	VI	VII
1	10000-25000	3.82%	24.20%	20.38%	18.47%	66.88%
2	25000-50000	1.27%	8.28%	5.10%	5.10%	19.75%
3	50000 & above	0.00%	0.00%	1.27%	1.27%	2.55%
4	5000-10000	1.91%	4.46%	1.91%	2.55%	10.83%
	Grand Total	7.01%	36.94%	28.66%	27.39%	100.00%

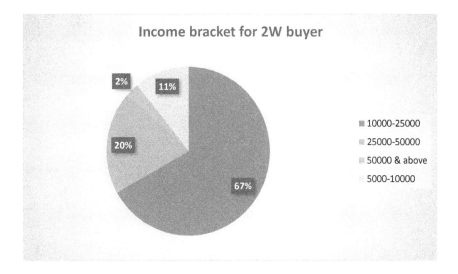

Chart No. 6.71 – Income bracket for 2W Buyer (Source: Field Investigation)

(Income bracket for 2W buyer) – It was observed that some one who is going to make a decision about buying of 2W , 67% of probability is he will have income of Rs 10000 to 25000 , only 20% felt that he will have income between Rs 25000-50000. Only 2% felt that the buyer will have income more than 50000 per month.

With reference made to *Table No. 4.9* below, two third of the respondents mentioned that the ideal income bracket to buy a 3W is INR. 25,000. Moreover approximately 29 per cent of the respondents mentioned bracket of INR. 25,000 to INR. 50,000. It is encouraging to know that the monthly income bracket of 25000 to 50000 is enough to have willingness to buy automobiles, many in the urban areas fall in this category, and hence the future for this segment looks good

Table No. 4.9 - <u>Most relevant income Bracket for buying 3W</u>

Income Bracket	Experience in years				
	0-5 years	15-25 years	25+ years	5-15 years	Grand Total
II	III	IV	V	VI	VII
10000-25000	4.46%	19.75%	16.56%	12.10%	52.87%
25000-50000	0.00%	8.92%	7.01%	6.37%	22.29%
50000 & above	1.27%	2.55%	1.27%	2.55%	7.64%
5000-10000	1.27%	5.73%	3.82%	6.37%	17.20%
Grand Total	7.01%	36.94%	28.66%	27.39%	100.00%

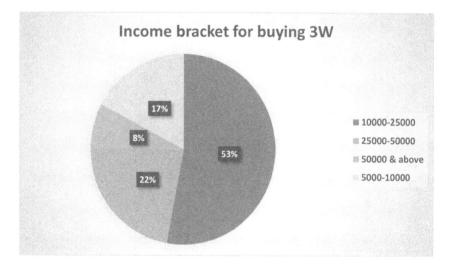

Chart No. 6.72 - Income bracket for 3W Buyer (Source: Field Investigation)

(Income bracket for 3w buyer) – The respondents felt that the probability of 3W buyer who will have income of Rs 10000-25000 is 53% , having income bracket of Rs 5000-10000 is 17% , income bracket of Rs 25000-50000 will be 22% , Only 8% felt that with income bracket exceeding Rs 50000 will buy a 3W

On the aspect of buying bracket for four wheeler, below mentioned *Table No. 4.10* provides tabulated results of opinions of the respondents recorded during the investigation of the present study. It is seen that, more than 62 per cent of the respondents have monthly income bracket more than INR. 50,000 for buying four-wheeler. The open ended limit saying more than INR. 50,000 provide certain kind of assurance in buying four wheeler. Price range for most of the cars sold in Indian market is INR 5 -20 lakhs, as most of the car purchase happens on loan only , the effective monthly installment of approx. 10000 to

25000 per month depending on the loan tenure. Hence the income bracket of INR 50000 is most relevant for a car buyer.

Table No. 4.10

Most relevant income Bracket for buying 4W

Sr. No.	Income Bracket	Experience in years				
		0-5 years	15-25 years	25+ years	5-15 years	Grand Total
I	II	III	IV	V	VI	VII
1	10000-25000	0.00%	1.27%	0.00%	0.64%	1.91%
2	25000-50000	3.82%	10.19%	12.74%	7.01%	33.76%
3	50000 & above	2.55%	24.20%	15.92%	19.75%	62.42%
4	5000-10000	0.64%	1.27%	0.00%	0.00%	1.91%
	Grand Total	7.01%	36.94%	28.66%	27.39%	100.00%

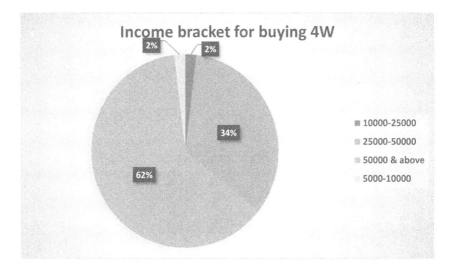

Chart No. 6.73 - Income bracket for 4W Buyer (Source: Field Investigation)

(Income bracket for buying Passenger car) – 62% felt that people with income bracket more than 50000 will buy passenger car , 34% felt that they will have income bracket of 25000-50000

In spite of this discussion on buying brackets, below mentioned tables provide popular utilization of these vehicles based on the quantified opinions of the respondents. This may have significant impact on the growth of automotive industry. The product is treated as a means of satisfying needs of customer's mobility Thus we can conclude that auto industry considers the applications and utility part, also the disposable income of the buyers in India type price sensitive market before launching the product. It is always essential to keep this in mind while developing and launching any vehicle. Once this aspect is understood to the required extent, Policy makers can make suitable policies, which are suitable for the specific segment.

In this view of matter, *Table No. 4.11*, provides insights on popular use of two wheelers. It would be seen from the table that, almost half of the respondents mentioned 2W is used for city travel and for less than 50 km distance as stated by 26 per cent of the respondents.

Table No. 4.11

Popular use of 2W

Sr. No.	Uses of vehicle	Experience in years				
		0-5 years	15-25 years	25+ years	5-15 years	Grand Total
I	II	III	IV	V	VI	VII
1	<50 km travel	0.64%	9.55%	7.64%	8.28%	26.11%
2	City Travel	5.10%	21.66%	13.38%	13.38%	53.50%
3	Stand by vehicle	0.64%	1.27%	0.00%	0.00%	1.91%
4	Urban household use	0.64%	4.46%	7.64%	5.73%	18.47%
	Grand Total	7.01%	36.94%	28.66%	27.39%	100.00%

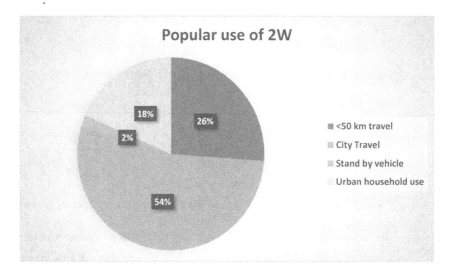

Chart No. 6.74 – Popular use of 2W (Source: Field Investigation)

(popular use of 2W) – 54% respondents felt that most popular use of 2W will be city travel, 18% voted for urban household use , and 26% felt it will be used for any travel needs which are less that 50km

From *Table No. 4.12*, it is seen that popular use of the three wheeler found as mentioned for city travel for passengers (as stated by 50 per cent of the respondents) and also it is being used for goods carrier pickups. The reason behind this utilization is low cost of transport.

Table No. 4.12– **Popular use of 3W**

Sr. No.	Uses of vehicle	Experience of Respondents				
		0-5 years	15-25 years	25+ years	5-15 years	Grand Total
I	II	III	IV	V	VI	VII
1	City travel passenger	5.10%	19.11%	12.74%	13.38%	50.32%
2	Family vehicle	1.27%	0.00%	0.64%	0.64%	2.55%
3	Goods carrier picks up	0.64%	12.74%	11.46%	9.55%	34.39%
4	Low cost transport	0.00%	5.10%	3.18%	3.18%	11.46%
5	Road side vendor	0.00%	0.00%	0.64%	0.64%	1.27%
	Grand Total	7.01%	36.94%	28.66%	27.39%	100.00%

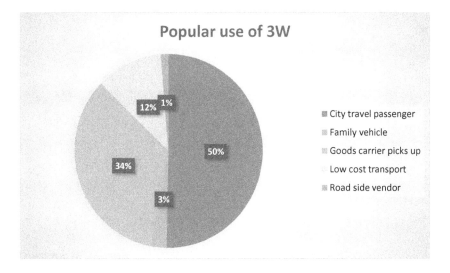

Chart No. 6.75 – Popular use of 3W (Source: Field Investigation)

(popular use of 3W) – 50% respondents felt that it will be used for city travel for passengers , 34% felt that popular use is for good carrier , 12% responded for low cost transport use

On the part of use of four-wheeler, it would be seen from *Table No 4.13* that, 91 per cent of the respondents have mentioned four-wheeler as a family car. The data shows very clearly that 4W are used as used as means of passenger travel particularly for family. The transportation of goods is strictly prohibited by the government through passenger cars;however, this could be lack of knowledge for respondents that LCV are also considered as part of 4W industries and 3.82 per cent respondents have stated this kind of use of four wheelers.

Table No. 4.13 - **Popular use of 4W**

Sr. No.	Uses of vehicles	Uses of vehicle				
		0-5 years	15-25 years	25+ years	5-15 years	Grand Total
I	II	III	IV	V	VI	VII
1	City travel for passengers	0.64%	2.55%	0.64%	0.64%	4.46%
2	Family vehicle	5.10%	33.12%	26.75%	26.11%	91.08%
3	Goods carrier picks up	0.64%	1.27%	1.27%	0.64%	3.82%
4	Road side vendor	0.64%	0.00%	0.00%	0.00%	0.64%
	Grand Total	7.01%	36.94%	28.66%	27.39%	100.00%

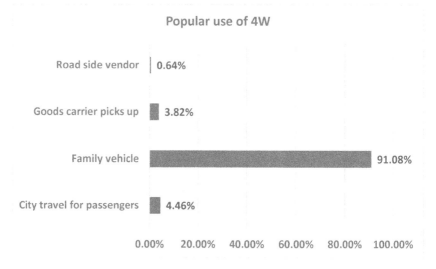

Chart No. 6.76 – Popular use of 4W (Source: Field Investigation)

(popular use of passenger car /4W) – 91% of the respondent felt that most popular use of 4W is family vehicle , only 3.82% felt that it is good carrier also

Moreover, bus and trucks are used popularly for bulk goods transport (59 per cent of the respondents); intercity travel-most probably for buses (21 per cent of respondents) and finally looked as intercity travel as mentioned by 16 per cent of the respondents (refer *Table No. 4.14).*

Table No. 4.14- **Popular use of commercial vehicle -Bus & Truck**

Sr. No.	Use of vehicles	Experience of Respondents				
		0-5 years	15-25 years	25+ years	5-15 years	Grand Total
I	II	III	IV	V	VI	VII
1	Bulk Goods transport	3.18%	24.20%	16.56%	15.29%	59.24%
2	Intercity travel	1.27%	5.10%	7.64%	7.01%	21.02%
3	Luxury vehicle	0.00%	1.27%	0.00%	0.00%	1.27%
4	School Bus	0.64%	0.64%	0.00%	0.64%	1.91%
5	Urban transport	1.91%	5.73%	4.46%	4.46%	16.56%
	Grand Total	7.01%	36.94%	28.66%	27.39%	100.00%

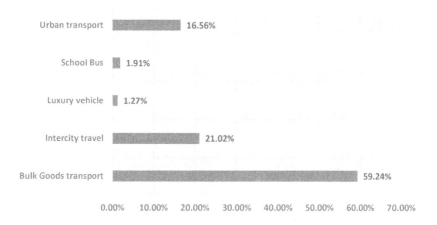

Chart No. 6.77 – Popular use of Bus and Truck (Source: Field Investigation)

(popular use o bus and truck) – 59% felt that bulk good transport , and 21% felt that intercity transport is the most popular use. 16% also felp that urban transport is the most popular use for commercial vehicles

In a summary, it may be noted that, four wheelers are used as family car; buses used for intercity passenger transportation, three wheelers are used goods transport as well as passenger transport because it is cheaper cost. Trucks are treated purely as means of commercial transport and mostly for goods.

Section-(d)

4.6 Economic Growth and Automotive Industry

More the sales will result increased revenue generation for auto industry. In this view of matter, a common question is always asked and that is, what is the possibility of buying two wheeler by bicycle owners when disposable income increases. The policy makers of two wheeler manufacturing industry is always interested in understanding this probability for estimating new segmentation of the emerging market. This aspect has been investigated in this study and tabulated results have been discussed with the help of *Table No. 4.15*.

It is seen therefore from the table that, almost 61 per cent of the respondents mentioned that, there is up to 50 per cent chance of buying two wheeler by bicycle owners once his disposable income will grow. Though, surprisingly need to note that, as per 18.47 per cent of the respondents stated that there is 100 per cent of chance for buying two wheeler by bicycle owners when disposable income grows.

Table No. 4.15 -

Probability that the bicycle owner will buy a 2W as his disposable income grows

Sr. No.	Probability	Experience of Respondents				
		0-5 years	15-25 years	25+ years	5-15 years	Grand Total
I	II	III	IV	V	VI	VII
1	Prob 10%	0.64%	7.01%	4.46%	5.10%	17.20%
2	Prob 30%	2.55%	3.82%	10.83%	8.92%	26.11%
3	Prob 50%	2.55%	7.01%	3.82%	4.46%	17.83%
4	Prob 70%	0.64%	10.19%	4.46%	5.10%	20.38%
5	prob 100%	0.64%	8.92%	5.10%	3.82%	18.47%
	Grand Total	7.01%	36.94%	28.66%	27.39%	100.00%

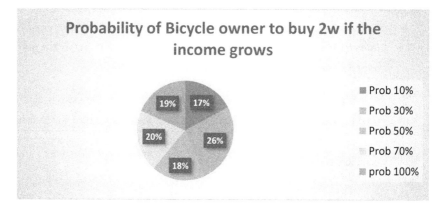

Chart No. 6.78 – probability of cycle owner to buy 2W (Source: Field Investigation)

This aspect also has been studied for the possibility of buying four wheeler by two wheeler owners as disposable income grows. Referring to the tabulated quantified results mentioned in the *Table No. 4.16*, it is seen that, approximately three fourth (71 per cent) of the total respondents mentioned, more than 50 per cent of chances for buying four wheeler.

Table No. 4.16 -<u>Probability that the 2W owner will buy a 4W as his disposable income grow.</u>

Sr. No.	Probability	Experience of Respondents				
		0-5 years	15-25 years	25+ years	5-15 years	Grand Total
I	II	III	IV	V	VI	VII
1	Prob 10%	0.64%	0.00%	0.64%	0.64%	1.91%
2	Prob 30%	1.27%	12.10%	5.73%	7.01%	26.11%
3	Prob 50%	2.55%	7.01%	10.19%	10.19%	29.94%
4	Prob 70%	0.64%	8.28%	7.01%	7.64%	23.57%
5	prob 100%	1.91%	9.55%	5.10%	1.91%	18.47%
	Grand Total	7.01%	36.94%	28.66%	27.39%	100.00%

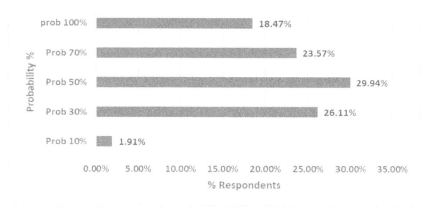

Chart No. 6.79 – probability of 2W owner to buy 4W

(Source: Field Investigation)

Apart from this segmentation possibility, an effort has been made to investigate probable factors essential for automotive industry growth. The tabulated results have been presented with the help of **Table No. 4.17**. Total five factors have been identified for further tabulation, namely; (a) exports and internal consumption; (b) industrial infrastructure; (c) purchasing power; (d) quick movement of goods and people as resource; and (e) road infrastructure. Though, ultimate analysis has led to observe that exports and internal consumption along with industrial infrastructure are the major factors that would be essential for growth of automotive industry.

Table No. 4.17 -Factors essentials for industrial growth

Sr. No.	Factors	Experience in years				
		0-5 years	15-25 years	25+ years	5-15 years	Grand Total
I	II	III	IV	V	VI	VII
1	Exports & internal consumption	3.82%	15.92%	8.28%	5.10%	33.12%
2	Industrial infrastructure	0.00%	10.83%	11.46%	9.55%	31.85%
3	PP (Purchasing power)	0.64%	4.46%	3.82%	7.64%	16.56%
4	Quick people and goods movement	1.27%	2.55%	1.91%	1.91%	7.64%
5	Road Infrastructure	1.27%	3.18%	3.18%	3.18%	10.83%
	Grand Total	7.01%	36.94%	28.66%	27.39%	100.00%

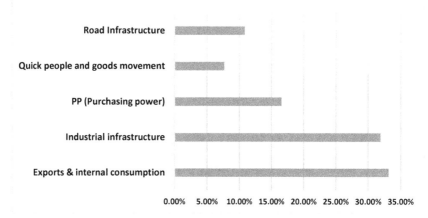

FACTORS ESSENCIAL FOR INDUSTRIAL GROWTH

Chart No. 6.80 – Factors essential for industrial growth (Source: Field Investigation)

(Factors responsible for industrial growth) – Out of all the respondents 33% felt that exports and internal consumption are essential for industrial growth , 32% felt its industrial infrastructure, 11% felt its road infrastructure & 16% felt its purchasing power which is responsible for industrial growth

Business cycles are essential part of any industry that have impact on demand and industrial production as well. In Indian scenario monsoon and tax structure also plays vital role. Automobile industry is also not exception for this. Though, based on the quantified results presented with the help of *Table No. 4.18*, it has to be pointed out that, economic cycles are most observed influencer of auto industry sale (as stated by 54 per cent of respondents) followed by monsoon (according to 28 per cent respondents).

Table No. 4.18 – <u>Factors responsible for cyclic nature of the Auto industry sale</u>

Sr. No.	Factors	Experience in years				
		0-5 years	15-25 years	25+ years	5-15 years	Grand Total
I	II	III	IV	V	VI	VII
1	Economic cycles	5.10%	15.29%	16.56%	17.20%	54.14%
2	Industrial production	0.64%	0.00%	0.00%	0.00%	0.64%
3	Infrastructure growth	0.00%	4.46%	2.55%	3.82%	10.83%
4	Monsoon	0.64%	15.29%	7.64%	4.46%	28.03%
5	Tax structure	0.64%	1.91%	1.91%	1.91%	6.37%
	Grand Total	7.01%	36.94%	28.66%	27.39%	100.00%

Factors responsible for cyclic nature of auto industry

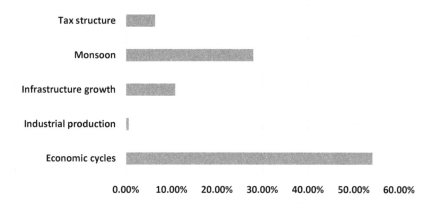

Chart No. 6.81 – Factors responsible for cyclic nature of auto industry (Source: Field Investigation)

(factors responsible for cyclic nature of auto industry)54% felt that economic cycles are responsible for the cyclic nature of automotive industry ,28% felt it was monsoon cycle, 10% felt it was infrastructure growth.

Growth of automotive industry is partially dependent on the economic growth of India. This has been wisely revealed from the primary data collected from investigation. The same responses have been tabulated and presented with the help of *Table No. 4.19*. Surprisingly need to note that, almost 85.33 per cent of the respondents mentioned it affirmative to the question on strong correlation between economic growth and growth of automotive industry in India.

Table No. 4.19 - **Do you think there is strong correlation between economic growth and growth of automotive industry in India?**

Sr. No.	Experience	Level of agreeableness					Grand Total
		Strongly Disagree	Disagree	Neutral	Agree	Strongly Agree	
I	II	III	IV	V	VI	VII	VIII
1	0-5 years	9.09%	0.00%	0.00%	63.64%	27.27%	100.00%
2	15-25 years	0.00%	1.72%	6.90%	48.28%	43.10%	100.00%
3	25+ years	0.00%	0.00%	22.22%	42.22%	35.56%	100.00%
4	5-15 years	0.00%	2.33%	13.95%	46.51%	37.21%	100.00%
	Grand Total	0.64%	1.27%	12.74%	47.13%	38.22%	100.00%

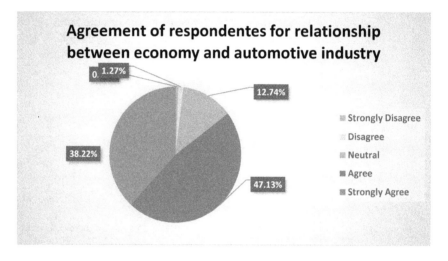

Chart No. 6.82 – **Relationship between economy and automotive industry** (Source: Field Investigation)

(Relationship between economy and automotive industry) 47% respondents agreed and 38% strongly agreed for the relationship between the both. 12% were neutral for this relationship.

Moreover, similar kind of response have been quantified and observed on the aspect of government spending on road infrastructure and increase disposable income will have positive impact on automotive industry in India. Total 85.35 per cent of the respondents supported this assumption and possibility. Further details have been presented with the help of *Table No. 4.20.*

Table No. 4.20 -<u>Do you think that rise in government spending on Road Infrastructure and increase in Disposable Income will have positive impact on automotive industry in India?</u>

Sr. No.	Experience in years	Responses			
		Can't say	No	Yes	Grand Total
I	II	III	IV	V	VI
1	0-5 years	0.64%	0.64%	5.73%	7.01%
2	15-25 years	3.18%	1.27%	32.48%	36.94%
3	25+ years	3.82%	0.00%	24.84%	28.66%
4	5-15 years	3.18%	1.91%	22.29%	27.39%
	Grand Total	10.83%	3.82%	85.35%	100.00%

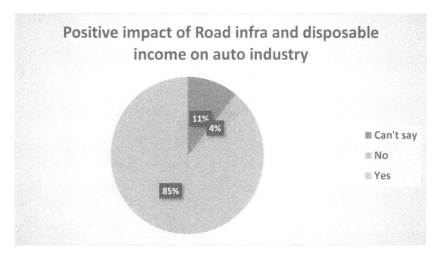

Chart No. 6.83 – Impact of road infra and disposable income (Source: Field Investigation)

(positive impact of rise in road infrastructure and disposable income on automotive industry) 85% respondents agreed on the strong co relation between these factors 11% responded cant say and 4% of them disagree on the relationship between these factors

In a summary, it can be stated that, government spending on road infrastructure and increase disposable income will have positive impact on automotive industry in India. Also increase in disposable income will help in enhancing prospective customers for automobile industry. Similarly, growth of economy and growth of automotive industry are complementary to each other. Hence, it has to be appreciated that change in one may cause change in other in positive manner, reflecting unit correlation.

Section-(e)

4.7 Challenges faced by Automotive Industry in India

Keeping in mind aims and objectives of the present study, challenges faced by automotive industry has been investigated and quantified results tabulated and presented in this section. Investigation has been initiated separately for four segments of this industry such as, two wheeler segment, three wheeler segment, four wheeler segment and industry of commercial vehicle manufacturers. To accommodate this discussion, four tables have been prepared in the view of explaining the challenges faced by the automotive industry distributed according to the segments mentioned above.

With reference made to the *Table No. 4.21*, challenges faced by two wheeler industry have been quantified and presented in tabular form. It would be seen from the table that, 66 per cent of the total responses have received for fuel price as a key challenge for two wheeler industry followed by city traffic (8.33 per cent) and other challenges as mentioned in the table below.

Ultimately, it has to be pointed out that, increase in disposable income may influence the decision of prospective twowheel buyers for buying four wheeler. On similar time, heavy traffic in city play as vital role for buying two wheeler. Though, safety of the two wheeler user is a constraint as compare to four wheeler users. All these aspects remain challenge for two wheeler industry.

Table No. 4.21 Challenges faced by 2W Industry

Sr. No.	Challenges for Two Wheeler Industry	No. of Respondents	Per cent
I	II	III	IV
1	Fuel price	96	66.67%
2	City traffic	12	8.33%
3	Pollution	12	8.33%
4	Emission	10	6.94%
5	Availability of finance options	9	6.25%
6	Taxes	5	3.47%

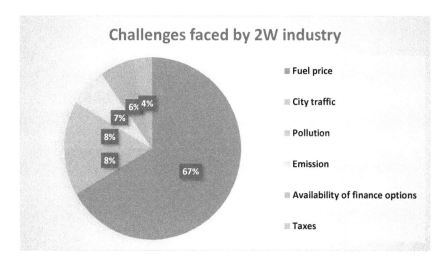

Challenges faced by 2W industry

- Fuel price
- City traffic
- Pollution
- Emission
- Availability of finance options
- Taxes

(Source: Field Investigation)

Chart No. 6.84 – Challenge faced by 2W Industry

(Challenges faced by 2W segment) 67% felt that rise in fuel prices was the biggest challenge for 2W industry, 8% felt that city traffic and pollution are also challenges faced

In similar fashion, quantified results of challenges faced by three wheeler industry has been presented with the help of *Table No. 4.22*. It would be seen from the table that, fuel efficiency stood as significant challenge (as stated by 30 per cent respondents) for three wheeler industry. Also competition of OLA and UBER along with restriction of mostly commercial uses has been weighted similarly by the respondents (slightly more than 19 per cent of respondents).

Table No. 4.22 Challenges faced by 3W Industry

Sr. No.	Challenges for three Wheeler Industry	No. of Respondents	Per cent
I	II	III	IV
1	Fuel efficiency	55	30.22%
2	Competition (OLA / UBER)	35	19.23%
3	Commercial use	35	19.23%
4	Public transport	19	10.44%
5	Space	15	8.24%
6	Shared mobility	13	7.14%
7	RTO Norms	10	5.49%

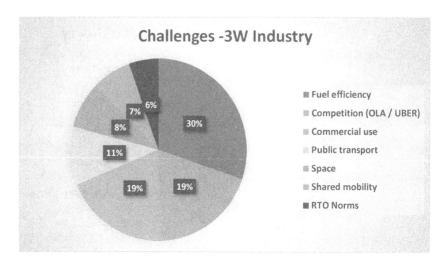

(Source: Field Investigation)

Chart No. 6.85 - Challenges faced by 3W industry

(Challenges faced by 3W industry)- 30% felt fuel efficiency was the challenge, 19% felt competition from OLA and UBER , 11% also felt that public transport is also a challenge as better availability of public transport could slow down the growth for 3W industry, small portion respondents also raised concern about RTO norms , shared mobility are also challenges

Most often automotive industry has been referred only for car manufacturing industry. Naturally the term has been used interchangeably. The challenges faced by this segment of auto industry has been tabulated and presented with the help of *Table No. 4.23*. It can be seen therefore that, fuel price is significant challenge with more than 40 per cent of weightage followed by interest rate and affordability with 20 per cent of weightage. Further details have been presented in the table below.

Table No 4.23 - **Challenges faced by 4W Industry**

Sr. No.	Challenges for Four Wheeler Industry	No. of Respondents	Per cent
I	II	III	IV
1	Fuel price	92	40.17%
2	Interest rate and affordability	46	20.09%
3	Government policy and taxes	34	14.85%
4	Fuel to electric	29	12.66%
5	Easy loan	28	12.23%

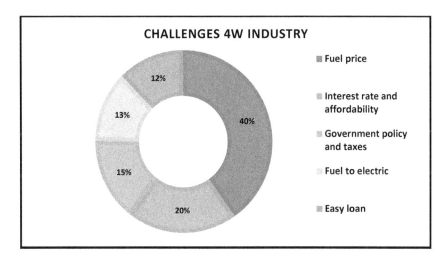

CHALLENGES 4W INDUSTRY

- Fuel price
- Interest rate and affordability
- Government policy and taxes
- Fuel to electric
- Easy loan

40%
20%
15%
13%
12%

Chart No. 6.86 - Challenges faced by 4W industry

(Source: Field Investigation)

(challenges for 4W industry) – 40% indicated that fuel prices was largest area of concern, 20% felt it was interest rate and affordability ,13% felt the fuel affordability for electric vehicles

Growth in industrial infrastructure is the main challenge faced by commercial vehicle manufacturing industry with weightage of 20 per cent. Similar weightage has been observed for fuel price. Further details have been offered with the help of *Table No. 4.24*.

Table No. 4.24 **Challenges faced by Commercial Vehicle Industry**

Sr. No.	Challenges for commercial vehicle Industry	No. of Respondents	Per cent
I	II	III	IV
1	Growth in Industrial Infrastructure	31	25.41
2	fuel price	29	23.77
3	Road infrastructure and safety standards	23	18.85
4	Govt policies and tax structure	18	14.75
5	Emission	12	9.84
6	Availability of finance options	9	7.38

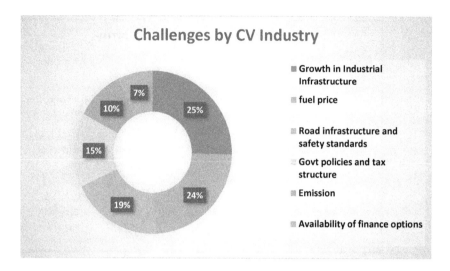

Chart No. 6.87 – Challenges faced by commercial vehicle industry

(Source: Field Investigation)

(Challenges faced by commercial vehicle industry) –24% felt it was fuel prices , and 25% felt it was growth in industrial infra, 19% also felt road infrastructure is also a challenge, 15% felt government policies and tax structure is a challenge

In a summary, it may be stated that, automotive industry is now transforming from the challenges such as, fuel efficiency, entry of shared mobility based competitors such as OLA and UBER, government regulations and increase in disposable incomes.

PART-II

4.8 Growth pattern of automotive industry in Indian Economy

The title of the present study is self-explanatory to provide objectives of this research work. Though, keeping in mind the objectives mentioned in the chapter of research methodology, comparison of the automotive industry with Indian economy is the primary concern of this research work. This aspect of comparison has been quantified and presented in this part of the chapter. Primarily, scenario of Indian economy and its growth has been provided with the help of six parameters, namely; (a) Gross domestic products- expressed in INR. in crores; (b) Road infrastructure- presented in running kilometers; (c) population of India; and (d) fuel price in India. Secondly, growth of automotive industry has been quantified using number vehicles produced in particular year. Moreover, it has to be pointed out here that, all the quantified details have been collected from valid sources for 14 years spread over between Year 2004 and Year 2017.

4.9 Growth of India GDP

As has been stated in above paragraph, quantified details on GDP of India for 2004 to 2017 has been presented with the help of **Table No. 4.25**. The GDP for particular year has been expressed in INR Crores. The column labeled as 'Growth in %) provides growth the Indian GDP as compared to previous year. In this view of matter, India has observed annual growth of GDP from at least 3.98 per cent to maximum of 24.10 per cent in the Year 2009. Though, average growth in GDP has been observed to be the magnitude of 14 per cent. In terms of USD the GDP growth will be in between 6 to 9 % , However as we have converted the numbers in INR crors , due to the depreciation of INR against USD the rate of growth in INR looks more in terms of percentage.

Table No. 4.25 Growth of Indian GDP

Year	USDB	Exchange rate USD-INR	INR CRORS	Growth in %
2004	721.59	45.32	3270246	Base year
2005	834.22	44.1	3678910	12.5
2006	949.12	45.31	4300463	16.9
2007	1238.7	41.35	5122025	19.1
2008	1224.1	43.51	5326059	3.98
2009	1365.37	48.41	6609756	24.1
2010	1708.46	45.73	7812788	18.2
2011	1823.05	46.67	8508174	8.9
2012	1827.64	53.44	9766908	14.79
2013	1856.72	56.57	10503465	7.54
2014	2039.13	62.33	12709897	21.01
2015	2103.59	62.97	13246306	4.22
2016	2294.12	66.46	15246722	15.1
2017	2652.76	67.79	17983060	17.95

Measure	Statistic
Mean	8863198
Standard Deviation	4584495
Minimum	3270245
Maximum	17983060
Count	14

4.10 Road length

With reference made to the *Table No. 4.26*, growth of Road Infrastructure has been quantified and presented. It would be seen from the table that, in the year 2009 highest rate of growth (8 per cent) has been registered by adding 3,61,917 KM of road infrastructure in a year. Though the lowest growth (1.88 per cent) has been observed in the year 2006. Average growth of road infrastructure has been noted to be the magnitude of 3.71 per cent per year since 2004 to 2017. This parameter has direct impact on automotive industry. It is observed that as the infrastructure grows, the sale of automobile also grows for all the variants.

Table No. 4.26 Road length

Sr. No.	Year	Road length (in KM)	Growth Per cent
I	II	III	IV
1	2004	3621507	Base Year
2	2005	3809156	5.18
3	2006	3880651	1.88
4	2007	4016401	3.5
5	2008	4109592	2.32
6	2009	4471509	8.81
7	2010	4582439	2.48
8	2011	4676838	2.06
9	2012	4865394	4.03
10	2013	5231922	7.53
11	2014	5402485	3.26
12	2015	5472144	1.29
13	2016	5600000	2.34
14	2017	5800000	3.57
	Descriptive Statistics		
	Measure		Statistics
15	Mean		4681431
16	Standard Deviation		729894
17	Minimum		3621507
18	Maximum		5800000
19	Count		14

4.11 Population growth

The growth of parameter called as population has been tabulated and presented in the *Table No. 4.27*. It has been observed that population growth in India has registered a steady growth of 1.13 per cent to 1.60 per cent per annum. The general trend of diminishing growth has been seen in the population growth. Highest increase observed in the year 2004 registering 1.60 per cent of growth as compared to previous year. An average growth in population for the period of 14 years has been observed to be the magnitude of 1.34 per cent. Ultimately, population is considered as prospective consumers of any economy. It also creates negative impact on the economy, like the total earning or working population will go down as percentage and per capita income goes down.

Table No. 4.27-Population growth in India

Growth of Population in India (in crores numbers)			
Sr. No.	Year	Population	Growth Per cent
I	II	III	IV
1	2004	112.6	Base Year
2	2005	114.4	1.6
3	2006	116.2	1.57
4	2007	118	1.55
5	2008	119.7	1.44
6	2009	121.4	1.42
7	2010	123.1	1.4
8	2011	124.7	1.3
9	2012	126.3	1.28
10	2013	127.9	1.27
11	2014	129.4	1.17
12	2015	130.9	1.16
13	2016	132.4	1.15
14	2017	133.9	1.13
Descriptive Statistics			
	Measure		Statistics
15	Mean		123.6357
16	Standard Deviation		6.84719
17	Minimum		112.6
18	Maximum		133.9
19	Count		14

4.12 Fuel prices

This is with reference to the responses gathered from primary respondents regarding challenges faced by automotive industry; fuel prices remains more challenge for automotive industry. This parameter has been observed more fluctuating over the period of time under consideration. The prices of fuel has direct impact of world economy. It has been observed varied between decreases of -14 per cent (in 2015) to 28 per cent of increase in 2014. Though clear understanding would be visible by inspecting next table containing annual production of vehicles.

Table No. 4.28- Fuel price increase

Increase in fuel price in India (in INR per Liter)

Sr. No.	Year	Petrol		Diesel	
		Price	Growth in %	Price	Growth in %
I	II	III	IV	V	VI
1	2004	36.49	Base Year	24.35	Base Year
2	2005	40.84	11.92	29.77	22.26
3	2006	46.76	14.5	33.65	13.03
4	2007	46.41	-0.75	32.85	-2.38
5	2008	48.65	4.83	34.04	3.62
6	2009	43.37	-10.85	32.76	-3.76
7	2010	50.98	17.55	38.51	17.55
8	2011	61.47	20.58	40.01	3.9
9	2012	68.97	12.2	43.47	8.65
10	2013	72.68	5.38	52.03	19.69
11	2014	73.7	1.4	66.79	28.37
12	2015	66.5	-9.77	56.85	-14.88
13	2016	66.7	0.3	54.1	-4.84
14	2017	73.24	9.81	60.47	11.77
	Descriptive Statistics of fuel price				
		Petrol		Diesel	
15	Mean	56		42	
16	Standard Deviation	13		12	
17	Minimum	36		24	
18	Maximum	73		66	
19	Count	14		14	

4.13 Automotive industry growth

It would be seen from the *Table No. 4.29* that, in accordance with the fluctuation obverted for fuel price production of vehicles also have been observed fluctuating. The combine output of commercial vehicles, four wheelers, three wheelers and two wheelers have been recorded and presented in the below table. Comparative aspect of growth patterns of vehicle production and fuel price has been presented with the help of chart below

Table No. 4.29-Automotive production and growth

Production of Automotive Industry and Overall Growth (Qty.)

Sr. No.	Year	Production of vehicles (Qty.)				TOTAL	Growth in %
		Four Wheeler	Commercial Vehicles	Three Wheeler	Two Wheeler		
I	II	III	IV	V	VI	VII	VIII
1	2004	989560	550080	356223	5622741	7518604	Base year
2	2005	1209876	707406	374445	6529829	8821556	17.33
3	2006	1309300	782166	434423	7608697	10134586	14.88
4	2007	1545223	539989	556126	8436212	11077550	9.3
5	2008	1777583	484141	500660	8009292	10771676	-2.76
6	2009	1838593	466393	497020	8395613	11197619	3.95
7	2010	2357411	721939	619194	10510336	14208880	26.89
8	2011	2982772	881144	799553	13349349	18012818	26.77
9	2012	3231058	832649	839748	15744156	20647611	14.63
10	2013	3087973	699035	830108	16883049	21500165	4.13
11	2014	3221419	698298	949019	18489311	23358047	8.64
12	2015	3465045	786692	934104	18830227	24016068	2.82
13	2016	3801670	810253	783721	19933739	25329383	5.47
14	2017	4010373	894551	1021911	23147057	29073892	14.78

4.14 Co relation coefficient

It will not call upon any clarification to understand the close correlation between growth of vehicles produced per year and the fluctuation in fuel price. As has been seen from the chart below, production of vehicles have been hampered because of variation in economic activity which has also impacted fuel prices as one of the indicator for global demand and supply cycle . Quantification of the aspect has been made and presented with the help of below by applying correlation coefficient .

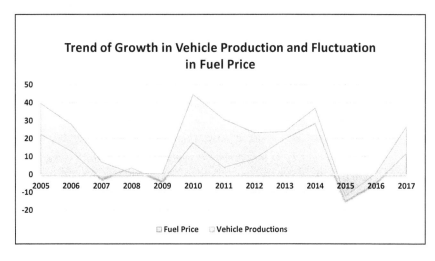

Chart No. 6.88 – Comparison between the vehicle production and fuel price fluctuation

4.15 Factor analysis

As stated earlier correlation coefficient has been calculated along with 't' test statistics for understanding its significance. All the detailed calculations have been presented with the help of *Table No. 4.30*. Without going into the further details, it has to be noted significantly here that, all the variables are correlated with significant linearity marked by asterisk (*). Also all the coefficients are observed to be more than 0.85 with 0.00 significance value showing to be significantly less than 0.05 resulting in accepting the correlation coefficient.

Table No. 4.30 - Comparison of Automotive industry and Growth of Economy ,(Using Correlation Co-efficient)

		GDP	Road Constru ction	Population	Price Petrol	Price Diesel	Vehicle Production
GDP	Pearson Correlation	1	.968**	.961**	.844**	.906**	.963**
	Sig. (2-tailed)		0	0	0	0	0
Road Construction	Pearson Correlation	.968**	1	.993**	.920**	.942**	.979**
	Sig. (2-tailed)	0		0	0	0	0
Population	Pearson Correlation	.961**	.993**	1	.922**	.922**	.976**
	Sig. (2-tailed)	0	0		0	0	0
Price Petrol	Pearson Correlation	.844**	.920**	.922**	1	.927**	.950**
	Sig. (2-tailed)	0	0	0		0	0
Price Diesel	Pearson Correlation	.906**	.942**	.922**	.927**	1	.938**
	Sig. (2-tailed)	0	0	0	0		0
Vehicle Production	Pearson Correlation	.963**	.979**	.976**	.950**	.938**	1
	Sig. (2-tailed)	0	0	0	0	0	
**. Correlation is significant at the 0.01 level (2-tailed).							

If we test the data using pearson correlation with GDP of the country which is considered to be 1 , all the parameters comparted are 0.9 which is very close co relation , also from the 2 – tailed analysis it is clear that all the figure's are less than 0.01 which again is the strong logic to prove that the data is co related

In summary of the section, it has to be pointed out that, Indian economy is developing economy and growing significantly. Moreover, Automobile industry is highly correlated with the Indian economy and having direct impact of fuel price fluctuation on total quantity produced for particular in automobile industry. Technical hypothesis have been tested on this aspect in Part-III of this chapter.

4.16- PART-III Testing of Hypothesis

In this section, efforts have been made to test hypothesis of the present study as mentioned below-

H_0: **The growth of Automotive Industry is NOT directly co- related with the economic growth of India.**

H_a: **The growth of Automotive Industry is directly co- related with the economic growth of India.**

For purpose of testing this hypothesis, primary data has been considered. As has been mentioned earlier, eminent experienced professionals have been contacted and survey has been implemented for purpose of collecting primary data. Considering the nature and structure of said hypothesis, question no **H0** has been considered suitable for testing purpose. Initial tabulation of the responses collected under this question have been tabulated and presented in the **Table No. 4.19** in **PART-II** of the present chapter.

The responses of the said question has been quantified and measured by applying Likert Five Point scale. Distributed between Strongly Agree (representing score and weight of 5) and Strongly Disagree (representing score and weight of 1). The median of the scale is '3', representing neutrality of the response. Keeping in mind this discussion, it needs to be pointed out here that, One Sample 't' test is found more scientific and appropriate for testing this hypothesis.

Now, arithmetic mean of the opinions regarding growth of Automotive Industry is directly co- related with the economic growth of India has been observed to be 4.21 on five point Likert Scale, which is considerably favorable to assumption made in present study. Considering all these aspects, technical hypotheses for the selected variable have been presented in below **Table No. 4.31.**

Table No. 4.31 Technical hypotheses for H1

Sr. No.	Referred Table No.	Question of Hypothesis	H_{null}	$H_{alternate}$
I	II	III	IV	V
1	4.19	On the 5 point scale standard average is 3 which stood neutral on the aspect of growth automotive industry is directly co-related with the economic growth of India. Now, can it be said that the observed mean is significantly differed from the standard average of 3?	There is no significant difference	There is significant difference

As has been mentioned earlier, considering all the aspects of the present hypothesis, one sample 't' test with 5 per cent level of significance has been observed to be appropriate for further procedure of the testing. Hence the output of testing has been presented with the help of *Table No. 4.32*.

Table No. 4.32- Descriptive Statistics

	N	Mean	Std. Deviation	Std. Error Mean
Supply of consumer durables increased due to free economy	157	4.2102	0.7598	0.0064

Table No. 4.33 - One-Sample Test

One-Sample Test	Test Value = 3					
	t	df	Sig. (2-tailed)	Mean Difference	95% Confidence Interval of the Difference	
					Lower	Upper
Supply of consumer durables increased due to free economy	19.95	156	0	1.21019	1.0904	1.33

On scrutinizing the results of calculations mentioned above in *Table No. 4.32 and Table No. 4.33* the inferences are as follows-

In case of hypothesis-H1, opinions of respondents regarding correlation between growth automotive industry and economic growth of India, one can safely conclude that because of the Significance value obtained show a tendency to be less than 0.05. In such case, the column labelled 'Sig. (2-tailed)' displays a probability from the 't' distribution with 156 degrees of freedom. The value listed is the probability of obtaining an absolute value greater than or equal to the observed 't'statistic, if the difference between the sample mean and the test value is purely random. Since, confidence intervals lie entirely above 0.0; in this case, one can safely say that observed level of agreeableness regarding 'The growth of Automotive Industry is directly co- related with the economic growth of India' is significantly (positively) differing from the standard mean of 3. Hence, in this case of the hypothesis-H1, hypothesis null may be rejected and result can be interpreted as the growth of Automotive Industry is directly co- related with the economic growth of India.

Finally, it needs to be mentioned specifically that, this research was under taken with the intension of contributing to the understanding of the growth of Indian Economy and the growth of automotive industry to offer probable solutions in the light of findings. This study has added to the current body of knowledge relating to managerial aspects of automotive industry, also it has provided insight into areas that warrant further exploration.

Chapter 5 - Findings, Suggestions & Conclusion

5.1. Summary of Findings based on Primary and secondary data

- Based on the usage type and number of wheels Automotive industry in India is classified in to six classes   1. Two-Wheeler 2. Three-Wheeler 3. Passenger Car 4. Commercial vehicle 5. Tractor 6. Construction equipment's

- Off road vehicles industry do not contribute to the volumes of the automotive industry, however it is based on the applications and hence the type of vehicles are based on various special applications

- Automotive industry can also be classified considering verticals as fuel used, actual usage, wheels used for movement, purpose, engine capacity

- International way of classification of automotive industry is based on the combination of usage and wheels used to run the vehicle

- Indian Automotive industry had a turnover of about 73 USD Billion with the contribution of 6% in the national GDP. It provided employment to 13.1 million people directly with highest FDI inflow of 25 USD Billion in 10 years from 2010 to 2020 as per IBEF and SIAM

- The automotive industry in India is on the growth trajectory, if we study the 14 years period from 2004 to 2017, we will find that total automotive industry experienced growth of CAGR 11%, the sub segments of automotive industry experienced CAGR (compounded annual growth rate) per the number in bracket. Passenger vehicles (CAGR 11%), Commercial vehicles (CAGR 4%), Three wheelers (CAGR 8%), Two wheelers (CAGR 11%), Tractor Industry (CAGR 11%), & off road industry (CAGR 16%). Post study of various category of automotive industry in India one can understand that 2W segment is the largest contributor in terms of volumes exceeding 80% of the total industry volume

- Automotive industry in India is spread primarily in the states of Maharashtra, Karnataka, Tamilnadu, Delhi NCR, West Bengal and new area of Gujrat. The wide spread of the industry is helping in wide spread of employment generation also helping in balanced regional growth

- 2007 and 2009 was the period during which, auto industry in India experienced a dip due to slow down in the economic activity, this is one of the indicator of linkage between the economy and auto industry

- The four major pillars of automotive industry are 2W, 3W, 4W and CV (commercial vehicles), the ratio between them remains almost constant thru out the span of study. If we have to arrange them in large to small numbers just for the volumes produced, largest number will be 2W segment and smallest will be from commercial vehicles industry.

- The total Two wheeler manufacturers are 12 , for Three wheeler 7 manufacturers , passenger vehicle is manufactured by 15 players , Commercial vehicle have 10 manufacturers , farm equipment has 13 manufactures and last but not the least is construction equipment's are manufactured by 10 manufacturers

- Top five companies manufacture almost 85% of the total production. Maruti Suzuki India Ltd is the largest JV Company in the automotive space between Suzuki India Ltd. The first company have almost 50% market share and the second largest have only 17% market share. That is huge difference between the first and the second

- Top five manufacturers of commercial vehicles manufacture 97% of the total commercial vehicles. Out of which first three hold, almost 80% market share and command the market.

- Bajaj auto ltd is the world leader in 3W manufacturing with 35 % market share followed by Piaggio Ltd. With 18%share, both the players put together control more than 80% market share.

- Hero MotoCorp is world's largest 2W manufacturer, followed by Honda and Bajaj. The top five manufacturers control more than 90% of the market share by volume

- Mahindra is emerging as a clear leader in the manufacturing of the farm tractors based on the numbers above. It is clearly visible that top five manufacturers contribute for more than 80% of the tractor production in India.

- India population continues to grow @ 2% average, in the recent years it has shown reduction in growth rate of population

- India has shown steady rise in per Capita income from Rs 4000 in 1985 to Rs 140 k in 2019

- Automotive industry spread is seen in Maharashtra , NCR region , Tamilnadu , Karnataka and near Jamshedpur , also the per capita income is higher in these regions compared to the national average .

- Infrastructure spend of India was less than 20 USD Billion which substantially grew to 275 USD Billion and have shown some dip in 2019 -2020 due to economic slowdown and Covid 19

- The agricultural dependency of Indian economy has moved from 50% to less than 20% over period 70 years from independence, at the same time the industrial segment have grown from 15% to 30% , and service sector from 30% to 55% during the same period

- As per automotive sector report published in 2016, Government of India have confirmed the strong linkage between employment and manufacturing auto. Employment generated by manufacturing each PV is 6, CV-13,Three Wheel -4, Two wheel – 1, Tractor -13, and Off road – 13 persons
- India spending on road infrastructure is 18% of GDP in from 2020 to 2025 , which is a good indicator as decided by government
- The automotive industry spread is seen across India , but largely in the state of Maharashtra , NCR region Tamilnadu and Krnataka at large
- Auto component industry supports automotive industry for all the components required. As per Automotive components manufacturers association (ACMA), auto components industry turnover is 51.2 USD Billion, contribution to GDP is 2.3% creates approx. 3 million employment
- Auto component industry consist of many components, ACMA report of 2017-18 indicates that total contribution of automotive industry was 345635 Crors. Out of the total turnover of the auto component industry 26% was from the engine related components..17% was with body and chasis , 14 % was with suspension , 12 % contribution was from interior systems, cooling systems contributed lowest.
- Indian auto component industry contributes a lot for exports as well, highest exports in 2017 were to Europe @ 3830 USD million and lowest were to CIS countries @140 USD million
- Total exports in 2004 was 1.4 USD billion and that in 2017 were 13.5 USD Billion. In these 14 years the exports grew @ 20.11 % CAGR
- The import study for auto components indicate that in 2017 the highest import was from China @ 27 %, 4.29 USD Billion. Lowest imports were @2% recorded from UK/Czech/France with the value of 0.32 USD Billion. The auto component imports were at 1.3 USD Billion in 2004 which increased to 15.09 USD Billion in 2017; effective CAGR growth was 19.13%
- India has second highest population growth in the world, In 1951 India had a population of 37.63 million with the yearly growth of 1.61% year on year. In 1974, the population was 60.88 Million with the highest growth rate of 2.36%. In 2017, the population reached 133.87 million however, the growth rate decreased to 1.07%
- China and India contribute for more that 50% of world population
- Top 6 countries in terms of population are china ,India , US , ,Indonesia , Pakistan, Nigeria. By all means these countries will act as engines for future growth.

- India GDP in INR is largely dependent on conversion rate of USD to INR . It has shown phenomenal growth from 2003 till 2019 , growing from 618 USD Billion in year 2003 to USD Billion 2868 in year 2019

- India carries close to 18% of the world's population, it still makes 3% of GDP, rendering it one of the world's most aspirational post-G8 economies.

- India has experienced constant devaluation of its currency in line with most of the Asian currencies over a period of time

- India has lowest density of commercial vehicles compared to any other country in the world. Having highest population to support it for further growth. India is correctly placed to encash this situation to grow further multifold in the space of commercial vehicles.

- The highest employment generation in India is from agricultural sector then service sector and around 20% is created by Industrial sector

- The traditional fuels are petrol and Diesel , however during 2009 and 2012 new fuels were introduced to India namely LPG and CNG , CNG continues to be the most competitive fuel in the current times @ RS 56 per Kgs against Gasoline and Diesel which have crossed Rs. 100

- Out of total usage of crude oil in India it has only 18% of the domestic production, balance 82% is import

- In 1985 1 USD was equal to Rs 10, Year 2018 saw the value going down to Rs78 , Now in 2021 its recovered at Rs 74

- Crude oil prices started from USD 20 per barrel in 1987 moved as high as USD 100 per barrel in 2013 , It came down to USD 40 during Covid times in 2020 due to low demand

- The complete comparison between the GDP , fuel prices , population , road infrastructure growth shows a strong co relation when studied for the data collected from 2004 to 2017

- The road length by end of FY 2019 was 155222 kilometres of state highways, 132500 kilometres of national highway, other roads contributed for 5207044 km.

- In the statistical report of 2016-17 published by Government of India it was seen that out of the complete length of highways around 2% are national highways , 3% belong to state highways , 10% were district roads and 70% of the roads belong to rural area.Total road length was 58 lakh KM.

- The data collected from 1970 to 201 shows growth in various type of road lengths. National highway length increased from 23838 km to 114158 km , state highway shown growth from 56765 km to 175036 km , district highway from 276833 km to 586181 km , rural from354530 km to 4166916 km , urban roads from 72120 km to 526483 km , project roads from 130893 km to 328897 km. Total road length adding all above move from 914979 km to 5897671 km

- The study of state wise infrastructure study indicates that , states which are industrially advance do have better infrastructure of roads, it has more length of roads
- World road statistics clearly indicate that US , Canada and Australia have excellent road infrastructure which exceeds more than 20 kms per 1000 numbers of populations , hoever the developed countries indicate that the Km per 1000 population is much lower below 5 km /1000 population in case of India , china and Indonesia due to higher number of population. This indicates the scope of further development of infrastructure and growth
- The Automotive industry profile clearly indicates that this industry in capital intensive and , large capital investment is considered as barrier for this industry, example VW had to invest Rs 4000 CRS and Daimler had to invest Rs 8000 CRS to put up a green field facility in India.
- Indian two wheeler industry manufactured 5622741 number of the vehicles in 2004 year. IN the year 2017 it manufactured 23147057 vehicles. The compounded annual growth for this segment of industry was 11% spread over the period of 14 years
- During year 2013 to 2017 , It is seen that the scooter segment grew faster than that of Bike segment
- The Hero moto corp. investor presentation indicates that Philippines have lowest level of 2W penetration @ 78 numbers of 2W /1000 Population ,where as India has 102 2W for the same density of population, Highest density is with Thailand which is at 291 2w /1000 population
- India manufactured 356223 numbers of 3W in 2004 and 1021911 in 2017.
- 3W density per one lakh people is highest in the cities like Pune , Raipur and Amritsar to the tune of 1062 per lakh population in Pune and Cities like Gangtok and Shimla have no population of 3W , state policies largely decide on population of 3W in the given state
- Passenger car segment manufactured 989560 vehicles in the year 2004 and in the year 2017 it manufactured 4010373 number
- In the passenger car segment of automotive industry hatchback contribute for approx. 50% of the share ,Sedans which have boot space contribute 24% and SUV which is slightly premium segment contribute for 26% of share.
- Commercial vehicle segment manufactured 5550080 numbers of vehicles in the year 2004 and it manufactured 894551 vehicles in the year 2017. However the nature of this industry is cyclic in nature and it's a real barometer of economy. when the industrial production was very low un like the other segments it had shown a dip in manufactured numbers in the year 2013 again at 699035

- As per the data indicated by OICA (International Organization of motor vehicles manufacturer) China has 1.17 commercial vehicles per Kilometer of road and India has lowest 0.2 Kilometer

- India tractor industry manufactured 179000 tractors in the year 2004 and 691361 tractors in the year 2017. It has shown a CARG growth of 11% over the period of 14 years from 2004 to 2017

- Mahindra continues to be leader in the over market share of tractor with 40% share , TAFE and Escorts have market share of 18% each, Sonalika with 12 % and other small players contribute all put together 12% share

- In JCB shareholders PPT it is observed that 68% of the construction equipment manufactured are earth moving machines. This indicates that the basic need for infrastructure development is addressed by this specific equipment

- During the study of construction equipment manufacturing data it is observed that as the infra spend from government increases this industry sales are going up. The trend was clearly seen from 2014 and 2018 data there was total rise of 59% in the production numbers during this period

- On the part of education of respondents, it would be seen from the table no. 5.1 that, almost 61 per cent of the respondents are graduated and 33 per cent are postgraduate. There are six respondents having doctoral degree 2 respondents are diploma holders.

- Out of the 157 respondents 10% has age between 20-30 years , 31% had age between 30-40 years , 36% had age between 40-50 years and rest 23% had age 50+ years

- Respondents had a good amount of experience which can be proved from the data that 37% of the respondents had experience between 15-25 years , 28% had experience 25years +, 27% had experience of 5-15 years

- On the economic growth indicators it was observed that 32% respondents indicated their choice as index of industrial production and 42% gave preference to per capita income

- During the field investigation for impacts of industrial growth , 62%indicated that GDP growth will be positively impacted , and 14% responded that the purchasing power of the population will go up

In this exciting journey of studying the automotive industry and its impacts on the Indian economy. We are able to clearly see the interdependency based on the trend analysis done and various statistical analysis done during the study. Before we jump in to the conclusion lets co relate the findings and suggestions to the Objectives of the study. The comparative study started with the definite objective, which was set up at the beginning of the study.

Objectives of the Study which cover the research topic of "A comparative study of economic growth and growth of automotive industry in India " are as follows

Objective 1 - To study the growth pattern of the Automotive industry in India

Objective 2 - To Understand the relation between the Economic Growth & Automotive industry growth pattern

Objective 3 - To Understand the challenges faced by these industry & provide suggestions to overcome the challenges

Objective 4 - Compare the vision plan & study the challenges faced by the industry to meet vision plan

In this chapter we will see if each of the objective of study was met with explanation

Objective 1 - To study the growth pattern of the Automotive industry in India

We can very well say that this Objective of the study was completely met. The data range which we could collect from the year 2004 to 2017. It is being collected from the most trusted resource called SIAM – Society of automotive manufacturers. SIAM is the most trusted organization for the automotive industry and it collects data from all the members on regular basis for the production and sales figures for automotive industry.

We also studied the data from ACMA (Automotive components manufacturers association), which could also give some co relation of the data being collected from SIAM. The trend analysis done in the statistical analysis clearly indicates the liner graph of the automotive industry growth trend. We not only studied the growth of automotive industry but also tried to understand the various factors, which are responsible for growth of each of the segment of automotive industry. As we have studied earlier that automotive industry consist of six main verticals namely, two wheelers, Three wheelers, Passenger cars, Commercial vehicles, Tractors and off road vehicles.

Segment	Driver
Passenger vehicles	Higher growth in GDP, income levels and stable prices
Two and three wheelers	Higher GDP growth, good monsoon, higher disposable income
Commercial vehicles	Pick up in industrial production, GDP, stable interest rates
Tractors	Good monsoon, stable interest rates

Factors affecting the growth of Auto sector

- **Passenger vehicle Industry** – Factors affecting growth of this industry are , Urbanization , disposable income , Job stability , stable prices of the vehicles. Passenger cars sales are driven by many factors, one of the primary factors is travelling together in comfort and with the convenience of time. It also helps in point to point connect. In the earlier day's car was considered to be luxury but looking at the todays pace of life It is a basic need. Faster and reliable mobility is need of the time. As people spend more and more time in car due to longer travel hours some basic amount of comfort is also required while driving the car

- **Two-wheeler Industry (2W)** – This segment of the industry is largely dependent on the entry-level people who normally convert from bicycle to Bike /scooter. In the earlier days bicycle were used in bulk as a media of faster mobility. In today's scenario in India the speed of actions is very key. Largely used by the labor class, quick mobility requirement, short distances from home to office, multi-tasking needs. Smaller roads in cities drive the sales for two wheelers.

- **Three wheelers (3W)** – 3W sales are largely dependent on the permits allowed by the government in the given city. These sales are still dependent on the government and not entirely by the market forces. 3W are used mainly public transport vehicles for small distance movements. This type of vehicle is also used as personal vehicles in the countries like Bangladesh and Sri Lanka. However in India its used only as the vehicle which is used for the public transport. Every state government decides the ratio to population for each of the city based on the same how many autos can be bought is largely decided. India is also a major hub for exports of 3W to various Asian nations and African nations.

- **Commercial vehicles (CV)** – The name says everything, largely used for Public and Goods transport and sales are dependent on GDP, Industrial output, intercity goods and people movements. Population. It also depends on the agricultural output and Monsoon Generally the life of truck is considered to be 5-7 years, after which the commercial vehicle needs to be replaced. There are many factors, which drive the commercial vehicles sales like good monsoon is key for agriculture relates good movement, school going kids' population for school buses. Commercial vehicle sales are also driven by availability of skilled drivers. Every commercial vehicle based on the engine size has a passing criterion for tonnage.

- **Tractor /Farm equipment**– India is world's largest tractor manufacturer. Mahindra and Mahindra is the world's Number one tractor manufacturer based out of India. Tractors are used as multi-tasking equipment by farming community. The sales of tractor are directly proportionate to the monsoon and good crop price, it remains largely uncertain due to the demand and supply situation in the farming industry. Also, the monsoon cycles are un predictable hence there is no assurance that every farmer will get the required water resources to run the show.

- **Construction equipment's(OFF Road)** – Sales of the construction equipment's largely dependent on the activity of construction. Road development infrastructure development. All these projects are largely decided by the central or state government depending on the fund's availability. Central government , state government and local municipal corporations do have various infrastructure projects for infrastructure spend. Hence this spend on the construction equipment complete depend on the spends done by these governing authorities.

Objective 2 - To Understand the relation between the Economic Growth & Automotive industry growth pattern

During the pre 1980 , Automobile was considered as luxury as mobility of people was limited and not required for day to day operations. However as India shifts its dependency more towards industrial production, the need for good and people transport have gone up dramatically. It is evident based on the following facts that Indian economy and Automotive industry in India are largely interdependent

- GDP contribution from Automotive and auto component industry
- Employment generation
- Infrastructure development around the automotive clusters
- Industrial Hub development around Pune ,Chennai , Bangalore , Gurugram and Ahmedabad (sanand)
- FDI received in the Automotive industry amongst the total manufacturing sector

Large numbers of the components used in the auto industry give opportunity for rotation of money multiple times , there are approximately 40000 small and big components in the car . Every component needs to be manufactured and assembled with another component, which is done manually, this increases the employment and hence wealth generation together. The entire increase in the economic cycle gives positive impact on the GDP and growth of demography as whole. Looking at the total automotive industry the impact is huge and gives very positive support for the Indian economy. The detailed statistical analysis was done using co relation coefficient shows most of the values of major economic growth factors as nearing 1 or 1 , which shows the high level of correlation in the aspects.

Objective 3 and 4 - To understand the challenges faced by this industry& provide suggestions to overcome the challenges looking at the vision document.

This objective was studied to the extent of the information provided by industry experts based on the segments of automotive industry below are the clear challenges which are common to the auto industry and some challenges are specific to the segment of auto industry.

During the primary data study, it was observed that the Common challenges of the automotive industry are as follows

- Infrastructure spends by Government and auto industry growth – while doing the trend analysis it was observedthat, there is definite interdependency between, the infrastructures spend by the government and growth of automotive industry. As infrastructure spend, is ongoing process. Once the infrastructure spend starts, there is definite lag time between the spend and actual cyclic impact on the economy for people to get the feel of growth in the disposable income and they start the spend. The solution for having wide spread growth is to have wide spread infrastructure spend.as seen in the trend of spends by the current and previous government. They have tried to create industrial infrastructure across India at various places. This has helped creating the auto clusters and have regional growths in place.

- The only solution to have balanced growth without being having problems related to Rapid urbanization is to have growth centers spread across the geography so as to create job opportunity for all across the geography and hence avoid problems related to rapid urbanization
- Multi skilling amongst the autoworkers and professionals – as we have stated early every Car has 40000 spare parts. It needs to be manufactured accurately and assembled precisely. This entire activity calls for huge amount of skill sets to be developed among the population. Even the driving skills for heavy trucks and off roader machines are very essential for the growth of this industry, as it needs a special skill to operate these vehicles

- Government is already spending on the required resources to get the skill sets for the auto industry. However, there is need felt to have more of a practical knowledge amongst the skilled population to make them employable. Direct industry exposure will actually help further to bridge the gap.

- Disposable income of Buyers – Disposable income of buyers gives direct impact for 2W and Passenger car industry. It was observed during the primary data study that higher disposable income helps in higher buying of the vehicles required for mobility. The cycle is completely interconnected. Regional infra development gives rise to regional growth , helps generate the employment and hence disposable income.

- The solution for increasing disposable income is already in place and needs to be nurtured further. Fueling the regional developments is the only way forward. Looking at the spread of automotive industry across India and the current employed population. The auto industry is playing this roll of self-propulsion very well.

5.3 Suggestions

It is very evident after going thru the Objectives at the start of the study and findings post the study is done.

Suggestion 1 – Government should give special status to automotive industry looking at the regional wide spread impact it makes on the economy

Suggestion 2 – Forming special economic zones for Automotive industry and its vendors so that special tax benefits can be planned for them.

Suggestion 3 – Looking at the import of automotive components data , India must think of localizing most of the parts so that It will save on to the forex revenues and the industry will become revenue positive.

Suggestion 4 – During the low cycles of the economy infrastructure spend will trigger the process for spend , Automotive industry responds well to this with the GAP of few years. This industry acts as link between the Governments spend to boost the economy and consumer spend. Hence Government must continue its spend on the public infrastructure, so that the cascading effect will help in employment generation and Automotive industry growth

Suggestion 5–The economic way of operating on the CNG Fuel will improve on affordability of car or commercial vehicle. It is required that larger CNG infrastructure will help on industry growth and lowering down the Forex spend

Suggestion 6 –India is a big country , spread of industries across the regions will help getting the required pay loads for return trips also and regional development will help avoid the rapid urbanization. Automotive industry clusters are seeing taking this load and needs a special attention from the government.

5.4 Data co relation and final conclusion

It is considered to be essential that primary and secondary data collected derive the same meaning to dis prove the Null hypothesis and approve the alternate hypothesis. In the 4th chapter we analysed the data and found that the correlation coefficient derived out of the pearsons test was exceeding 0.9 (nearing +1), this clearly indicates the strong co relation between the data. Alternatively in the 2 tailed test , the value of P was less that 0.001 , which means that the null hypothesis was rejected and alternate hypothesis was accepted / approved. Finally we can conclude that the 4 major objectives of the study which were defined at the start of the study were completed and alternate hypothesis was approved, rejecting the Null Hypothesis establishing the strong correlation between Indian economy and Automotive industry in India.

5.5 Key words and their long forms

M&HCVs = Medium & Heavy Commercial Vehicles

LCVs = Light Commercial Vehicles

CVs = Commercial Vehicles

UVs = Utility Vehicles

PCs = Passenger Cars

PVs = Passenger Vehicles

MoRT&H = Ministry of Road Transport & Highways

SIAM = Society of Indian Automobile Manufacturers

ACMA = Automotive Components Manufacturers Association

SAFE - Society for Automotive Fitness & Environment

OICA- Organization of Motor Vehicle Manufacturers

IMMA- International Motorcycle Manufacturers Association

VDA- German Association of the Automotive Industry

JAMA- Japan Automobile Manufacturers Association

SMMT- The Society of Motor Manufacturers and Traders

TAIA- The Thai Automotive Industry Association

MAA- Malaysian Automotive Association

GAIKINDO- Indonesian Automotive Industry Association

AAF- ASEAN Automotive Federation

5.6 Bibliography

Books

1. C. Jeevanandam /Foreign Exchange/2009 /Sultan Chand & Sons
2. Francis Cherunilam /International Economics/2008/Tata McGraw Hill Publication
3. Paul Samuelson and William Nordhaus /Economics /2010,Author /McGraw Hill, INC
4. Ramesh Singh /Indian Economy/2016 /Mc Graw Hill Education

Reports

1. Annual report 1998-1999 SIAM (Society of Indian Automotive manufacturers for statistics related to automotive segment manufacturing)
2. Annual report 1999-2000 SIAM (Society of Indian Automotive manufacturers for statistics related to automotive segment manufacturing)
3. Annual report 2000-2001 SIAM (Society of Indian Automotive manufacturers for statistics related to automotive segment manufacturing)
4. Annual report 2001-2002 SIAM (Society of Indian Automotive manufacturers for statistics related to automotive segment manufacturing)
5. Annual report 2002-2003 SIAM (Society of Indian Automotive manufacturers for statistics related to automotive segment manufacturing)
6. Annual report 2003-2004 SIAM (Society of Indian Automotive manufacturers for statistics related to automotive segment manufacturing)
7. Annual report 2004-2005 SIAM (Society of Indian Automotive manufacturers for statistics related to automotive segment manufacturing)
8. Annual report 2005-2006 SIAM (Society of Indian Automotive manufacturers for statistics related to automotive segment manufacturing)
9. Annual report 2006-2007 SIAM (Society of Indian Automotive manufacturers for statistics related to automotive segment manufacturing)
10. Annual report 2007-2008 SIAM (Society of Indian Automotive manufacturers for statistics related to automotive segment manufacturing)
11. Annual report 2008-2009 SIAM (Society of Indian Automotive manufacturers for statistics related to automotive segment manufacturing)
12. Annual report 2009-2010 SIAM (Society of Indian Automotive manufacturers for statistics related to automotive segment manufacturing)
13. Annual report 2010-2011 SIAM (Society of Indian Automotive manufacturers for statistics related to automotive segment manufacturing)

14. Annual report <u>2011-2012</u> SIAM (Society of Indian Automotive manufacturers for statistics related to automotive segment manufacturing)

15. Annual report <u>2012-2013</u> SIAM (Society of Indian Automotive manufacturers for statistics related to automotive segment manufacturing)

16. Annual report <u>2013-2014</u> SIAM (Society of Indian Automotive manufacturers for statistics related to automotive segment manufacturing)

17. Annual report <u>2014-2015</u> SIAM (Society of Indian Automotive manufacturers for statistics related to automotive segment manufacturing)

18. Annual report <u>2015-2016</u> SIAM (Society of Indian Automotive manufacturers for statistics related to automotive segment manufacturing)

19. Annual report <u>2016-2017</u> SIAM (Society of Indian Automotive manufacturers for statistics related to automotive segment manufacturing)

20. Annual report <u>2017-2018</u> SIAM (Society of Indian Automotive manufacturers for statistics related to automotive segment manufacturing)

21. Annual report <u>2018-2019</u> SIAM (Society of Indian Automotive manufacturers for statistics related to automotive segment manufacturing)

22. Annual report 2009-2010 , Ministry of statistics and program implementation

23. Annual report 2010-2011 , Ministry of statistics and program implementation

24. Annual report 2011-2012, Ministry of statistics and program implementation

25. Annual report 2012-2013 , Ministry of statistics and program implementation

26. Annual report 2013-2014 , Ministry of statistics and program implementation

27. Annual report 2014-2015 , Ministry of statistics and program implementation

28. Annual report 2015-2016 , Ministry of statistics and program implementation

29. Annual report 2016-2017 , Ministry of statistics and program implementation

Online Pdf reports

30. Automobile components: Structures and prospects , 27th March 2017, CARE (Credit analysis and research Ltd)

31. Automotive sector report India by EMIS , March 2016

32. Auto Components report by IBEF , Jan 2016

33. Atul Auto annual report 2016-2017

34. Annual report Bajaj Auto Ltd 2016-2017

35. Automobiles –Advantage India report IBEF (India Brand Equity Foundation) , Feb 2019

36. Automobile : The economic outlook and employment situation , By PWC , Aug 2013

37. Auto fuel vision policy 2025 , Government of India , May 2014

38. Automotive Mission plan 2016-2026, Department of Heavy Industries

39. Agricultural and allied industries report , IBEF , May 2018

40. Asia Pacific Automotive sector , August 2016 , webreports published on Mergent

41. Basic road statistics of India , 2016-17 , Ministry of transport and Highways , Government of India

42. Connected car in emerging markets by VISTEON Dec 2016

43. Construction Equipment's, By IBEF , Jan 2017

44. CRISIL report on Automotive industry May 2013

45. Department of industrial policy and promotion , Department of heavy industries , Automotive sector achievements report , 30th Dec 2016

46. Economic survey of India 2017-2018

47. Economic liberalization in India , A report by CII, 6th August 2011

48. Electric two wheelers in India and Vietnam , repost by ADB (Asian development Bank) , 2009

49. Eicher Investors presentation Feb 2016

50. Growth of automotive industry and its economic impact : An Indian perspective by Vandana Singh , ISSN 2455-1627, Aug 2017

51. Global auto Industry by OICA, www.OICA.net

52. Global commercial vehicles outlook , by Power systems research , Nov 2014

53. Go Green with FDI in Indian two wheeler Automobile Industry by Avinish sharma , Institute of Business management , GLA Mathura , ISSN 2249-6920, Aug 2013

54. India, The galloping elephant by VDMA India services Pvt. Ltd

55. Indian HD truck market , 29 Nov 2016 , Frost and Sullivan

56. Indian Auto components industry performance review , FY 2018 ,ACMA (Automotive components manufacturers association)

57. Impact of GST- Automotive sector , PWC report , Feb 2019

58. Indian Auto Industry 2.0 , Innovation , NPD and Globalization imperatives , March 2019 by CII and Grant Thornton

59. Investment Opportunities in India , Feb 2016 , Make in India

60. Indian Tractor industry by ICRA , June 2016

61. Investors presentation , Escorts Nov 2017

62. Indian commercial vehicles industry ,by ICRA , March 2016

63. India two wheeler sector , Credit Suisse ,29 August 2012

64. India two wheeler industry by ICRA , Oct 2014

65. Indian passenger vehicles industry : strategic analysis with focus on big four firms by Karunakar B., NMIMS journal of economics and public policy , April 2017

66. KPMG'S Global Automotive executive survey, 2015

67. Making India world class manufacturing hub, Earnest and Young and CII joint report, 6 Feb 2016

68. Motorised two wheelers in India cities by EMBARQ India, March 2014

69. Opportunities in Indian Automotive components Industry, Business Sweden, April 2015

70. Overview of the Indian automotive components industry, By Atish Mukhopadhyay Tata Strategic management group, 2011

71. Production and sales trends if automobile industry in India by Jimmy CortonGaddam. Assi. Professor, GITAM University, Bangalore school of management studies, Bangalore, Published in Global journal of commerce and management Perspective, July – Aug 2013

72. Report on Indian Automotive industry by SESEI (Seconded European standardization expert in India)

73. Role of automotive industry in employment generation in India:An analysis of TATA motors and Mahindra and Mahindra, New man international journal of multidisciplinary studies, ISSN:2348-1390), By Santosh Kumar Maurya, Neharu Gram bharati university Allahabad

74. Scaling the Indian automotive aftermarket, path to profitable growth, McKinsey & Company, 16th Nov 2012

75. Seven Automotive growth areas you must know about to succeed, QUBE by Just auto, Author Mr.Calum Macrae, 2013

76. State wise annual sales of Tractors,2000 to 2017, By Tractors manufacturers association

77. Step on the gas steer into the future of the automotive industry in India, June 2014 by WIPRO and Dun and Bradstreet India

78. The Indian Automotive industry, By KPMG, Jan 2010

79. Truck Manufacturing by Marketline, Oct 2015

80. Two and Three wheelers in India, June 2009, Innovative transport solutions, IIT Delhi

81. Two wheelers By Motilal Oswal, Dec 2013

82. The future of work in the automotive sector in India, The centre for internet and society

83. World Diesel engines by Freedonia, April 2014

84. World Buses by Freedonia, March 2015

Online sites

85. http://www.mospi.gov.in- Annual reports

86. http://www.marutisuzuki.com- Annual reports

87. https://www.emis.com- Automotive industry production reports

88. https://censusindia.gov.in- Reports on Populations and demography in India

89. http://www.dipp.nic.in- India industrial production reports

90. http://morth.nic.in/- statistics on India road infrastructure

91. www.siamindia.com- Society of Indian Automotive manufacturers for statistics related to automotive segment manufacturing

92. www.acma.in- Automotive components manufacturers association for data related to imports and exports of auto components industry

93. www.icicidirect.com-

94. www.mahindra.com- Annual reports and Balance sheet for Passenger car and tractor industry study

95. www.frost.com- Reports on Automotive industry

96. Earnest and Young - www.ey.com - Reports on Automotive industry

97. www.team-bhp.com- Production reports verification for automotive production numbers

98. www.tatamotors.com- Annual reports

99. www.bajajauto.com- Annual reports

100. www.eicher.in- Annual reports

101. www.toyotabharat.com- Annual reports

102. www.tvsmotor.com- Annual reports

103. www.ashokleyland.com- Annual reports

104. www.smlisuzu.com- Annual reports

105. www.statista.com- Automotive industry production reports

Production data

106. International Organization of Motor Vehicle Manufacturers

5.7 Papers Published with ISSN / ISBN No

Sr No	Paper Name	Journal Name	ISSN/IBSN Number
1	GST Impact on automotive industry in India	International research journal of Multidisiplinary studies	ISSN - 2454-8499
2	Mat mount and Insulation solutions for BS6	BS-VI and real driving emissions , Path forward ,	Automotive industry Funded conference
3	Make in India , Opportunities and Challenges with special focus on automotive industry	International conference on make in India , opportunities , challenges and its impacts	ISBN-978-93-24457-17-5
4	A comparative study of growth of automotive industry in India during 2000 to 2016	Sate level workshop on research methodology	ISBN-978-93-24457-21-4
5	Modern and Traditional marketing	International Journal of advance and Innovative research	ISSN -2394-7780
6	Zonal level , University level and State Level Participation of Avishkar in 2017		
7	Self-reliant India and employment generation with Automotive industry- Chetana Collage Mumbai	UGC - Shodh Sarita Vol 8 ,Issue 29 , March 2021	ISSN 2348-2397
8	mpacts of Covid 19 on the Automotive Industry in India - Laxicon Pune	UGC - Shodh Sarita Vol 8 ,Issue 29 , March 2021	ISSN 2348-2397
9	Rise of Electric Mobility/ alternate fuel use, resulting in Import substitute for Crude oil- Tirpude Nagpur	UGC-Kala Sarovar /Vol-24-No 2- 2021	ISSN 0975-4520

- Chief Guest at INTAGLIO , Management fest at Anekant Institute of Management Studies
- Guest Lecture on Digital Marketing at ISMR Business school , Phursungi , Pune
- Paper Published along with presentation on Modern marketing methods at VPMS Bedekar Collage

5.8 ANNEXTURE

QUESTIONNAIRE- A Survey on Growth of Automotive Industry in India

Dear Auto sector professional, My Name is Prasad Soman, having more than 22 years' techno commercial experience with Auto Industry in India. I am persuading my Ph.D. on the Indian auto sector at Pune University; the project will focus the overall development of the automotive sector in India over the last 10 years. Looking at the enabling factors and the challenges, which the sector has encountered. The important milestones in the development etc. correlate this study with Barometers of Indian Economy and to look at the possible road map for future of this sector. I look forward to your valuable personal views as an Auto industry professional engaged with the industry over the years in various capacities. You have been involved with the development, growth of the industry as an industry professional and seen the development closely. Hence, your inputs are very important in this study. I thank you in advance for giving your valuable time and inputs for my project work. I would share the findings of the project work with you on its completion. Your valuable inputs will be used only to support the findings during my thesis of Ph.D. at Pune University. The nature of the study in purely academic & will not be used for any commercial purpose.

QUESTIONNAIRE

1) **Name of the Respondent**

   ----

2) **Mobile No of the Respondent**

   ----

3) **Email of the Respondent**

   ----

4) **Age Group of the Respondent**

   Select Any One.

- 20-30
- 30-40
- 40-50
- 50+

5) **Education qualification of the respondent**

Select Any One.

- Diploma
- Graduation
- Post-Graduation
- PhD

6) Number of Years' experience of the respondent

Select Any One.

- 0-5 years
- 5-15 years
- 15-25 years
- 25+ years

Objective section

(Please tick the most relevant option in below questions)

7) Tick the most relevant indicator for economic growth

Select Any One.

- Index of Industrial production (IIP)
- Infrastructure
- Per Capita income
- Agriculture income
- Foreign direct investment

8) Growth in industrial production will give rise to factors below

Select Any One.

- Automobile sales
- Disposable income of people
- GDP growth
- Increase in purchasing power
- No impact

9) Increase in road infrastructure will affect factors below

Select Any One.

- Rise in Automobile sales
- Rise in Industrial investment
- Catalyse GDP growth
- Rise in employment
- Improve Economic efficiency

10) Factors responsible for growth of Automobile industry

Select Any One.

- Industrial growth
- Disposable income
- Road Infrastructure
- Rapid Urbanization
- Intercity mobility needs

11) Factors affecting commercial vehicle sales

Select Any One.

- Agriculture growth
- Industrial growth
- Urbanization
- Fuel prices
- Road Infrastructure

12) Most relevant income Bracket for buying 2W

Select Any One.

- 5000-10000
- 10000-25000
- 25000-50000
- 50000 & above

13) Most relevant income Bracket for buying 3W

Select Any One.

- 5000-10000
- 10000-25000
- 25000-50000
- 50000 & above

14) Most relevant income Bracket for buying 4W

Select Any One.

- 5000-10000
- 10000-25000
- 25000-50000
- 50000 & above

15) Popular use of 2W

Select Any One.

- City Travel
- <50 km travel
- Stand by vehicle
- Urban household use
- Leisure travel

16) Popular use of 3W

Select Any One.

- City travel passenger
- Family vehicle
- Goods carrier picks up
- Roadside vendor
- Low cost transport

17) Popular use of 4W

Select Any One.

- City travel for passengers
- Family vehicle
- Goods carrier picks up
- Roadside vendor
- Low cost transport

18) Popular use of commercial vehicle -Bus & Truck

Select Any One.

- Intercity travel
- Bulk Goods transport
- Luxury vehicle
- School Bus
- Urban transport

19) Probability that the bicycle owner will buy a 2W as his disposable income grows

Select Any One.

- 10%
- 30%
- 50%
- 70%
- 100%

20) Probability that the 2W owner will buy a 4W as his disposable income grows

Select Any One.

- 10%
- 30%
- 50%
- 70%
- 100%

21) Factors essentials for industrial growth

Select Any One.

- Road Infrastructure
- PP (Purchasing power)
- Quick people and goods movement
- Exports & internal consumption
- Industrial infrastructure

22) Factors responsible for cyclic nature of the Auto industry sales (tick the most relevant)

- Monsoon
- Industrial production
- Tax structure
- Infrastructure growth
- Economic cycles

23) Do you think there is strong correlation between economic growth and growth of automotive industry in India?

Select Any One.

- Strongly Disagree
- Disagree
- Cannot say.
- Agree
- Strongly Agree

24) Do you think that rise in government spending on Road Infrastructure and increase in Disposable Income will have positive impact on automotive industry in India?

Select Any One.

- Yes
- No
- Can't say

Subjective section

1) State top two challenges for growth of two-wheeler industry

   ----

2) State top two challenges for growth of Three-wheeler industry

   ----

3) State top two challenges for growth of Four-wheeler industry

   ----

4) State top two challenges for growth of Commercial vehicles industry

   ----

5) Suggestions & Comments

A Thesis on

"A Comparative study of Economic growth and Growth of Automotive Industry in India"

Submitted to the Savitribai Phule Pune University in Fulfilment

of the Degree of Ph.D. (Doctor of Philosophy) in Commerce &

Management

Under the board of Business Administration

Submitted by

Mr. Prasad Prabhakar Soman

Under the guidance of

Dr. Padmawati Sanjay Ingole

(M.Com. M.A., B.Ed., Ph.D., SET)

Head of Dept. of Commerce

Prof.Ramkrishna More Arts Commerce and Science College. Akurdi, Pune

411044

RESEARCH CENTRE

Prof. Ramakrishna More Arts Commerce and Science College, Akurdi,

Pune 411044

Date – September 2021

CPSIA information can be obtained
at www.ICGtesting.com
Printed in the USA
LVHW080148121122
732945LV00045B/3404